THE FIRST COLLECTION OF HUMOR BY WOMEN

TITTERS

Edited by

DEANNE STILLMAN

and

ANNE BEATTS

Design and
Art Direction by
JUDITH JACKLIN

Managing Editor:
PENNY STALLINGS

COLLIER BOOKS
A Division of Macmillan Publishing Co., Inc.
New York
Collier Macmillan Publishers
London

Macmillan Publishing Co., Inc.
866 Third Avenue, New York, N.Y. 10022
Collier Macmillan Canada, Ltd.

Library of Congress Cataloging in Publication
Data
Main entry under title:
Titters: the first collection of humor by
women.
    1. American wit and humor. 2. Women—
Anecdotes, facetiae, satire, etc. I. Stillman,
Deanne. II. Beatts, Anne.
PN6162.T54 1976b   817'.5'408   76-8015
ISBN 0-02-040700-9

First Collier Books Edition 1976

Titters is also published in a hardcover edition by Macmillan Publishing Co., Inc.
Printed in the United States of America

Cover photo by Lynn Goldsmith.

INTRODUCTION

"Since when did women get funny?"
—the guy at the stat house

Nobody will admit to not having a sense of humor. It's something that everybody has, like parents. No sense of direction, no ear for music, poor eye/hand coordination, color blindness—these are handicaps that people will admit to publicly. But who among us will say, "I have no sense of humor. I wouldn't recognize a joke if I tripped over it"?

Nobody. Nobody, that is, except women. More than one woman has actually been heard to announce, when confronted by some floundering male attempt to amuse, such as making-believe his shoe is a telephone and trying to contact the Coast on it, "I just don't think that's funny. But then, I have no sense of humor"—a statement that usually goes unchallenged.

Women aren't supposed to be funny, particularly. It's not part of the feminine role-model, the set of stereotypes that got dished out to us along with our pablum. "As soft and as funny as a nursery"—whoever heard of that? The best we could do was, "Nancy with the laughing face," and even then it was never clear what Nancy found to laugh about. Maybe she was just a grinning idiot.

It's more likely, though, that she was broken up by male antics. That was definitely allowed, even on *Saturday Evening Post* covers, where the tow-headed little boy with the frog and slingshot in his back pocket was eternally cutting up for the benefit of the freckle-faced little girl in pigtails who was stifling admiring giggles behind her hand—when she wasn't running in terror from the frog or the slingshot.

Okay. At this point the protests begin. Wait a minute, you say, it wasn't always like that. What about Ruth Draper? Dorothy Parker? Anita Loos? What about Carol Burnett? There have always been funny women!

Well, what about them? Just because women really *are* funny doesn't change the prevailing attitude. And the prevailing attitude has been, and to some extent continues to be, "Chicks just aren't funny." As chicks who have put in a lot of years in the chuckle racket, we can testify to that.

We don't want to bore you with case histories of oppression. This is meant to be an introduction, not a political manifesto. But after years of telling our favorite jokes, witticisms, funny ideas, satirical remarks, and boss slashes to men, and having them respond, "I just don't think that's funny"—notice, no corollary statement about lacking a sense of humor here—we began to get suspicious. How many people have to think something's funny before it's funny, we asked ourselves. Ten? Twenty? Two hundred? And does it matter who they are? What if they're, say, convicts? "Oh, that doesn't matter, even if two hundred of them are laughing, they're only convicts. Everyone knows that felons have no sense of humor."

What if two hundred women thought something was funny? Or two thousand, or two hundred thousand, and men still didn't? What did that mean? Maybe it meant that men had no sense of humor where women were concerned? Or that when women were the ones cracking the jokes, men just didn't feel like laughing—because they imagined that next they'd be chased after with the frog and hit by the slingshot?

But what really cinched it for us, Anne Beatts and Deanne Stillman (Deanne Stillman and Anne Beatts, let's get that order right, AB) was that *we* thought it was funny. We broke each other up. "Hey, that's really funny," we said to each other, not "Chicks just can't get it on when it comes to humor." Oh, sure, each of us pretended that she had known all along she was one hell of a funny woman. But it helped to have someone else think so, too. And that's how *Titters* was started, by a majority of two.

So, does that mean that *Titters* exists only as a means of crashing the male-dominated humor biz? Of course not. *Titters* is meant to make you laugh, whoever you are. And here we feel we should add a caveat, the way they used to in ads for horror movies in the fifties: it may shock you. There are certain things in *Titters* that will probably shock certain segments of the public, such as men, or feminists, or people who don't like to see certain four-letter words—the word "foot," for example—in print.

We don't mind that. The days of pigtails and hair ribbons and laughing discreetly behind our hands are gone and good riddance. If it's now okay for women to write poems about menstrual blood, why shouldn't it be okay for women to make jokes about women who write poems about menstrual blood? Well? Why shouldn't it?

Please do not reveal the ending of this picture to anyone after you have left the theater.

You see, we think women should be allowed to be outrageous, or even silly. After years of watching men play the fool, it's a great release to be able to hold our shoes to our heads and go "hello, hello?" The book may be called *Titters,* but giggles, guffaws, and belly-laughs are in it as well. Come in, the Coast . . . hello? I'm sorry, I can't hear you, I have a tampon in my ear.

Then is nothing sacred? Maybe something is, but personally we doubt it. The way we see it, humor is basically reflective—like holding a fun-house mirror up to nature. Someone we know once defined the role of the satirist as "pointing out that the emperor's not wearing any clothes

—I'm not saying he should have clothes on, I'm just saying he's not wearing any." Well, that's about the size of it—which is to say that if it's part of *Titters,* it's part of life. We didn't think of it. We just thought of making fun of it. Some people say you're not supposed to do that. We say it's spinach and we say the hell with it.

Is there such a thing as women's humor? Hard to say. Is there such a thing as women's mathematics? There might be such a thing as feminist humor, though nobody seems able to point to many examples. "Why did the feminist cross the road?" was the best we were able to come up with, and we never did think of an answer.*

In any case, *Titters* is not a book of women's humor. It's a book of humor by women, all kinds of women, and that means most of the subjects it deals with are things women in general find interesting. As a result, the book might be slightly overburdened with jokes involving the word "cuticle." There are no jokes in *Titters* about the following: jock straps, beer, trains, mothers-in-law, dumb blondes, cars, boxing, the Navy, chemistry, physics, stamp catalogues, spelunking, pud-pulling, or poker.

Why not? Because those subjects concern men, and, as such, have received their fair share of chuckles elsewhere. Sure, we could have chosen to parody *Field & Stream* and John Updike instead of the Tampax instructions and Lillian Hellman—and maybe we will, someday. (Watch for *Daughter of Titters, Titters Revisited,* and *Titters, Student Nurse.*)

What's more likely, however, is that men, flighty creatures of impulse that they are, will begin following our lead—and find themselves in deep trouble when they try to write parodies of makeup ads based on knowledge of the single word "mascara." Women's culture, you see, is secret because it was for so long a sub-culture to the dominant masculine one. As a result, we know far more about what the guys really talk about in the locker room than they know about what any four women, chosen at random, say to each other when there are no men around.

So, if you're a man, *Titters* may hold some surprises. You may even think some of it is "just not funny." We can't help that. We didn't do it for you, although we hope you'll enjoy reading it. We did it for ourselves.

Then what got into *Titters,* anyway? Anything the editors thought was funny.

Who are the contributors and where do they come from? Well, after a worldwide search conducted by our qualified humor talent scouts, we discovered that, by sheer coincidence, most of the world's greatest humorists live within a one-mile radius of *Titters* headquarters. No, that does not mean the book is too regional. One of our contributors lives in Minnesota.

We're both under thirty, but our oldest contributor is seventy. Our youngest is nineteen.

Are there any men in the book? No, not unless you count the guys who set the type. There were men who asked us if they could be in the book. We said no, not unless they went to Denmark for a sex change. As far as

we know, none of them went.

Why have the editors written so many of the pieces? Why not?

Why is Candice Bergen in the book? Because she got to know Anne Beatts, who writes for NBC's "Saturday Night" show, when she was the guest host.

Why isn't Zsa Zsa Gabor in the book? Because she can't speak English.

Who's Penny Stallings? The managing editor.

Do most books have their own managing editor? No.

Who's Judith Jacklin and what did she have to do with *Titters*? She designed the book, art-directed the book, took some of the pictures, drew some of the pictures, spec'd the type, modeled for some of the pictures, and whenever we went over to her house she was always cutting up these little strips of paper and pasting them down on something.

What's the difference between parody and satire? It says in the dictionary that parody is "a satirical imitation of a work of literature or music," while satire is "a literary work in which irony, derision, or wit is used to expose folly or wickedness." Do the editors know the difference? You be the judge.

Our favorite color is black.

No, we have not had big arguments. Once we spent three hours screaming at each other about the proper use of the word "furnace." See if you can find where.

No, *Titters* is not a CIA attempt to co-opt the women's humor movement. Nobody's offered us any money lately.

Is humor a dead end? Don't know yet (see answer to above).

At last count, about three *Titters* contributors were lesbians. No, we do not know why this falls below the national average.

If there's no outlet for humor by women, where did the editors dig up all these parodies and satires? From various places. Most of *Titters* was written, drawn, or photographed expressly for us. When there were existing pieces which we liked and thought should be in the book, we reprinted them.

What do we say when people tell us "Chicks have no sense of humor?" Different things (usually some variant on "Neither do you, pizza-face!").

What do women really want? Sometimes a cigar is just a cigar.

One more question—*Titters* contains parody and satire, poetry, journalism, one-line jokes, comic strips, cartoons, cut-outs, samplers, and paper dolls. But why no limericks? Frankly, we received many limericks. None of them were funny, so we decided to write one ourselves.

(Limerick to Come)

Deanne Stillman
Anne Beatts

---

*If you think you know the answer to that one, please send it special delivery to: The Editors, *Titters,* c/o Macmillan Publishing Co., Inc., 866 Third Avenue, New York, N.Y. 10022.

TABLE OF CONTENTS

JUGS

HOOTERS

BONGOS

Knockers, Melons, etc. photographed by Lynn Goldsmith. Art by Barbra Bergman.

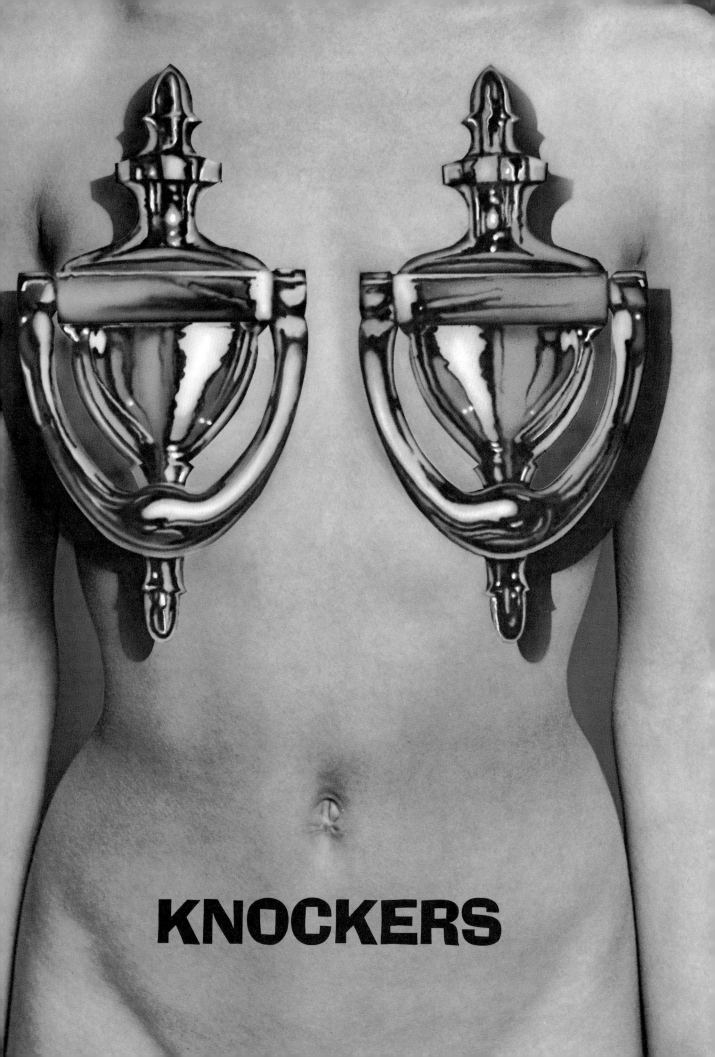

KNOCKERS

The Total Slave

by Marabel Moron

My name is Marabel Moron and when I married my husband, Chuck, ten years ago, I naturally assumed that our marriage was made in heaven. We were both, I thought, prepared to give our all to each other, but my knowledge of what that entailed was virtually nil. I thought a good marriage meant sharing your dreams and achieving them together, hopefully raising a family, and, of course, inseparable love.

In the beginning, things looked very good for Chuck and I. We both seemed to march to the sound of the same drummer. During our engagement, he spent all his evenings with me studying his law books at my apartment, and in between cases, I listened for hours while he spoke of his dreams and desires. Of course, when he talked of his work, in all its legal terms, I didn't understand a word of what he was saying, but I let him go on because I loved him so. I thought, how lucky I am to have found such a talkative man. In many marriages I had seen, there was no communication between the couples at all. In ours, at least, one of us spoke.

Chuck talked and talked. The night he asked me to marry him, it was my birthday, and he took me for an expensive dinner at one of the big hotels. While I was trying to savor every last taste of the luxurious meal, he talked. Afterwards, when we drove out to the ocean, with a full moon and a starlit sky, he talked. Though he did have some sweet little thoughts for me, he really wasn't being romantic at all. But, content to be with the man I loved, I leaned back into his arms, and, thanks to a full stomach and the peacefulness of the surroundings, I fell asleep.

I have no idea how long I managed to stay asleep, but when I awoke in the back seat Chuck was saying, ". . . and that's what I want in a wife." My darling man, with his analytical mind, had been outlining the qualities he found essential in a wife! What did he want? I had missed it all.

When he quickly asked, however, "Will you be that girl?" my drowsiness faded instantly and I replied, "Of course, yes, yes, yes!" We pulled our disheveled selves together and he led me back to the front seat, where he took a velvet jewelry box out of the glove compartment and, with a gleam in his eye, placed a gigantic diamond ring in my lap.

He was asking me to be his wife! Forever! How happy I was. But there was one unspoken thought that kept marring my pleasure for the rest of that evening and through many sleepless nights that followed. What were all those things he said he wanted in a wife? I couldn't bring myself to admit to him that I'd slept through it all. If only I had, perhaps I could have saved us the misery which was to come.

My first hint that something was amiss came on our honeymoon. Oh, we were carefree and suntanned, sipping cocktails in the afternoon, dining in the moonlight, and loving in the dark, but, without a doubt, a change had taken place in our relationship. For one thing, Chuck stopped talking and began grunting. He seemed distant and preoccupied. In answer to my questions, he would get up and walk away. Sometimes, he would get up and walk away when I was still perched on his lap, letting me slip abruptly to the floor. One day, shortly before our return home, I had to pull a newspaper away from him and say "Hey, remember me?" He seemed perturbed but smiled. I realized, but not soon enough, unfortunately, that I was nagging him about his not talking instead of just allowing him to act as he pleased. Perhaps he'd been the silent type all along and had just forced himself to talk during those months preceding our marriage in order to win me over. A love like that certainly doesn't deserve to be rewarded with nagging and overreaction. As it says in that great book, the Bible, "What he giveth in love, you must taketh in love, even if it beith small potatoes." I resolved to stop pestering Chuck for conversation and keep whatever small talk I might have to myself.

Through the next few years, Chuck and I were polite to each other and said little things like, "Pass the salt," or "You have spinach in your teeth," but I couldn't help feeling that something in our marriage had gone wrong. I could talk to just about anyone else but my brain couldn't come up with one intelligent remark to say to my own husband. Though I didn't want to believe it at the time, there was a good reason for Chuck not to want to talk to me. All day long at the office he had to converse and be nice to people, so why should he be expected to have to act like that in his own home just for my benefit? It's only natural he should seek a little peace and quiet. Even the Bible says, "A man deserveth to act the way he pleaseth in his life and home." What kind of wife had I become that would deprive her husband of his most basic need, to be the king in his own castle?

I read every marriage book I could get my hands on, took self-improvement courses, and started memorizing the Bible. Again and again, certain points kept coming up, things I recognized immediately as having been missing from our marriage. For instance, Chuck had never told me I had a belly like a sheaf of wheat. Slowly at first, I began to apply what I had learned to our life together —with stunning results. Little by little, I was winning my husband back. He became attentive to me again, laughed again, and for the first time in ages, talked to me again about his work. He was never one to go all out buying me gifts, even before we were married, but almost at once, he began showering me with presents—a new refrigerator-freezer, wallpaper for the den, a whole new set of aluminum cookware, even a Kitchen Magician.

This brand new love between us, as a result of my new-found knowledge, revolutionized our marriage so much that I had to pass on my findings in the three-lesson Total Slave course outlined in the following pages. If by reading and applying these principles you become a Total Slave, with your husband happier than ever before, my efforts in this writing will have been rewarded. If only every woman in America could become a Total Slave then I could stop gadding about the country and stay home like Chuck wants me to!

Lesson 1

Many wives have admitted to me at various Total Slave sessions across the country that the main reason they are unable to meet their husbands' needs and listen attentively to his every interest is that by the time he comes home from work in the evening, rightfully expecting dinner, good conversation, and sex, they are totally beat from their full day of housecleaning, child care, and shopping. Perhaps you're like many women, who say, "Too bad about him. He doesn't give a damn how tired I am." Yet I have known dozens of bitter and frazzled housewives who have been transformed into calm, gentle, and thought-free Total Slaves! By redeeming your time, you can beat the 6:00 P.M. wash-out blues.

First, write down everything you have to do during the day. Everything. Making the beds, washing the dishes, dusting his gun collection, vacuuming the living room, scrubbing the floor, laundry, grocery shopping, the lot. Don't worry if the list seems endless. Then, number everything in order of importance. Of course, when your husband asks you to do something special, like cleaning out the bathtub with your tongue, he expects it to be done, so make sure anything of this nature is given top priority on the list. Also, try to put the most unpleasant tasks up front, as the sooner they're gotten out of the way, the better you'll feel. A Total Slave can't function properly with nagging thoughts of toilet duties hovering over her head all day.

Tomorrow, begin with the first item and stick with it until it's accomplished. Then start on number two and so on down the list. Early in the day, as you see items checked off, you'll begin to feel a sense of real accomplishment. Don't worry if you can't complete everything; you can always go back to it after your husband goes to sleep.

Finally, stop everything, if you haven't finished already, by 4:30 P.M. With your husband due home in only an hour and a half, it's time to start preparing for him. Dinner, of course, should have been one of your top priorities, and already planned and prepared, so as not to take up the valuable time you now need to ready yourself for the man you love. Bathe, shave, perfume yourself silly. Freshen up your little mound with his favorite aroma. Fix your hair and makeup, and dress up in that sexy outfit you only wear to the doctor's office. Light the candles, put on the music, and bend over, waiting patiently for your husband to enter. He will be thrilled. Every man appreciates order, and he'll be especially glad to find it in his own home.

Lastly, be prepared for the unexpected. You might have finished all your wifely chores by noon, prepared a delicious dinner, soaked in bubbles for an hour, and dressed to kill, only to have your husband phone and say he'll be home from work a month late. Knowing full well that life is full of changes, I try not to panic when a monkey wrench is thrown into my day. In the Bible, James says, "When all kinds of trials and tribulations crowd into your lives, my brothers, don't resent them as intruders, but welcome them as friends."

Lesson 2

No matter what your husband is, accept him as that. Some women may say, "Well, I hate my husband, so why in hell should I accept him?" Well, this attitude is wrong. First of all, the Bible says that wives should love their husbands. If you've lost that love, you should ask God to restore it.

The changes I've seen in some couples once the wives have made up their minds to completely accept their husbands are remarkable. One wife told me, "Now he's so much more loving and generous. He wants to give me money all the time! I'm going to start taking it just to make him happy!"

Your man too needs to feel important, loved, and accepted. If you won't accept his idiosyncracies, who will? A Total Slave caters to her man's special quirks. Love your man and hold him in reverence, it says in the Bible. *Reverence,* according to the dictionary, means "to respect, honor, esteem, accept completely, praise, adore, and admire." Nothing less will suffice.

Try this test for a week. Starting tonight, determine that you will accept and admire your husband. Let him know you care. Put your magazine down and look at him. Applaud him when he performs the simplest of feats, such as remembering your name. Let him know he's your hero.

Tell him you love his body. If you choke on that phrase, practice it in front of a mirror until it comes naturally. Even the ugliest man has certain qualities worth admiring. Pick out his most masculine characteristics and let him know they please you, even if all you can come up with is symmetrical feet.

One woman once said to me, "I feel guilty using feminine wiles on my husband. It seems dishonest. Anyway, his body is not all that great. He's gotten fat and bald, it's disgusting. Why should I lie to build him up?" It's not using feminine wiles to put your husband's tattered ego back together again. It's the very nature of love. In addition, if you have an ugly, flabby husband who does nothing but stay home drinking beer all day and taking the Lord's name in vain, that just may be the result of you having usurped his role somewhere along the line. Your nagging may have taken the getup out of his go, and now he has no desire to keep working for you. If so, he needs your compliments to restart his engine.

Finally, after accepting and admiring your husband, you must adapt to him. Probably the most recurrent problem in any marriage is the conflict over who gets his or her way when the viewpoints differ. Every couple has this problem. The Biblical remedy states: "You wives must submit to your husband's leadership in the same way you submit to the Lord." God planned for woman to be under her husband's rule.

Ask your husband tonight to write down the twenty most important changes he'd like to see take place at your house. Read the list, write it down one hundred times (no carbons!), and then set out to accomplish these changes with a smile. Be a "Yes, of course, dear," woman every day. (One Total Slave I know, who really wanted to make the changes part of her, made a tossed salad with the first ten copies of her husband's list. With the simple addition of a little salt and pepper, it was amazingly easy to get down.)

Lesson 3

How long has it been since you said to your husband, "Take me, I'm yours"? When was the last time your husband came home to find you waiting in bed for him? Giving your husband his due of sexual pleasure is essential to any good marriage. Remember, you are the one woman he selected to live with. He chose you ahead of all the other girls. You owe it to him to show that you appreciate that honor, and nothing can demonstrate it better than keeping a sexually-charged household.

First, you must set up an atmosphere of sex. From the minute you wake till you fall asleep that night in his arms, let your husband know you are his for the taking. Even in dreamland you can make yourself available by always sleeping with your legs open.

Let your husband know you miss him every time he leaves by walking to the car and perhaps even running with it until it disappears from sight. I made it all the way to the train station with Chuck one day and you can't imagine how happy he was.

When he's at the office, away from you, make it your business to remind him you are waiting at home—anxiously. Call to say you are lying on the floor of the kitchen, naked, with legs spread, and will stay in that position until he arrives. When he does come home and comes after you, respond, don't just endure. While he still may be able to get pleasure with you limp as a dishrag, his ego needs to know that you too are ecstatic over the act. Move a lot, sigh, and claw his back. If he should drop off to sleep before you are finished, be careful not to wake him up. Practice these techniques at home alone with a duffle bag so they become second nature. They must not preoccupy you when you are with your husband, as your only consideration then should be his satisfaction. In the Bible it says, "One thought only hath a wife, if that, and it be her husband's pleasure."

Of course, to really please the man of your life, you must be physically pleasing to his eye. Saying "Take me" with Noxzema on your face and spoolies in your hair may only drive him out the door at an even earlier hour. Make sure you always look good enough for him to want to stay. *Never* allow him to see you looking bad. Should you have a cold and be pale, or suffer from a runny nose, stay down in the basement until you've recovered. Tell him you love him but couldn't endure him seeing you like that, and he'll be thankful for your consideration.

If the same old gowns or negligees have become second nature to him, dream up some new costume to wear each time he arrives home. The scantier, the better. One wife, who greeted her husband at the door wearing only a leash and a muzzle, said, "It's unbelievable, the change that came over him. He loved my outfit so, he's asked me to wear it all the time."

The rewards for all this are many. There is, of course, the ultimate reward which you will one day receive in heaven. In fact, everything you do for your husband, your master on earth, is but paving the way for that glorious moment when you may anoint the feet of Jesus Christ. But there are immediate rewards as well. Your every day will be filled with purpose and your life for the first time will take on a true worth. As one happy Total Slave from West Virginia put it: "I've never known such fulfillment. Stu just thinks the world of me now, and to prove it, he has even consented to my using bigger apples on my head. I always trusted his aim, but still— what a nice way of saying I love you."

Fran Lebowitz's Page

The New York Times Magazine
**Part Two/Fashion of the Times:
In Recent Years**

It's no good trying to pin this thing on one person. Believe me, I've tried, and I tell you it just can't be done. No sooner have you finally and absolutely decided on Judy Collins when out of nowhere the name Alan Watts comes looming up at you like The Ghost Of Krishna Past. Well, all right—Judy Collins *and* Alan Watts. You begin to relax. You light a cigarette. You lean back. And then like a bat out of hell—*Herman Hesse*. You rub your eyes. Run your hand nervously through your hair. Open a window. But it's no go. The floodgates are open. The damage is done. Neil Young. Peter Fonda. Kate Millet. Timothy Leary. John Sinclair. The names descend upon you mercilessly. A hard rain has fallen. Another sleepless night.

You pour yourself a drink. Turn the pillow cool side up and try to think back to a gentler era. An era when *The New York Times Magazine* Part Two/ Fashion of the Times had more to do with Fashion than it did The Times. When it was filled with impossible looking models posed in impossible looking positions. Seven-foot-tall girls with monumental cheekbones spread-eagled against the Seagrams building on a moonless night. Page after page depicting a world entirely populated by Great Beauties that no one could ever meet dressed in clothes that no one could ever wear. Every so often there would be a flurry of little illustrations flawlessly executed by a wood nymph. The only words allowed were those such as *look, bloused, flowing, smartly,* and *tailored.* You decided to drop out of high school and move to New York.

Then came the word *lifestyle.* Not a word at all, really—rather a wordette. A genuine case of more is less. The sum of the parts being greater than the whole. You get my drift. People started saying *lifestyle,* writing *lifestyle,* and singing *lifestyle.* And not a single one of them thought to point out that the word *life* and the word *style* are, except in rare cases (and chances are that *you're* not of them), mutually exclusive.

The change was gradual, but in a few short years models had all but disappeared from the pages of *The New York Times Magazine* Part Two/ Fashion of the Times. They were replaced by people. People with life-styles. Research chemists from NYU Medical Center. Divorcees rebuilding shattered lives. Lesbian mothers. Teachers of incorrigible children. They all live in fifth floor walk-ups. They all have stories to tell. And they all look like they make their own clothes out of contact paper and nylon cord.

The change in *The New York Times Magazine* Part Two/Fashion of the Times has had the following effects:

1. Girls who are seven feet tall and possessed of monumental cheekbones apply light foundation makeup to their cheeks in an effort to make them appear puffier, and walk around all slouched over hoping to be taken for city planners.

2. Wood nymphs capable of executing flawless fashion illustrations do graphic design for Public Health brochures-containing information on home abortion.

3. I have left New York and gone home to finish high school.

On the Revival of the Stage Name: A Strongly Worded Request

It is primarily the fault of Simon and Garfunkel. Their success, despite or perhaps because of the use of their real names (remember, that was the sixties), encouraged a lot of other performers with equally cacophonous appelations to do the same. This has been particularly true of Jewish girl singers. There are many such girls. They are usually the opening act in the nightclubs that cater to the trade trade. They are usually too fat or too skinny and they talk about it. A lot. The stunning success of the girl friend of a well-known Hollywood hairdresser convinced a lot of these girls that they could get away with looking like that. The more recent achievement of The Divine Miss M. didn't help any, either. It is now practically impossible to set foot inside any place that has a cover charge without being confronted by a girl you think you went to camp with. And while it was certainly no picnic having such a girl in The Bluebirds, it is even less of a treat to sit at a table and watch her sing "It Must Be Him." Especially when you know full well that not only was it never Him—it was never *anybody.* I mean, here is a girl who during the course of her adolescence received six phone calls—four from people who *knew* that she was available to babysit Saturday night and two from the allergist's nurse to change her appointment. This is not my idea of a star.

The Word *Lady:* Most Often Used to Describe Someone You Wouldn't Want to Talk to For Even Five Minutes

For years and years, people who had them referred to their girl friends as their girl friends. With the advent of an unattractive style known as being hip, many people stole the term old lady from perfectly innocent black jazz musicians and began using it in regard to their own girl friends. Then came women's lib, and quite a number of people apparently felt that the word *old* was sexist. These people began to call their girl friends their ladies.

This particular group is not alone in its affection for the word *lady.* It is also in great favor among those who think that what Bob Mackie does for a living is design clothes. These people like to go on television talk shows a lot and refer to absent overweight nightclub singers as terrific ladies or absent underweight variety show hostesses as beautiful ladies.

Lest you get the impression that I am totally opposed to the word *lady,* I rush to assure you that I think it is a perfectly nice word when used correctly. The word *lady* is used correctly only when used as follows:

1. To refer to certain female members of the English aristocracy who have been so designated by Queen Elizabeth or any of her predecessors.

2. In reference to girls who stand behind lingerie counters in department stores, but only when preceeded by the word *sales.*

3. To alert a member of the gentle sex to the fact that she is no longer playing with a full deck. As in, "Lady, what are you—nuts or something?"

4. To differentiate between girls who put out and girls who don't. Girls who put out are tramps. Girls who don't are ladies. This is, however, a rather archaic usage of the word. Should one of you boys happen upon a girl who doesn't put out, do not jump to the conclusion that you have found a lady. What you have probably found is a lesbian.

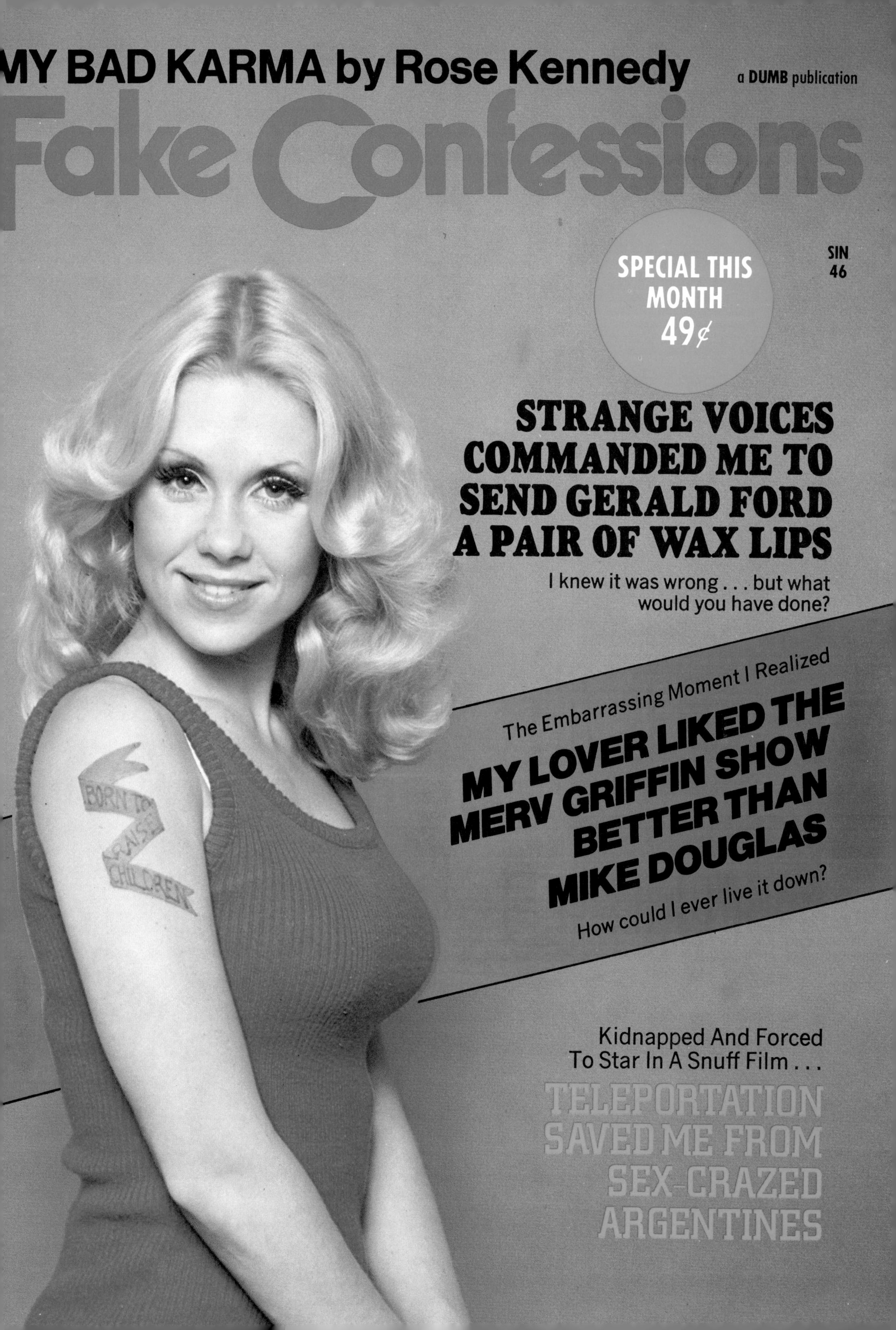
MY BAD KARMA by Rose Kennedy
a DUMB publication
Fake Confessions
SIN 46
SPECIAL THIS MONTH 49¢
STRANGE VOICES COMMANDED ME TO SEND GERALD FORD A PAIR OF WAX LIPS
I knew it was wrong . . . but what would you have done?
The Embarrassing Moment I Realized
MY LOVER LIKED THE MERV GRIFFIN SHOW BETTER THAN MIKE DOUGLAS
How could I ever live it down?
Kidnapped And Forced To Star In A Snuff Film . . .
TELEPORTATION SAVED ME FROM SEX-CRAZED ARGENTINES
BORN TO RAISE CHILDREN

Editors
ANNE BEATTS and
DEANNE STILLMAN

Art Director
JUDY JACKLIN

Staff
**NANCY DUGGAN, MARJORIE GROSS,
MAUREEN LA JOY, ANNA
UPPSTROM, MAUREEN RAEDY,
PENNY STALLINGS, TRACY YOUNG.
DIANA LAGUARDIA**

Fake Confessions

OCTOBER   VOL. 80   NO. 603

IN THIS ISSUE

Cover photo by Lynn Goldsmith

COMING NEXT WEEK

My Marriage was a Nightmare:
MY HUSBAND TREATED ME AS IF I WAS HIS MOTHER

A Candid Account of One Woman's
Brave Battle with Life

GIRLS!

I STARTED GETTING

ALL MY MEAT

REVOLTING NOVELETTE

by Maureen La Joy

"What are those bloody fingerprints doing on the back of your white sweater?" *My husband suspects something* (*and why, oh, why did I wear white?*), I thought frantically. How to explain the prints, when I'd just come from a prime affair at the meat market? My mind began jittering, like hamburger on the griddle, searching for a quick, plausible excuse.

"Oh, those," I began nonchalantly, my brain still working at the speed of hot fat shooting from a sausage, "um, I accidentally backed into an accident victim, who was rushing from his smashed car to the hospital. I happened to be standing on the sidewalk, near the hospital, backing away from an aggressive fly, when we collided. And that's how I happened to get bloody fingerprints on my white sweater." I took a deep breath, waiting, praying for him to believe me.

"Well, I'm certainly glad nothing *weird* happened," my husband, Tom, sighed with relief.

I had gotten away with it this time, but how long could I continue to deceive the man I loved? When and why had it started? Certainly, rising meat prices had no place here, but what other justification had I? I removed a hot dog from the refrigerator, and while I munched on it I began to reminisce.

I'd been overpoweringly attracted from the first to Butch. There's always been something about men in white that signifies "service" to me—and Butch, standing behind the meat display wearing his stained, soggy butcher's apron, clutching a cleaver with bits of meat sticking to it, symbolized the ultimate in service to me. Because I, like most people, am really turned on by meat. Perhaps even more than others, I just don't know. But that first day I watched Butch slapping around a center cut pork chop, I had to have him. And when we spoke for the first time and I noticed the three beautiful stubs for fingers (I've always had a penchant for missing appendages), I was lost.

I can't remember now who initi- (Continued on page 58)

FROM THE BUTCHER

Nothing anyone could say would help me ...
I threw myself down on our king-sized bed
and drenched the pillows with my tears ...
My head ached and my heart pounded
as over and over
I asked myself the searing question ...

WHY WAS I THE LAST TO KNOW

MY SON WAS A PEEPING TOM

It was a beautiful autumn day and the vibrant colors of the leaves reminded me of the crayon-and-construction-paper scribbles Kevin had brought so proudly home from school yesterday. I felt a pang of guilt. Why had I scolded him when his muddy feet tracked up my freshly-washed floor, instead of taking time to appreciate his handiwork?

Today I'd make it up to him, I resolved as I turned away from the kitchen window to check the clock. Two-thirty—just enough time to slide a tray of cookies into and out of the oven before Kevin bounded off the school bus and up the walk.

Just then the phone rang. It was Mr. Saunders, Kevin's grade-school principal. "I don't know how to put this, Mrs. Philips," he said haltingly. "During recess today, your son Kevin was found hiding in the shrubbery beside that sexy Mrs. Dennison's house. Right outside her bathroom window."

Kevin? Sexy? Mrs. Dennison? Bathroom window? My brain was in a whirl. "Wh-wh-what do you mean?" I managed to stammer out.

"We have reason to believe he may be a Peeping Tom," the principal said.

My breath began coming in short, un- *(Continued on page 24)*

...FROM THE BUTCHER
(Continued from page 14)

ated the affair, Butch or I. Perhaps if I'd limited my meat purchases to only one or two a day, we wouldn't have become so terribly embroiled. Thinking back on it, I find it incredible that Tom suspected nothing—with me making separate trips to the meat market for each part of the chicken, buying a quarter pound of hamburger at a time, dashing out at bedtime because "I think our leg of lamb for tomorrow is too short," and endless other expenditures as excuses for seeing Butch. Tom didn't even protest when I had two additional full-capacity freezers brought in. Even though I felt incredibly guilty about it, I couldn't help myself.

Finally, Butch's and my love was consummated. It happened one morning when I came to the store to buy thirty pounds of chipped beef. Butch motioned for me to come behind the counter, indicating that he had some interesting rib-eye steaks he wanted to show me. Before I knew it, we were entangled in each other's limbs. "You have such tender loins," he told me gently as I traced his wishbone. As overcome with emotion as I was, I didn't have the heart to tell him that his rump was a little tough. We spent that night in each other's arms (I left home on the pretense that we needed another strip of bacon and explained to Tom when I came home at 6:30 A.M. that I had to hunt all over town for it). Like an unsuspecting lamb ready for slaughter, he believed me. Butch and I spent countless other nights, afternoons, and mornings together.

If there was any time whatsoever that Tom would have caught on to what I was doing, it should have been when I started demanding that fresh meat be brought into our bedroom before I would make love. Tom was a little hesitant at first, especially about the special cuts soiling our sheets, but he loved me and finally conceded. All along he's done more than the average husband would do—and I can't leave him. Which means if I wish to stop leading this double life, I've got to give up Butch.

I can only hope that I can have the courage to stop deceiving my husband, and I pray that my story can help the millions of people in America who have the same problem.

Who Was That Gentleman I Saw You With?

by Mrs. Lorne Michaels

Thank you, thank you. It's great to be here. It's great to be anywhere. But seriously . . . I'm dying to tell you what happened to me last week. I'm on the road, right? And I'm beat. So I go back to my hotel room, and what do I find but these two absolutely gorgeous guys—so help me, perfect strangers—lying naked in my bed. So I say to them: "Look, you're very lovely, but I'm sorry—I'm a respectable married woman and I can't afford to have my name linked with scandal. One of you will have to go!"

And I just wanna tell ya . . . men! Are they dizzy, girls, or are they dizzy? Take last night. I'm with this sweet young fluffbrain I picked up at the bar. He must've been drinking a Cardtable Cocktail because one sip—and his legs curled up.

Really, I'm just teasing about him. He was a fine, upstanding guy . . . and not bad lying down. He lived south of the border, but I knew he'd come across. I nicknamed him "Television" because he gave the best reception at night. I don't mean to imply he made his living immorally, but you could say he was hard-pressed for cash.

Men. They're all alike. Would I lie to you, ladies? They all think they're God's gift to women. Take my husband . . . please! No kidding. Isn't marriage a great little institution? That is, if you don't mind living in an institution. No, really, marriage gives a woman a new leash on life.

But seriously . . . my friend Tilly is what I call lucky in love—still single! You could say she never made the same mistake once. Tilly says weddings are funerals where you can smell your own flowers. I remember once, Tilly put an ad in the paper for a husband. She got hundreds of replies, all saying the same thing: "You can have mine!"

Husbands! Ya never know what they're gonna get upset about next. Like the time mine came home early and caught me in bed with a midget. Boy, did he fly into a tizzy! So I said to him: "What's wrong, honey, I'm tapering off, aren't I?"

Look, I figure what they don't know can't hurt them. I mean, my husband's a homeloving guy. Whenever I'm away, he's home loving another woman. You know, a few months ago, Tilly took me aside and asked me: "How long have you been wearing those jockey shorts?" So I told her: "Ever since my husband found them in the glove compartment."

And how 'bout those men drivers? Talk about out of control! They drive like they own the sidewalks! My husband loves his car so much he's taken it to England. He wants to see what it's like to drive on the left side of the street . . . legally. So I've only got three weeks to live. Then he gets back in town. . . . And I just wanna tell ya. . . . Anyway, it never worked out between me and the little man. He kept complaining I treated him like dirt. Just because I hid him under the bed. He stuck with me this long only because I had a will of my own. And it was made out in his favor. No hard feelings, though, really he was a great little housekeeper. When we got divorced, he kept the house . . . and won custody of the bank account. One week I was taking in Reno, the next week the washing.

Say—speaking of ex-husbands, I just bumped into one of mine. So I asked him: "Hey, honey, wanna make love just for old time's sake?" So he says: "Over my dead body!" So I say: "Sure, why change anything?" . . . And I just wanna tell ya . . .

Hey, before I have to run, I wanna leave you with this. Ya know what "assault" is—it's what men should be taken with a grain of. Seriously, though, my husband's a beautiful person.

You're all very beautiful and I love you very much. God bless. And good night.

Alice Makes A Few Calls

by Laraine Newman

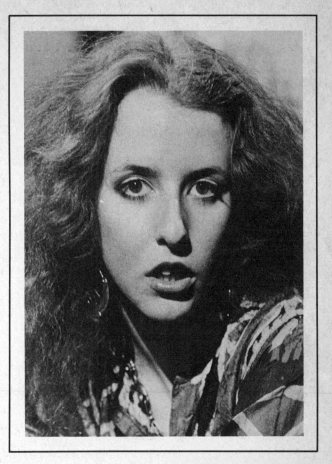

(Alice *enters, looks in mirror.*) Well, I think Ken Russell is jerking himself off.... (*She makes a phone call.*) Hello, Francesca? Woah, it's really weird that you're home because I've been really depressed (*sigh*). ... Well, I haven't spoken in a week and it's so bizarre because I had this dream last night that you were home and you are. Blows me away. I'm so psychic that it's frightening. I saw this weird woman on Hollywood Boulevard who told me I had mystic eyes. She was so strange, I could see her aura when she was picking up trash in the gutter.... No, I wasn't hungry. Anyway, it really upset me because I thought, there but for affluence go I (*takes bite of candy bar*).... I got so depressed that I just sat in my closet with the lights out and stared at the walls.... That's not true, I don't always call you when I'm depressed. You know, it's really weird, but I just accept people for what they are.... What? With Justin? Okay. Well, tell him he'd better give me back my tarot cards. They're not cheap. Okay. Good-bye. (*She makes another phone call.*) Hello, Winona? ... Woah, I'm so blown away.... Well, because no one understands me. ... Well, I just got back from Cafe Figaro.... Yes, with Phil, only I won't be seeing him any more. He's such a toad.... Well, you know that phobia I have about being used as a prop for someone's arm, like I was "the prize"? Well, I started to feel like Phil wasn't really into my head and if he was then he would risk losing me by being honest, so I ate an entire Camembert cheese and I didn't brush my teeth and I spoke really close to him and I told him my satellite theory.... You know, the one where I am the center of my universe and people are relegated to being satellites revolving around me, and he must have thought I was really weird, but he didn't say a word. I was so disgusted I ran out of there without paying my part of the check. I swear to God, I hate men. I'm really becoming a hermit. I think I'm going to fast (*takes another bite of candy bar*). I really want to get him out of my system. You want to hear some of my poetry? It's about going back to the womb....It'll only take a second. "Cloisters." (*Recites.*)

> Penny in the pocket of a camel hair coat
> Sound of your heater hissing and kissing
> The mingling of street noises
> It is left up to me as to whether it is
> A confrontation or a lark.

What? ... Oh, well, no, it's okay. I was just kind of crawling the walls because I realized that I tried to kill myself.... Well, I burned the hell out of my feet and hands. I was cooking artichokes and I took the pot off the stove without a potholder and dropped the pot on my feet. I really think that no one is on my level, like I don't think you know, no, you couldn't possibly know, but being beautiful is really a nightmare and there's no escape. Sometimes I'd just like to take a razor blade and slice my face up. I think I'm a genius.... Winona? ... Hello? (*She hangs up and makes another phone call.*) Hello, Cathy?

Fig Newtons and Gun Control

by Emily Levine

I'd like to do something I've never done before. I'd like to do a snappy opening. Normally, I don't do a snappy opening. I am not a snappy person. I like to think things over.... I'm sure I could be snappy. I could be like everybody else. I could tell a joke. You could laugh. Okay, then, here we go:

A man walks into a restaurant. He says to the waiter, "Hey, waiter, what was that I had yesterday?" And the waiter says, "I don't know, but you got it again!" Or the waiter says something else. Something funny. I don't care. I don't have enough information to care. Before I would make an investment like caring, I would need to know, who is this man? Why isn't he eating at home? What about the waiter? What are his needs? What kind of restaurant is this? Who can afford these prices? What about Chappaquiddick? Why does the man have a limp?

Wait a minute. I made a mistake. I left something out of the joke. Okay. You never saw me before:

Hi. A man with a limp walks into a doctor's office. And he says to the doctor, "Hey, doc, whatsa da matta wid me?" And the doctor says, "Well, you know what you had last week?" And the man says, "Yes." So the doctor says, "Well, you got it again!"

So—you don't like jokes. Oh, good. I have a lot of material that's not funny. See, we'll get along. I knew I

should have just come up and been myself and forget the snappy opening. That's what I intended to do and then, just before I came up, someone in the bar was trying to be helpful, I guess, he said, "Hey, just go up there and be yourself!" And I got confused. I mean, I don't feel as if I have a choice. Who else am I going to be? Lorna Luft? Princess Lee Radziwill? You don't be Princess Lee Radziwill overnight, you know. It takes two days to learn her act.

Sure, I have days when I wish I could be somebody else. I would be Candice Bergen. I would be Jennifer O'Neill. I would be Tatum O'Neal. I'm not proud. I'd be Eugene O'Neill and be depressed all the time. I wouldn't care. I'd be Somebody. Because it is so hard to get to be Somebody all by yourself.

I don't usually whine publicly in this fashion, but something happened today which really set me off. First of all, I went to a funeral. Now, this is something I never do. I never go to funerals. I don't even make friends with people who die. I mean, what's the point? But, anyway, I go and listen to this eulogy. The guy says, "We could go on and on about this man, this husband, this father, this brother, this friend, this lover, this stranger, but why bother? He's dead, he's gone, that's the end of him." Which I felt was unnecessarily abrupt. But he went on to explain that the purpose of the service was not to extol the dead but to console the living...whose time clocks were running out. And suddenly I got very nervous. I realized the awful thing about dying, why people don't like it. See, one day you die. Now, that part's all right. Nobody's going to quibble over that. It's the next day. The next day, through no fault of your own, through nothing you have done, you don't have any more potential! That's it. The curtain comes down and God poses the musical question—was it a hit or a miss?

Now I go home and I'm thinking of all those things I haven't been yet. Compassionate, generous, true to myself. I mean, I have plans to be all this, but right now I'm on a diet. I can't do two things at once.

But as long as you're going to be something you're not, make it really something you're not. I mean, forget all that I'm Okay, You're Okay, He Loves Me, He Loves Me Not stuff. Get down to the real stuff. Like what I would really like to be that I'm not, deep down inside, is I would really like to be not broke. See, I feel that I personally have had all the good times you can have being broke. I have been to the Central Park Zoo. I have been to a block party. I have been to the free Tuesday night dinner at Saint Luke's. It's very good. But not good enough. The next good time I have is going to cost Somebody a million dollars. This is how I feel.

Not that I think money is all there is to life. I would also like Power. Quite frankly, next to using big words in front of a lot of people, there's nothing I like better than telling other people what to do. Don't you ever feel that things would be different if you were in charge? I sometimes think that there is not a problem in the world I personally could not solve with a box of Fig Newtons and a gun.

I just threw that in. I mean, that's not really me. I'm really very nice. Meanness does not come naturally to me. I have to work on it. I'm basically very sweet. As a child, I was just the sweetest thing you ever saw. I used to wish on stars. This is when you could see them. I used to wish that the whole world would be beautiful and everyone in it would love each other and there would be world peace. I was also smart. I figured with a speech like that, if I didn't get my wish, at least I'd be prepared for the Miss America Pageant.

But I have changed a little from the sweet little girl I was. You have to. First off, you have to go to school. That will do it to you. I mean, school was a very negative experience for me. No matter what school I went to, in whatever state, in whatever country, all they had to teach was negative knowledge. It was all things like: "All that glitters is not gold"; "Money doesn't grow on trees"; "Don't throw the baby out with the bathwater"; "You can't have your cake and eat it too and lose weight." The only positive thing they had to say was, "You learn something new every day." But who wants to learn that negative shit?

Of course, it has its effect. As I say, I've changed. When I wish on a star now, I don't wish that the whole world would be beautiful or that there would be world peace. I wish for no root canal work. This is what my dreams have been reduced to.

Usually, around here I sing a little song. Or do something clever, like put my foot to my ear (a genuine gymnastic feat). Whatever I do, it's much easier to find an ending onstage than it is on paper. So I'm stopping here because I'm tired and I don't want to miss tonight's "Creature Feature." Thank you all, and good night.

The Latest, Up-to-the-Minute, Real, Confidential Inside Low-Down on What's Happening (And I Don't Mean Maybe)

Greetings, everyone. . . . Our town the scene of another star-studded wing-ding. . . . Host of glamorous celebs included Raquel Welch, who's giving up her movie career to become an actress . . . and Totie Fields, who just bought a new water bed . . . Lake Tahoe. . . . Also arriving: Howard Cosell, the new Ed Sullivan . . . the only difference between Howard Cosell and Ed Sullivan is that they've buried Ed. . . . All eyes were on Cher Bono Allman, who was dressed in a skimpy outfit made entirely out of the lint from her navel . . . Cher's motto: If you haven't got it, flaunt it! It wasn't difficult to interview Julie Andrews because she's so perfect you don't believe she was born . . . she was torn off at the perforation . . . if the pope ever got married it would be to Julie Andrews. Julie said: "I am so perfect . . . the other day Bella Abzug told me she thought God was a woman and I am so excited because I think it's me . . . I am so perfect I never have to go . . . but when I do go—rosepetals." . . . Florence Henderson says she's the pure type, doesn't have blood flowing in her veins . . . she has Listerine. . . . Good news for music lovers: Mr. and Mrs. Osmond have promised to stop breeding . . . I predict Greta Garbo will come out of seclusion and reveal herself to be just another old person . . . and we asked Charo how she can coochi-coochi being married to an old man like Cugat.

. . . She said, "It's easy. I sneak out the back." . . . And this is Rona Barrett in Hollywood; saying, "If you can't say something nice about a person, I want to be the first to hear it."

Household Hints

by Phyllis Diller

I'm very good at household hints. I'll give you an example. Supposing you are a housewife and you have goofed. Well, let's put it this way—it's 4:30 and you're still in bed. And you know, that's gettin' pretty close to overtime. And when the beast comes home, the beauty better be ready. So here's the way you play that. You put a little O'Cedar wax behind each ear. It makes you smell tired. It works . . . and I've developed something to do with leftover sauerkraut. See, you can only do it in December, though. Silver it and hang it on the tree. It stinks but it's beautiful. You see, I consider this creative home-making when things happen and you take it . . . well, all right, our stove broke down one day—I mean way down —well, to the basement. Well, there was something heavy in it . . . a cupcake. So I tell you what I did. I heated his dinner in the dryer. And I admit it was a mess. But it was hot. So I realized that I would have to treat him rather graciously which was gonna be pretty unnatural— at that time of day. So I read a couple of chapters of *Peyton Place* and a little Norman Vincent Peale. And I even put on a dress . . . over my bluejeans. And when I say I kissed him—he thought he was in the wrong house. Until one of the kids bit him. The way we know they're growing up, the bite marks are higher. So I brought him in the house, I sat him down, I put this food in front of him and right away he starts with the beef—he says, "Okay, what is this stuff on top? You know I hate coconut." I said, "Eat it, it's lint." How did I know he had given up lint for Lent?

Men Dress Me With Their Eyes

by Cassandra Danz

Yes, I am Cassandra Danz. Men dress me with their eyes.

When I went to high school, there were three kinds of girls: there were the gorgeous girls, who got a lot of dates; there were the average girls, who got an average number of dates; and then there were the homely girls, who put out and got the most dates of all. I was none of these. I was the groupie for the chess team. I would run around the room yelling, "Mate, mate!" It didn't do me any good. I didn't go out too much, so I got to watch a lot of old movies on television: 1940s movies, Joan Crawford movies, war movies . . . I would identify with the women in those movies. Criminal women, for example: "You wonder why I did murder? What woman wouldn't do murder, with this!?" (*Pulls back hair to reveal imaginary scar.*)

Or those movies where the heroine goes to see Sherlock Holmes in London:

"Mr. Holmes, Mr. Holmes, you must help me!"

(*With heavy British accent*) "I'm afraid I can't. You see, I'm working on a plan for British Intelligence to use against the Nazis. It's one of the most diabolical tortures ever conceived by the mind of man. See this centrifuge? I place two white mice in the centrifuge, turn it on, watch it spin, put it in reverse, and watch them throw up!"

"Oh, how horrible!"

"Yes, I hate Nazis. And I hate mice, too."

Remember the old Tarzan movies?

Tarzan: *(Tarzan yell)*

Jane: Oh, God, schwartzes!

Tarzan: Hey, mamacita *(rude kissing noises),* que linda, chiquita, etc.

Jane: Who are you?

Tarzan: Me Tarzan.

Jane: Well, you certainly are a natural man, aren't you? I suppose now you'll carry me off into the escarpment, take me against my will, fight lions for me, jump off precipices into lagoons for me, and in general protect and care for me for the rest of my life!

Tarzan: Mmmm. Jane heavy trip. Tarzan want quickie.

I loved the film biographies of singers, usually played by Susan Hayward, in the fifties. They were always about women who fell into degradation, but came back. I call my version *The Lillian Froman Story:*

"I'm Lillian Froman, and this is the story of my life. It hasn't been a pretty one. I started in show business when I was five years old, but time passes quickly. *(Sings "When the red, red robin comes bob-bob-bobbin' along." etc. Turns around three times, each time singing song as if older, to indicate the passage of time.)* Pretty soon I became a star. Thank you. *(Bows)* Thank you very much. It was then that I began to drink. Even my mother noticed."

Mother: *(screaming)* You're a lush! *(Mimes opening a window)* My daughter's a drunk! *(Pleadingly, to Lillian)* Is it me? Is that what's making you drink? Well, I'll leave. *(Mimes packing)* Look, I'm packing my things. *(Mimes opening door)* Look, I'm walking out the door. *(Mimes closing door, muffled voice)* Look, I'm out the door. *(Away from mike, small voice)* Look, I'm in Chicago.

"After my mother left, things went from bad to worse. I began to do cheap tricks to gain the sympathy of the audience. *(Sings "When the red, red robin" again, only this time flapping crutches)* I'd sing on crutches."

"Pretty soon I found myself in a Skid Row bar."

Lillian: Give me a glass of whiskey, Joe.

Joe: Why, say, I remember you! You're a has-been! Weren't you Veronica Lake?

Some of the old movies that you never see on TV, though, are the old Movietone newsreels. Movie buff that I am, I just happened to get hold of some rare footage of Eleanor Roosevelt:

"I'm very happy to be here in Zululand. You know, some of my best friends are Zulus. None of you understand a word of this, do you? Well, since you don't understand an effing word I'm saying, I can tell you the truth. Franklin can walk. He even dances, good as you or I. And as long as I'm letting my hair down, I might as well confess that I'm sexually attracted to your leader, King Oo-ga-la-la. And what the hell, Franklin's ten thousand miles away, probably screwing his secretary. *(Sees camera)* Oh, that damned Movietone News. *(Recovering)* And so, in conclusion, let us work for world peace, an end to poverty, and the beginning of fraternity for all mankind."

Regina Margaret Mulcahy

Characters: Walter Cronkite
Regina Margaret Mulcahy

Walter Cronkite: Walter Cronkite for "Meet the People." Tonight's edition—"The Issues Of The Seventies." Our setting: a random doorstep in Heartland, U.S.A. Our subject: Regina Margaret Mulcahy, Middle American. In our continuing effort to promote truth in broadcasting, the program you are about to see is unedited and uncut. And now, with all America watching, but unknown to her, let's meet Regina Margaret Mulcahy.

Regina Margaret Mulcahy: Who is it? What do you want?

Walter: I'm Walter Cronkite for "Meet the—"

Regina: I can't hear you—look, would you crummy kids shut up in there! Shut that TV off, Margaret Mary, or I'll marinate your mouth for ya.

Walter: Unedited and uncut—

Regina: I'm warning you, Vinny Mulcahy—I'll break your face—this is Mommy talking, sweetheart! Yeah, what do ya want?

Walter: I'm Walter Cronkite for "Meet the—"

Regina: Listen, mister, that's your story. My husband, he don't like me talkin' at the door to strangers.

Walter: Well, I'm not a stranger, Mrs. Mulcahy—

Regina: You could be a mugger or an attacker. It's happened before. You know, men follow me up and down the street all the time.

Walter: Well, Mrs. Mulcahy, I—

Regina: It's a curse—I'm born with it—you know what I mean?

Walter: Yes—uh—

Regina: All week long people have been knockin' at this door—a guy sellin' brushes, that Ding Dong lady pushin' makeup—

Walter: Ding Dong Lady?

Regina: Yeah, ding dong, ding dong. I got an attic full of hormone cream.

Walter: I see, well, Mrs. Mulcahy—

Regina: Yeah, I'll answer questions . . . anything you want—hey, will you shut up in there? Vinny, you're a mean, crummy, rotten, punk kid! You hear me? You're a lousy stinkin' crumbum kid . . . that kid is trouble—you know what I mean? Hey! don't you talk that way to your mother—God will punish you—

Walter: All right, Mrs. Mulcahy—let's—

Regina: Oh, he's got a lot of hate and hostility in him.

Walter: I see, uh—

Regina: I don't know where he gets it . . .

Walter: Right—uh, Mrs. Mulcahy—

Regina: You're not my kid—the gypsies left ya!

Walter: O.K., Mrs. Mulcahy, let me just ask you some of these questions—

Regina: Anything ya want to know, just ask Regina Mulcahy. I'm the leader on my block, you understand?

Walter: Mrs. Mulcahy, how do you feel about sex education?

Regina: Yecch! Bite your tongue—filth, dirt, and garbage!

Walter: I see I've obviously hit a sensitive sp—

Regina: I'm a homemaker and a mother. What are you . . . a Communist?

Walter: No, no, I'm not a Communist—

Regina: Well, you got a moustache. I don't want to hear none of that dirty, filthy, sex junk talk. I think it's embarrassing the way the kids talk today.

Walter: Embarrassing? What do you mean?

Regina: Well, when I was a kid, whatever happened underneath the boardwalk was your own

Middle American by Anne Meara*

business.

Walter: I see, O.K., look, uh—

Regina: Listen, my mother gave me good advice, Walter—

Walter: Really?

Regina: "Regina," she told me, "there's one thing you got to remember to do in this life."

Walter: What was that?

Regina: Always wear clean underwear—

Walter: Uh, I see—

Regina: You never know when you're gonna get hit by a truck!

Walter: Uh, Mrs. Mulcahy, let's move on—

Regina: She was no dumbo. My mother knew the score . . .

Walter: Uh, yes, I understand that—

Regina: Well, I think it's disgusting, teachin' the kids that sex education stuff.

Walter: I see. You feel, then, that sex education is dangerous, Mrs. Mulcahy?

Regina: Dynamite—you're playin' with a hot potato and it can also cause a lot of heartbreak and tragedy. Don't kid yourself . . .

Walter: Uh, well, Mrs. Mulcahy, we seem to be running out of time—

Regina: Well, when does my time come, huh, Walter?

Walter: Uh, I don't know, Mrs. Mulcahy—

Regina: When do I get a chance to have fun out of life—when? When? When does mommy get to freak out, huh, Vinny?!

Walter: Uh—Mrs. Mulcahy—

Regina: I'll give you alienation, Vinny—I'll alienate your teeth from your mouth!

Walter: Uh—Mrs. Mul—

Regina: That crummy kid up there. He don't know the meaning of the word gratitude—you know what I'm talkin' about, Walter?

Walter: Yes, uh—

Regina: Never a thank-you to his mother!

Walter: No thank-you, huh?

Regina: I laid out my life like a dishrag for those kids to walk over—

Walter: I see—

Regina: No gratitude, Vinny! Well, you'll find out when it's too late, Vinny—when I'm dead and buried and in my grave—then you'll cry—but it'll be too late! I'll be dead—I'll show you—ha, ha, I'll be dead—murderer! You're killing your mother (sobbing)!

Walter: You're no good, Vinny! You're no good! You're a rotten kid, no good ki—

Regina: Hey, listen—shut up—who do you think you're talkin' to?

Walter: Gee, I'm sorry, I—

Regina: That's my kid up there—that's my baby boy!

Walter: Sorry, I just got involved—I didn't mean—

Regina: Hey, Vinny, don't listen to this punk. He's not even from our neighborhood.

Walter: Uh, Mrs. Mulcahy, we're running out of time. What are your hopes for the future?

Regina: I got a lot of hope . . . I'm still breathin'!

Walter: No, I mean, what would you like to see happen in the seventies?

Regina: A lot of changes.

Walter: Changes—what do you mean by that?

Regina: First of all, I hope every cockroach in this town commits suicide!

Walter: Yes, thank you. This is Walter Cronkite for—

Regina: I'm not finished! I hope the King family runs out of holidays!

Walter: Thank you, uh, Walter Cronkite for "Meet the People." Be with us—

Regina: I hope Dr. Joyce Brothers has a nervous breakdown!

Walter: Uh, ladies and gentlemen—

Regina: I hope Marcus Welby is sued for malpractice!

Walter: Yes, and join us once again—

Regina: I want what everyone else wants, Walter. I want an all-out attack against cancer, poverty, and hate—I want peace!

Walter: Thank you and good night. . . .

---

*With a little help from Jerry Stiller.

31

Monologue Comedy ^Routine

by Rebecca Reynolds and ~~Richard Belzer~~

Him: Blank.

Her: Knock, knock.

Him: Blank blank?

Her: Katmandu!

Him: Blank blank blank blank blank blank blank!

Her: Why didn't you tell me you'd heard it?

Him: Blank blank blank blank blank blank blank blank blank blank blank?

Her: No, I don't know the difference between a Martian hooker and a peanut butter sandwich.

Him: Blank blank blank blank blank blank blank blank!

Her: Very funny. Last time I heard that one, I fell off my dinosaur!

Him: Blank blank blank blank blank blank blank blank blank blank blank blank?

Her: Okay, I give up. What does your dumb cousin Elma do with her birth control pills?

Him: Blank blank blank blank blank!

Her: She does? Well, that's really dumb!

Him: Blank blank blank blank blank blank blank blank blank blank blank?

Her: All right. Tell me why the old gypsy woman disowned her son, the vampire.

Him: Blank blank blank blank blank blank blank blank blank blank blank!

Her: Oh no, not because he was getting to be a pain in the neck! What else is new?

Him: Blank blank blank blank blank blank blank.

Her: Okay, give me the bad news first.

Him: Blank blank blank blank blank!

Her: Well, what's the good news?

Him: Blank blank blank blank blank blank blank blank blank!

Her: I don't get it.

NB: Rebecca Reynolds, a young woman comic, customarily performs with her partner, a Richard Belzer. However, Mr. Belzer refuses to allow any of his material to be reprinted in *Titters*, and has advised the editors that he would file suit to prevent such an action. Therefore, the following appears with deletions.

Him: Blank, blank!

Her: Who's there?

Him: Blank blank blank blank blank blank blank.

Her: Sri Chinmoy and Bill Dana who?

Him: Blank blank blank blank blank blank blank blank blank!

Her: That's a great one! Okay, now I've got one for you.

Girl Sprout Handbook

Introduction

Do you know about Grace Kelly? She was a simple girl from the east coast of America. As a young woman, she traveled by Greyhound to Hollywood, California. Like all good Girl Sprouts, she knew the meaning of service. And because she was so sincere, she soon became a motion picture star. Later, a real prince married her and she became a princess. Do you know the story of the American divorcee, Wallis Simpson? She tracked and stalked and blazed trails in Anglo-American relations for the Girl Sprouts of today. In 1936, the King of England abdicated his throne for her. And what do you know about Clare Boothe Luce, the first woman ambassador to Italy? She knew the meaning of "Be Prepared," and she never missed an opportunity to better herself.

Each of these famous women could be considered a true Girl Sprout. Each embodied the true spirit of American womanhood. Each, upon reaching puberty, flew up and received her sanitary protection kit and traditional Red Wings Badge. The ideals of Girl Sprouting helped all these women meet and overcome difficult challenges to their advancement. The Girl Sprouting experience can help you, too. There is a place for every girl in the Girl Sprouts of America.

Your Path in Girl Sprouting

Tenderfoot Rank

You may think Tenderfoot is a strange name. It was used in pioneer days. The early women settlers had to hike for many hours before they found a campsite. While their husbands fiddled with the early compasses, the women followed behind carrying all the belongings. Because the women had bought their shoes a size too small, their feet soon ached. Their husbands laughed and called them "tenderfeet."

1. Learn the Girl Sprout Promise.

    On my dower, I will try:

    To do my duty to God and my Daddy,

    To help other people most times of the month,

    To obey the Girl Sprout Laws.

There have always been special promises, pledges, oaths. Scarlett O'Hara Butler took an oath when she founded the Girl Sprouts in Atlanta, Georgia, in 1865. "As God is my witness, I'll never go hungry again," she pledged. Swearing to do something and seeing it through by whatever means are two of the most important things a Girl Sprout can learn.

2. Learn the Girl Sprout Laws.

    A Girl Sprout's honor is to be trusted.

    "Marry you, Bill? . . . Oh, I'd be honored. You know there's nothing I'd rather be than a plumber's wife. . . . But I'm afraid I was pledged at birth . . . to a shipping magnate."

    A Girl Sprout's duty is to be useful and to help others.

    "Oh, I know you can cook your own dinner, Bob . . . but I'd like to, really. . . . Besides, it'll give me something to do . . . while you turn in the term paper I wrote."

    A Girl Sprout is a friend to all and a sister to every other Girl Sprout.

    "I'm so glad you're seeing Sally. She's such a lovely girl. . . . Too bad about the insanity in her family."

    A Girl Sprout is courteous.

    "Don't be silly, Tom. I love giving you a blow job. I'm just one of those people who looks morally and physically repulsed when they're happy . . . I'm just funny that way."

    A Girl Sprout is a friend to animals.

    "Dougie's pet frog? . . . On GRIND in the blender? . . . Your spaghetti tongs missing? . . . It's horrible, Mom, horrible . . . what kind of person would do such a thing?"

    A Girl Sprout obeys orders.

    "Of course you should have your freedom, Mike . . . I agree completely. You go out with whomever you want . . . and I'll go out with your best friend, John."

    A Girl Sprout is thrifty.

    "Let's see . . . you had the tuna and I had the egg salad . . . Yours comes to $1.56¼ cents, with tax."

    A Girl Sprout is clean in thought, word, and deed.

    "But . . . why would anybody want to touch you where you go to the bathroom?"

Proficiency Badges

Adventuring in the Wily Arts

The following badge may be applied toward a wily arts major in the First Class rank: Slyboots.   *Daddy's Girl*

To earn this badge do six of these activities including three that have a star.

   1. Make a study of lap sitting. Find out Daddy's dressing side. Favor that side.

   *2. Know how to do four of the following: wink, giggle, blush, cuddle, fawn, plead, wheedle, whine.

   3. Visit the tie section of a men's clothing store and be able to distinguish the ugliest tie on the rack. Know how to charge it to Daddy and give it to him on his birthday. Make and include a hand-drawn card showing two stick figures, a large man and a small girl, holding hands beneath a round sun with projecting rays. Have the girl saying to the man, "I only love you, Daddy." If you are not near a men's clothing store, look for a tobacconist or pharmacy. Do the same activities, but this time choose a pipe, or after-shave.

   *4. Draw up a list of reasons why Mommy is not really necessary to your family life. Present it to Daddy and discuss with him the possibility of Mommy's going away; you and he living alone; or getting married.

   5. Plan ways to start a game of tickle.

   6. Find out all you can about Mommy's tennis instructor. Share your information with your father through photo-touch-ups, anonymous notes, crank calls.

   *7. Know how to throw up or cry on cue.

   8. Make an inventory of your wardrobe. Using number seven, act out a short scene portraying in words and action two characteristic ends you might seek if you don't get Easter shoes.

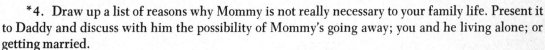

To earn this badge, do all of these activities. This badge will be more interesting if you do the   *Faking*
activities in the order listed.   *Orgasm*

   *1. Practice by candlelight: rhythmic deep breathing, sporadic pelvic movements.

   *2. Select suitable music and beat the time and tempo with your pelvis. Drown out the sound with your breathing. Do it double time. Then triple time.

   *3. Demonstrate the difference between a moan, a sob, a sigh.

   *4. Explore five separate kinds of rouges and know which best simulates a rash on your chest.

   *5. Show your ability to rake your nails down someone's back without drawing blood, but leaving scratches.

   *6. Learn to use your pubococcygeal muscles. Exercise them by picking up fruits, vegetables, your umbrella.

   *7. Explain and use the following terms correctly: *oh yes; oh no; now, now; fuck me; I'm coming; oh God.*

   *8. Learn the words: "I never knew it could be like this." Use them convincingly in a discussion with a friend.

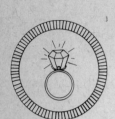

Artifice and Craft

To earn this badge do eight of the activities including three that have a star.

    1. Before working on this badge, list the things you think make a good provider. Discuss your list with your broker after completing the badge to see if there are any changes.

    *2. Learn how to use and care for the following tools: false eyelashes, push-up bra, Erace, blonde wig, violet lenses, lip bleach, Suspants, Supphose, Visine, chin strap, Lady Schick, chap stick, night brace, posture truss, perma-tweezer, Man Tan.

    3. From a list of the main occupations of young men in your community, choose several which seem most lucrative. Find out the names of young men now holding those jobs.

    4. Show you can greet and make friends with another person without use of verbal communication. Demonstrate your ability with: back lighting, a see-through nightie, a bedroom window.

    *5. Explain the importance of: culottes, hand-jobs, petti-pants, curfews, dry humping, your period, hatpins.

    6. Know how a forgotten scarf or a borrowed book can insure a date for drinks.

    7. Show your ability to play well and lose at a sport such as tennis, badminton, ping-pong, bowling, poker, gin, chess. Be able to win at bridge, always.

    8. Learn a sidelong glance or a come-hither look.

    *9. Plan and take part in a debate on the evils of marriage. Making clear your need to be free, discuss the unlikelihood of your ever being satisfied sexually by any one man.

    10. Tell how fifty aspirin or a blunt razor blade could affect your marital status. Give reasons for the use of each. Compare the different types of stomach pumps and how they are used.

Married Life

The following badges from other fields may be applied toward a married life major in the First Class rank: Backseat Driver, Bargain Hunter, Meddling, Henpecker, Group Sex, Social Climber, Tongue Wagger, Other Woman, Change of Life.

Better Half

Before starting this badge, it is suggested that you complete the Daddy's Girl and Artifice and Craft badges.

Do six of these activities including four that have a star.

    *1. Find out all you can about double-indemnity life insurance. Learn what is meant by co-respondent and alimony prison.

    2. Prepare a needling exhibit showing: a country club you don't belong to, a successful man you turned down, a coat you've had since your honeymoon.

    3. Practice spoiling a punch line.

    4. Talk with a person who is buried in a newspaper or glued to a football game. Ask him whatever happened to: the great guy you married, his hair.

    *5. Dramatize going home to mother.

    6. Be able to recognize dishpan hands; housemaid's knee; crowsfeet.

    7. Make a study of daytime drama, coffee klatsches, Mah-Jongg.

    *8. Discover how long it takes Valium 10 to work in your system. Use what you have learned or the words, "I have a headache," to describe two ways in which you would deal with your husband's rights.

    9. Enroll in extension courses at whatever university is nearest your town. Plan and prepare to get a teaching degree or a B.A./masters in Fine Arts. In a discussion with a neighbor, explain how arthritis in your knuckles and your husband's/childrens' jealousy forced you to drop out.

    *10. Collect some good stories that will help other people to know more about your husband's weak spots. Tell them in a public place.

Before starting this badge, it is suggested you complete the Lecturer, Moralist, and Grouch badges. To earn this badge do ten of these activities including eight that have a star.

*1. Know how to harp on three of the following: playing with food, wearing rubbers, drinking milk, feet on the sofa, indoor stoop tag, cleaning a cage.

*2. Demonstrate use of a home telephone. Show that you can: intimidate a younger caller; forget to take a message; listen on an extension.

*3. Be able to overcook a vegetable.

4. Show that you know how, where, and when to read a personal diary, go through a pants pocket, rifle a dresser drawer.

*5. Know four countries where children are starving.

*6. Demonstrate cleaning an ear or giving an enema.

7. Make an exhibit showing six forms of mental retardation caused by masturbating or watching television.

*8. Learn the importance of: piano lessons, military school, brussels sprouts, hand-me-downs, sensible shoes, thank-you notes, Wash 'n' Dries, clean underwear, prunes.

9. Show the correct way to pack a lunchbox. Explain the value of including a lunchmeat, a bruised fruit, something that melts in hot weather. Forget to include a napkin.

10. Dramatize taking a rectal temperature or giving a Tonette.

*11. Investigate the vocations open to women who do not have children, and compile a book of pictures and information on what you gave up to be a mother. Include in your book mention of journalism, show business, firm breasts.

*12. Make up a story showing how a person ruined her life. Illustrate, using three of the following: soiled white gloves, a Negro, a public display of affection, an actor, too much makeup, New York City, bad posture, a pinned hem, sleeping late, a college weekend, shoes without stockings, not learning to type, raising your voice, your own apartment.

To earn this badge do eight of these activities including four that have a star.

*1. Know the first aid treatment for skinned knees, banged shins, broken toes, nosebleeds.

2. Hold a discussion with an inanimate object such as a library stairs, standing ashtray, wing chair. Apprise it of your ability to hold your liquor. Read it the riot act. Encourage it to put up its dukes.

3. Plan to spend an afternoon rewiring a lamp. At the end of the day explain (a) why the lightbulb is in the freezer, (b) when the fuse blew, (c) how the lampshade became your hat.

4. Tell how expensive perfume can serve as emergency mouthwash.

*5. Explore the effects of: sherry, Champale, Gallo burgundy.

6. Record your voice on a tape recorder. Practice slurring your speech or slowing it down to a tedious drawl. See how deep you can make your voice. Can you make it as deep as: a truck driver's, a construction worker's, Ethel Merman's?

7. Explain how each of the following is essential to your family's nutrition: T.V. dinners, Chinese food, Chicken Delight.

8. Plan a trip to your local liquor store. Before going, arrange to: misbutton your blouse, pack your daughter's piggy bank, back the car out over the dog.

*9. Prepare and demonstrate the use and care of an ice bag.

*10. Know the definition of an alcoholic. Know you're not one. Dramatize telling your family and friends you can stop drinking any time you want. Dramatize trying. Dramatize failing.

Words by
Mimi Kennedy

(I'M) HAVING YOUR BABY

Slow (with a double time feel)

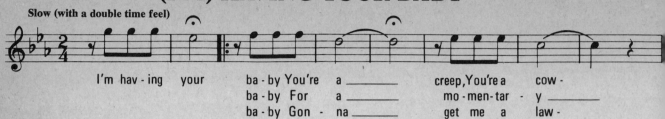

I'm hav - ing your ba - by You're a _____ creep, You're a cow -
ba - by For a _____ mo - men - tar - y
ba - by Gon - na _____ get me a law -

ard, and I wish _____ I'd nev - er known _____ you I'm hav - ing _____ your ba - by And
thrill threw a - way _____ my rep - u - ta tion Yes, I'm hav - ing _____ your ba - by Been
yer and let the _____ whole world know it That I'm hav - ing _____ your ba - by You

look - ing back now, I wish _____ I'd on - ly blown _____ you, Oh, gee
three months now since my _____ last o - vu - la - tion Let me
reap what you sow and you're _____ the one who sowed _____ it, Oh, gee

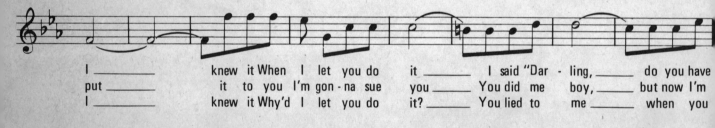

I _____ knew it When I let you do it _____ I said "Dar - ling, _____ do you have
put _____ it to you I'm gon - na sue you _____ You did me boy, _____ but now I'm
I _____ knew it Why'd I let you do it? _____ You lied to me _____ when you

it _____ on?" but you _____ said, "Screw it!" _____ So I'm hav - ing your
gon - na do you I'm gon - na screw you _____ By hav - ing your
said you with -   drew _ it So I'm _ hav - ing

your ba - by I'm a wom - an in trou - ble but it's no great dis - as - ter I'm hav - ing your ba - by For

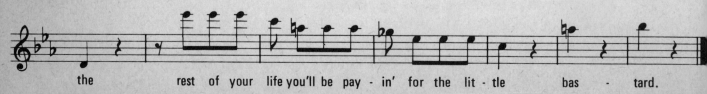

the rest of your life you'll be pay - in' for the lit - tle bas - tard.

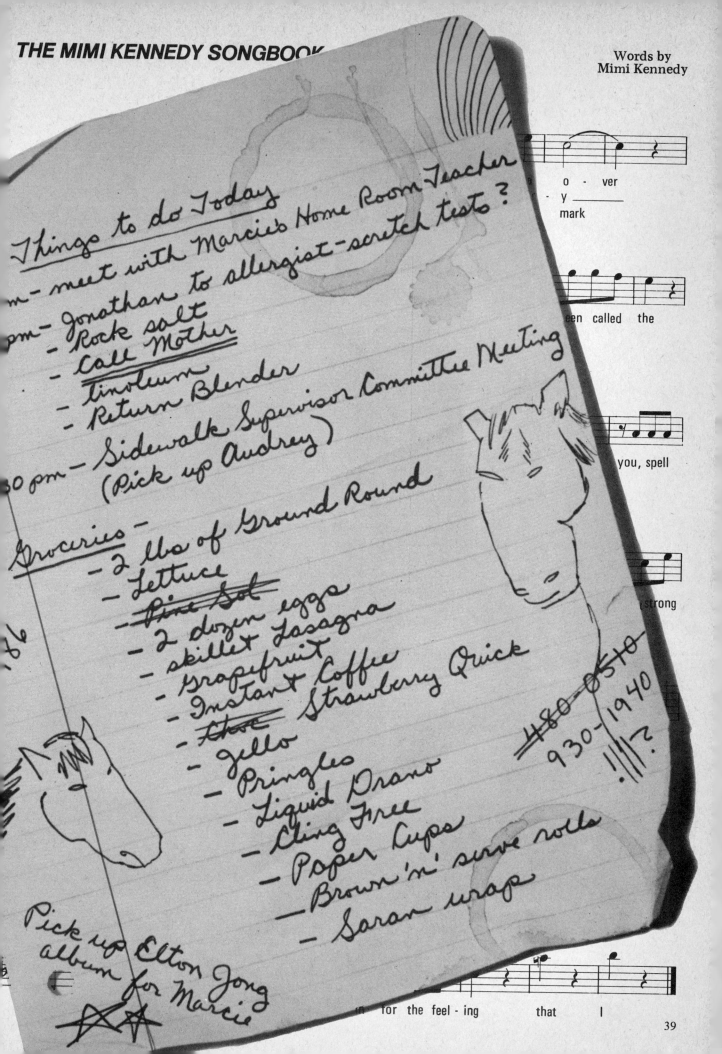

Words by
Mimi Kenned[y]

I AM DOG

Watch me foaming at the mouth,
You can't keep me in the house!
As we form our rabid packs for our revenge
We can tell each other's kind
With one sniff in the behind
And we know now we will never heel again!

Ohhh, yes! I am wise, but it's wisdom born of pain
Yes, I've paid the price with distemper and with mange
This is no craze—here come the dog days
I am strong
I am invincible
I am dog!

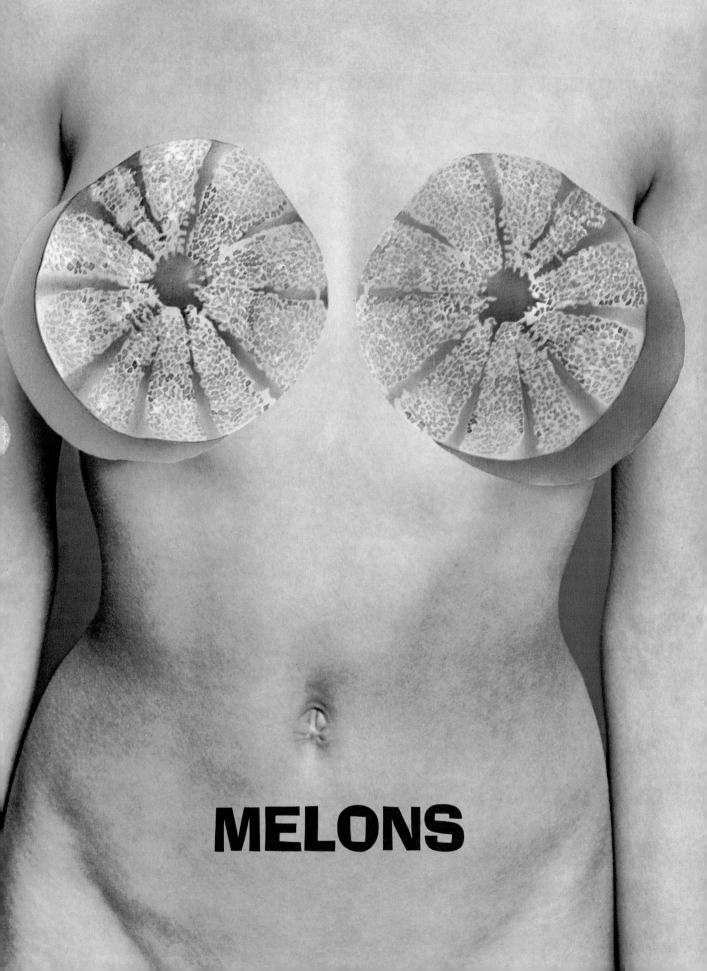

MELONS

Better Dead Than Read

Poetry by Women Poets Who Have Killed Themselves...or Ought to...

by Tracy Young

The surest way of securing a place in the big literary salon in the sky is to bump yourself off. Several of our more prominent women poets were mere cult figures before rigor mortis set in. Thus, the main pre-requisite for becoming a successful woman poet would seem to be a healthy attitude towards mortality vs. immortality—an awareness of the fact that you're nobody till you're dead. After all, God is dead, and look at all the great stuff She wrote!

Trying to Gossip with a Man

by Adrienne Poor

Here at home it's a war zone.
That's why we're armed.

Sometimes your eyes shimmer like napalm
burning their way through my thin skin
forcing me to look away or at least
reach for my aviator shades

How many other diversions we've neglected for this chat:
    Bartok records, underground movies where your mother is
always the star, Zabar's on Saturday afternoon, the language
of divorce agreements, overdrawn checks, weekdays in bed
videotaping our fantasies.

Now I feel like a schmuck
trying to chat with you
like one of the girls
like they told me in my c-r group
where everything is possible.

I try to talk about my new perm,
but your deadened eyes burn with a cool fire
that goes out of control in the
CO_2 of my remarks.

Pals

by Marge Piercing

We sat on a park bench.
he said, take a used razor blade
and cut off your nipples
they bug me.
I said okay.

Birds flew south and leaves fell.
he said, stick your face in my crotch
that way I won't have to see
how ugly you are.
I said okay.

I dig your act, I said.
because you don't hassle me with bullshit.
right, you are, he said,
smart chick.
have you started sucking yet?

Pop

by Sylvia Plotz

Oh Pop, you prick.
How you barnstormed through my life, headless horseman
of authority.
How empty you were, and how cruel.
You broke my toys.
You wanted boys.
Oh Pop, you bastard.
How you tyrannized me from your easy chair.
How frightening you were, and how bald.
Well, tough shit for you, Pop, 'cause Martin Bormann
is in Argentina
and Mommy is in love with me!

Sisterhoodlums

by Robin Gorgon

"The liberation of women," said the wife of an
ex-guerrilla, "is the price of patriarchy."
 I heard that on the TV news, right after a rerun of "As the
Third World Turns"; and got angry all over again.
 Mad! Mad! Mad! Revolution makes me mad!
 Mad enough to go out on the sweltering streets and spray
Feminique in some pig's eye.
 Mad enough to rub two bras together and burn this
city down.
 "A pregnant whale died in childbirth last month." I read
that in *The Feminist Geographic*.
 It was a blind item, buried between a couple of ads.
 Mad! Mad! Mad! Pregnancy makes me mad.
 Mad enough to go out and raze a sperm bank, just like the
sisters in Santa Barbara.
 Mad enough to stop having my period.

On My Daughter's First Menstruation

by Ann Sexless

O, little one, O golden girl.
The other day, when you were at your cello lesson,
I stole into your room—just to take a look.
Your Teddy bear, your rocking chair,
Were all like silent witnesses
When I found the blood-stained panties you'd hidden in a
  drawer.
O, little girl, O golden girl,
You never did want to grow up, did you?
So you passed out of your childhood all alone.
You didn't tell, you didn't smell
You didn't buy some Kotex.
You just pretended the whole thing never happened.
O, little girl, O golden girl,
Another mother would have died of shame
Another daughter would have been so proud.

Rape of the Revolution

by Nappi Giovanni

One fine day
my main man came by and I had on this white muslin gown
and he sits down and says, "The Blacks . . ."
so I take my long turquoise fingernails
and he—not mindin' at all—says "dig this bro . . ."
and I scratches lightly on his wrist as
I slip the gown over my head
and he raps on about "fightin' in the streets . . ."
while I tickle his stomach
he goes on—as he always does—Mr. Street Mouth, big hero—
and I unzip his platform boots
and he says some more "we'll tell them mothuhs . . ."
and I just slip his T-shirt off
pull down his pleated pants
"this situation's a bust . . ." he says
til he notices he's buck naked
and he says
"Nappi—you tryin' to rape the revolution or somethin'? . . ."

Concept by Anne Beatts and Lowena Hymovitch

Ms. print   by Mara McAfee

OK, HENRY...GET OUT YOUR RAZOR BLADE...MESSICK'S DONE IT AGAIN!

YES SIR!

THE DAY BRENDA STARR GOT A BELLY-BUTTON...

WHY DO I HAVE TO DO THIS TO THE WORLD'S MOST BEAUTIFUL PAPER DOLL?

SORRY, BRENDA-BABY, BUT IT'S MY JOB!

I UNDER-STAND, HENRY...

...IT'S JUST THAT I FEEL SO EMBARRASSED...WHEN I HAVE TO WEAR A BIKINI...

BUT AS THE ENGRAVED PLATES ARE ON THEIR WAY TO THE PRESSES... A DIRTY BIRD FLIES IN THE WINDOW...

Roll Me Over,

TIME: 1955

PLACE: A brand-new salmon-and-gray Chevy.

The radio was on and Dean Martin, who was a whole octave above whiskey and rye, was singing "Memories Are Made of This." My pants were hanging on the gear stick, my garters were pulled askew like crossed eyes. I was trying to figure out when my last period had started, and since I can't count unless I use my fingers, I had to stop playing with Joe Simpson's erection.

I was certain that I had gotten the curse the day after I turned in the term paper on the War of Jenkins's Ear, but I couldn't remember when *that* was. All I knew was that I was sitting in the sorority lounge making up footnotes for the quotations I had invented when Kathleen Hanrahan rushed in screaming that somebody would have to drive her to confession right away because she had just French-kissed with Pat Gilhooly and if she happened to die in the middle of the night she'd go to hell.

Which *must* have been Pat's birthday because Kathleen had been wondering what to give him and we had all recommended a real kiss for a change. So my period must have started two days after that.

Joe Simpson rolled over on top of me. "Do you want to?"

I screamed as I felt an unmistakable nudge on my bare stomach. "Don't let any get on me!"

"Let's get in the back!" he panted.

"When is Pat Gilhooly's birthday?"

"What?"

"Because that was two days before my period started and I think it's a bad time because I'm in the middle now and I'm afraid I'll get P.G."

"Don't worry," said Joe, reaching for his wallet. "I've got something."

"Those things break," I protested.

"No, they don't. They're tested. It's scientifically impossible. The law of averages . . ."

"I don't want to. I'm a virgin."

"You don't have anything to worry about, then. A girl can't get P.G. the first time she goes all the way. It's statistically impossible."

"No, I don't want to. I'm afraid."

"You little C.T.! You just like to lead a guy on!"

"That's a G.D. lie!"

"Aw, B.S. You're frigid!"

"I am not, you S.O.B! It's just that I'm not that kind of a girl."

I grabbed my pants, stuffed them in my purse, and retreated with something less than dignity, because my behind stuck to the leather seat and I had to peel it off with a loud scrape like someone removing a mustard plaster. I rushed like a gazelle into the sorority house so that I could pour Lysol on my stomach before it was too late.

When I entered my room I found my roommate, Lillian Ballinger, sobbing hysterically while Jennie MacPherson tried to comfort her.

"What happened?" I asked.

Jennie bit her lip. "It got on her."

Lillian wailed in a higher key, stood up and spread the folds of her voluminous ten-gore skirt.

"Look! How do you get this stuff off? It's like S-N-O-T! I'm P.G., I know it!"

The door burst open, and Pauline Cunningham came in holding a skirt by the tips of her fingers.

"Does anybody have any spot remover? I'm all out."

Lillian bawled still harder and reached into her pocket for a Kleenex, but pulled out her pants instead. She dried her eyes on them.

"He promised he wouldn't let any get on me, and suddenly it was all over the place!" She looked down in astonishment at her pants under her nose and dropped them with a scream.

Jennie opened her purse. "Here's a hankie," she said, except it wasn't. It was her bra. She stared at it, stunned for a moment, then tossed it back in her bag.

"They say if you let it dry you can scrape it off," Pauline said thoughtfully, eyeing her skirt.

Lillian threw herself down on the bed and kicked her feet in impotent fury.

"I'm P.G., I know it! And he promised!"

Every age has its identifying symbol. The twenties are represented by a ticker tape, the thirties by the Blue Eagle, and the forties by a swastika. To most people, the fifties are summed up nicely by Ike's grin, but to me, the perfect logo for my salad days would be a black taffeta halter-neck cocktail dress covered with semen.

I spent most of the decade suspended in such a state of horniness that every time Joe McCarthy screamed "Point

Lay Me Down

by Florence King

of order!" all I could think of was a penis, but unfortunately I couldn't do anything about it because I was living in the heyday of the hymen. You didn't have to be Jewish to be Marjorie Morningstar, the only penetrated hole was the one in Adlai Stevenson's shoe, and anyone who talked about bangs meant Mamie's hair style.

When the fifties opened, the two watchwords that were constantly dinned into us were, "Stay as sweet as you are," which was ideally somewhere between Jeanne Crain and June Allyson, and, "What will you say when you get married?" which our mothers screamed at us as they locked up their Tampax supply after catching us reading the brochure.

The hymen obsessed everyone, though it was never called by its proper name. It was referred to as your *innocence,* your *purity,* your *goodness,* your *maidenhead,* your *mark,* as in *mark of Cain,* and your *shield,* which never failed to make me think about the picture of the dead Spartan soldier in my history book. *Dulce et decorum est* not to get laid. We were told that "men can tell" and warned not to wipe ourselves too hard, which led to untold confusion about the logistics of sexual congress. We were told everything about the hymen except where it is, what it is, and the whimsical fact that the human female shares this pearl beyond price with no other species of living creature except the elephant, the ass, and the pig.

Like Diogenes in search of one honest man, I spent an inordinate amount of time locked in the bathroom searching for my hymen. Though we were not allowed to wear any makeup except a little pink lipstick, at about age thirteen or so, most of us received the gift of a compact to make us feel grown up. These compacts seldom saw reflections of a shiny nose because we were too busy steaming up the mirrors with our genitals during our look-see reconnaissance sessions on the toilet.

With the heraldic tables in *Burke's Peerage* firmly in mind, I probed carefully for my shield, hoping that I had not wiped myself hard enough to produce a bend sinister on what my future husband would expect to find *engoulé gardant.* I searched high and low—literally—but there was nothing sufficiently steely and unequivocal.

I was terrified that I had somehow ruined myself for marriage when I noticed the clitoris. I didn't know it was a clitoris; I referred to it as The Bump, but as I studied

its reflection in my compact, everything became clear. *This* was the famous maidenhead! It had to be; it was the only thing I could find that looked like a little head. I felt much better then, scratched out the first draft of the suicide note that I had inadvertently written on the back of my Latin homework,and called my girl friend to tell her about my discovery. "You know the bump? Well, intercourse," I said, "is when the man presses the bump with his thing and then the bump falls off."

I stuck to my clitoral theory for very good and logical reasons, I thought, because every time I got hot, I noticed a very pleasant, tickly sort of itch in my Bump. This proved beyond a doubt that I was right, after all, and I told my girl friend about it. "Itching," I said, "is when you want a man to do it to you. If the bump is the part that feels good, that must be where it happens," little knowing that twenty years later an organization called Women's Lib would be saying something similar.

Then a movie called *The Great Caruso* came out, and I went into heat with headlong, wanton abandon. One night I started humping the loose spring in my mattress and pretending it was Mario Lanza. I was fifteen, and from that moment on, I harbored a conscious desire for sex, which, in the fifties, was like harboring a conscious desire for the Hope diamond or a true chip off the old rugged cross.

As things turned out, I ended up being deflowered in the doctor's office, where the light finally dawned.

I had been suffering for some time from severe menstrual cramps, and usually fainted once every period. My mother took me to the doctor, who said that in order to make a thorough examination, he would have to "break through." He patted my shoulder, then offered my mother a seat when she started to cry, and told us not to worry because he would give me a certificate of virginity.

"She can show it to her husband when she marries," he explained. "That way, he'll know that he didn't get damaged goods."

I nearly took a flying dive out of his office window because I was certain that my mark of purity was now a mark of the bed spring. When he cut off my bump, he would realize that I had "done something to myself," would refuse to issue a certificate, and then—what? My mother would have a fit, that's what, and my father would get That Look on his face, the same look he always got

when he turned the pages of my baby book, the same look he got the day I started to menstruate. Then, when he recovered, he would do *something;* I wasn't quite sure what, but being sued for restitution of my allowance was one thing that passed through my terrified brain.

The next day I climbed into the stirrups and put my arms over my eyes in resignation while the doctor froze the area and started snipping away. I couldn't imagine what he was doing way down where he was because he was nowhere near The Bump. At last he said, "That's got it," and stuck his finger in me, whereupon I exclaimed, "Oh! Now I get it!"

"How's that, honey?" he muttered.

"Er, nothing."

He patted my foot, shook his head, told me to drink lots of hot tea, use a heating pad, and avoid getting my feet wet. "There's one thing that really cures cramps, and that's having a baby," he informed me, patting my bare foot again. "Now you stay as sweet as you are, honey. Here's your certificate."

It was most impressive except that it started out with "To Whom It May Concern," which sounded ominously like a collective summons to the Seventh Fleet, and it bore a notary's seal, since his nurse was so endowed. When we got home my mother announced that I had a certificate of virginity. By this time, the walls of our living room were covered with my certificates; I had one for every honor society and accelerated course imaginable, and my father had proudly framed them all. As soon as he heard the key word *certificate,* he automatically started poking around in his tool chest for nails and wire until my mother stopped him. My grandmother, who did not believe in intellectual women, snorted and said: "Well, she's got a piece of paper for everything else, she might as well have one for that."

I entered college in 1953 at the age of seventeen. My introduction to campus life was a picnic during orientation week at which the boys sat on one side of the grove and the girls sat on the other while we sang "Roll Me Over, Lay Me Down, and Do It Again," punctuated by salvos of giggles and/or guffaws, depending upon which side of the grove you were on. The only real cruising that took place was intrasexual, as the sorority and fraternity wigs looked over the freshman class.

My sexual frustration would have been unbearable except that, like all fifties co-eds, I visualized automatic marriage at twenty-one along with voting and legal booze. As we all well knew, "men might run around with bad girls, but they don't marry them," so we were willing to wait four years for a lifetime of simultaneous orgasms three times a week, which is what all the manuals promised us. We did not doubt for a moment that the wedding march would follow on the heels of "Pomp and Circumstance," preferably within the same week. This was known as Finding Somebody, and we considered it our birthright. I fantasized myself floating out of the bathroom in a white negligee saying "Here, read this" to a nebulous bridegroom with an ascot around the neck of his silk dressing gown, but meanwhile I wanted all the permissible fun I could get short of Going All the Way.

In high school I had done nothing but kiss, so when I got to college I was determined to find out what "the other things" felt like. In other words, I wanted to do Everything But, sometimes known as Making Out. Our mothers warned us against this practice, saying "A boy will go as far as a girl will let him" and "He's just testing you."

Since we all wanted to be tested as much as possible, we had to draw up unwritten laws for our ostensibly illegal activities, like Mississippi's famous "black market tax" on illegal liquor.

With a talent for partitioning unrivaled since the Congress of Vienna, we divided ourselves into a rigidly classified set of love play areas known as Above the Waist, or Up Top; Below the Waist, or There; and finally that *casus belli* that masqueraded under the *nom de guerre* of Inside Me.

French-kissing was no big deal; everybody did that except Kathleen Hanrahan, who used to kiss Pat Gilhooly through a handkerchief. The first real *pas de deux* that had to be negotiated was Above the Waist/Over the Clothes, or, Beginning Petting.

My first venture into this field occurred with Jack Garrett, who asked me for a date as we bent over the formaldehyde vat in zoology lab fishing out our fetal pigs.

In keeping with the partitioning rules, I had to wait three dates—a total of three weeks—before I got my bust fondled. I couldn't permit even a kiss on the first date; on the second I was able to allow a long but dry buss, and on the third date it was okay to neck in the car, which included French-kissing, and if the girl didn't pull away it was a signal that the boy could Go Further.

It seemed to me that I waited an interminable length of time to get what I wanted. We French-kissed through three verses each of "O Mein Papa," "Hernando's Hideaway," and "The Barefoot Contessa." Since the latter was the theme of a movie about a man who didn't have a penis, I began to wonder if Ava Gardner and I had a penchant for eunuchs.

Finally, I felt the hand creep up, whereupon the strains of "Papa Loves Mambo" were drowned out by the fortissimo crackle of my taffeta bodice. We might as well have shaken hands because I didn't feel a thing. Besides the taffeta dress, I was wearing a bra with circular-stitched cups to achieve that collie-muzzle point so popular in the fifties, plus camisole-style slip.

Jack didn't try to go further, so I gave it up as a bad job and said, "I think I'd better go in now," which meant Stop. The next day in zoo lab, he steadfastly refused to look at me, which wasn't surprising because he dropped his pig and splashed formaldehyde in his eyes.

I tried Above the Waist/Over the Clothes a few more times, taking care to wear something a little more suited to such abandoned intimacy, but even my most wanton bra had lined cups and enough lace to outfit the Pope for Easter Sunday high mass. Obviously, this stage of making out was comparable to something the boys referred to as "washing your feet with your socks on," so I decided to press on to Above the Waist/Under the Clothes, or Intermediate Petting.

According to unofficial sorority ground rules, this practice had to be initiated on a special occasion, a "big date" such as a semiformal frat party. In a mood of cynical premeditation which I chose to call common sense, I wore a strapless bra that I could merely unhook and toss aside. However, since it was a semiformal affair, I had to wear a cocktail dress, and since it was 1954, all my cocktail dresses had halter necklines.

That was the night I almost hung myself. The halter neckline was everyone's nemesis and nearly caused several bizarre mishaps, but I set an unchallenged record for insuperable conundrums by turning into a Chinese puzzle in the front seat of Pete Farrington's car.

Pete had been rubbing my bare back long enough to discover the zipper in my dress. He lowered the tab, and I made ready to slip the yoke over my head, which would have allowed the dress to fall conveniently off the entire top half of me. I had my head halfway through the halter when Pete, overcome with lust, grabbed my bra and, instead of unhooking it, followed my example and yanked it up around my neck in an attempt to pull it over my head. The bra caught me under the chin, mumps fashion, the dress got stuck on my earrings, my hair ended up in my mouth, and I scratched my nose on my sorority pin. Pete tried to remedy matters by twisting the bra to free it, a solution somewhat akin to using the albatross as a tourniquet. I ended up jack-knifed forward, tossing and jerking my head like a horse wearing a martingale.

Pete leaned over and said, "Are you all right?" at which precise and sublime moment, the car door opened and I had the first of my many compromising encounters with Ira the Terrible, the campus warden.

Ira was a retired cop who roamed around looking for cars without any heads in them. His rule of thumb was to bypass any car in which he could see two heads, more or less side by side in the *front* seat. If you slid down below window level, or if he saw you in the back, he would yank open the door, shine his flashlight in and say, needlessly, "What's going on here?"

I felt a blast of cold air, then the car was flooded with light and Ira's gravelly voice started barking out questions.

"What's going on here? What're you kids up to? What in the hell is wrong with *her*?"

"She . . . had an accident," Pete mumbled.

"Sit up, girlie!" Ira ordered, and tapped me on my bare back with his icy flashlight. I gurgled out a yell.

"I can't move!"

"What didya do to her, buddy?"

"I didn't do anything," Pete said in a quavering voice. "She must have pulled a muscle."

"Yeah? A muscle in her *what*? Look here, girlie, you can't stay like that all night. Where do you live? Start that car, buddy, I'm escortin' the two of you back to her dorm."

The next time I wore a cardigan sweater and a strapless bra and successfully negotiated Above the Waist/Under the Clothes. After doing this with a number of different dates and comparing notes with my sorority

sisters, I had reason to believe that the boys had their unofficial ground rules, too. Invariably, when you unveiled yourself they would stare pop-eyed at you and gasp, "God, they're beautiful!" This was a set piece that never varied, as standard a line as Helen Trent's "We can't go on like this."

After the recitativo, they took a flying lunge and grabbed handfuls of flesh with such ferocity that they almost knocked you out of the car. They either didn't know about nipple power or they didn't care; in keeping with the belle idea of the era, their main interest was cleavage, as in Marilyn Monroe, Diana Dors, and Zsa Zsa Gabor. If you didn't have a natural cleavage, they squeezed you together until one formed, then sat there and stared at it.

Getting one's nipples kissed, or as we genteelly put it, "He kissed me up top," resulted in hideous purple and green bruises that we called hickeys. Providing the housemother was out of earshot, we spied on one another and when we caught sight of one, we shrieked, "Ooooh! Shirley's got a hick-eee, Shirley's got a hick-eee," followed by a hysterical salvo of giggles.

Physiology being what it is, the first time I wet-nursed, I met Ira again because Wade Griffiths slid down in the seat the better to reach me with. Suddenly the door burst open and there was Ira with his blinding *flambeau*.

"All right, you kids, straighten up and fly right. Start that motor, buddy, I'm escortin' you back to her dorm."

Below the Waist/There, or intimate fingering, was serious business reserved for a boy you were practically going steady with. It was considered a good way to round off a really special date, such as a formal dance; consequently, you almost got smothered to death because yards and yards of material came flying up in your face. Flounced tulle, linings, underskirts, petticoats, crinolines, and a six-tier steel hoop. When you finally got your pudenda excavated, the next problem was negotiating a garment known as a Merry Widow, or, as we sometimes called it, the Iron Maiden. It was a combination half-cup strapless bra, waist-pincher, girdle, garter belt, and pants, all in one. It was constructed of black lace over black satin over starched canvas and reinforced with fifteen strips of steel. It tended to amputate the wearer at the hip, leave deep red welts, cut off all circulation in the legs, and maintained a constant threat of spontaneous circumcision because it had a detachable crotch piece that rode up the middle of your vulva and girted you within an inch of your life.

However, the crotch piece was very convenient for heavy petting because all one needed to do was unsnap four snaps and *voilà*. After you finished, it fit into an evening bag without any telltale bulges, unlike full-fledged pants. Always, after a big dance, the laundry room in the sorority house sported a wall-to-wall clothesline full of drying crotch pieces.

Some of the boys knew about the clitoris and some did not, but even the most enlightened sports were so used to masturbating themselves in hearty male fashion that they rubbed me raw. One date actually started slapping me with his palm. There was a set script to fingering, too. As soon as he touched it and felt the lubrication he would say, "You're passionate, aren't you?" Of course you didn't dare say yes because that was an extremely dangerous word to toss around in the fifties. Maidenly prudence was served by a shuddery sigh, whereupon the boy gasped and said, "Oh, God!"

Once the game was afoot, you had to concentrate on trying to keep his finger in the right place while you both kept one eye peeled for Ira. To the accompaniment of telltale oleaginous sounds the deathless dialogue was recited:

"Here?"
"Higher!"
"There?"
"Lighter!"
"Like this?"
"Up top!"
"Does that feel good?"
"Lower!"
"More?"
"Higher!"
"Like that?"
"Right there! Oh, right there!"
"Do you like that?"
"Oh, don't stop! Don't stop!"
"I think I hear Ira."

A girl wearing four-inch spike heels and having a climax in the front seat of a car can do a lot of damage. There were an awful lot of broken heaters; Lillian Ballinger stripped the gears once and Jennie MacPherson put her foot through the windshield, but once again I walked away with the honors and straight into campus legend.

It was the night of the spring formal, and Joe Simpson had found the right place for a change. When I climaxed, I jerked as though I had sat on a live wire. My feet flew up and somehow, some way, my heel got caught in the horn rim. The horn blasted away, and as I struggled to free myself, it got stuck. I panicked and twisted my ankle under the steering wheel in an effort to get untangled, and a numbing pain shot up my leg. I yelled bloody murder and buried Joe Simpson under a cascade of flounced tulle, linings, underskirts, petticoats, crinoline, and my six-tier steel hoop. By this time I was practically standing on my head and my legs were splayed out as far as they would stretch. The noise brought Ira out of the bull rushes with his flashlight at charge. He yanked open the door, rammed the torch in and hit me right in the bare crotch.

"What's going on here!"
"The horn's stuck," Joe yelled.
"*I'm* stuck!"

Ira ran to the hood, threw it open, and yanked at the wires. The noise cut off but I was unable to repair my dignity because I was paralyzed. Ira peered in, then quickly turned his back.

"Cover yourself, girlie."

By twisting out of my shoe, rolling over onto my stomach and doing something flappy that vaguely resembled the Australian crawl, I got free.

"All right," I signaled, and Ira turned around.

"Oh, no," he muttered. "It's you again." He stuck his flashlight into his belt and jerked his thumb in the direction of the sorority houses.

"Start that motor, buddy, and follow me."

If nothing untoward happened, fingering always ended with a breathless and somewhat awed male question: "Did I make you happy?" No one ever said *come*. The accepted reply to this peerless euphemism was another peerless euphemism: "Something happened to me." It was also okay to gasp, while you were kicking a hole in the heater or demolishing the dashboard, "It's happening!"

Then it was all over but the shooting—literally. Satisfying the boys was something we did with the utmost reluctance because we were all scared dreckless of sperm. If it got *on* you, anywhere *near* you, you *could* get pregnant, it *had* happened. A sheaf of horror stories made the rounds of the sorority, all about girls who got pregnant in swimming pools because a boy had ejaculated near them, and one chilling tale of woe about the New York water shortage and the girl who, in a spirit of civic responsibility, had used her brother's bath water after him.

As a result, we seldom masturbated the boys. We satisfied them by letting them rub against us. In the frat house we let them get on top of us but in cars it was done side by side, frontal view. To be on the safe side, we always put our pants back on and pulled our skirts down. When the boys started to go stiff and tremble we screamed, "Don't let it get on me!" and pulled away with all the strength we could muster.

The man who ran the dry cleaning shop drove a Cadillac. Sometimes the boys managed to get their flies open on time and finished on the floor, while we plastered ourselves against the door and pulled our feet out of the way. Edith Whitmore was scared silly of even being in the car when it happened, and one night she ran all the way up to the gym.

I masturbated a boy for the first time while sloshed to the gills during our senior year Homecoming dance. This was an almost insurmountable problem in the dressy fifties because I was wearing eighteen-inch white kid gloves that fit like skin. Once you got them on, which took twenty minutes per hand, you couldn't get them off again, but fortunately the manufacturer had had the foresight to include six little pearl buttons on the insides of the wrists so that ladies could drink, smoke, go to the bathroom, and, presumably, masturbate their dates at formal dances.

By this time I was sick of partitioning and divvying up the various portions of myself in the mad ballet of Making Out. I started to feel a little schizy around the edges; it became eerily like the Treaty of Versailles, with one of my breasts awarded to Greece and the other awarded to Turkey, and access to my vagina weighed as if it were a kind of Dardanelles. I got fed up, decided to write thirty to the whole business, and lost my virginity with the aid of two rubbers, three Norforms, coitus interruptus, and a douche.

I didn't get P.G. □

THE SYLVIA PLATH COOKBOOK

by Anne Beatts

"...I spent the rest of Christmas making my first simply beautiful golden-brown turkey with your bread dressing, creamed Brussels sprouts and chestnuts, swedes (like squash, orange), giblet gravy and apple pies with our last and preciously saved own apples. We all three had a fine feast in the midafternoon, with Little Frieda spooning up everything. Then a quiet evening by the fire...."

—Letter to her mother,
from *Letters Home*: Correspondence 1950–1963
by Sylvia Plath, edited by Aurelia Schober Plath

ROAST TURKEY

Clean, stuff, and truss your bird. (Allow 8 cups of stuffing for a 10 lb. turkey.) Place turkey, breast side up, on a rack in an open roasting pan. Rub the skin with soft butter or salad oil. Continue to baste while cooking. Roast at 325 (Regulo 3) until tender. Test for tenderness by moving the drumstick gently. To carve, remove turkey to a warm platter, insert the carving fork across your breastbone, holding it firmly in the left hand, and, taking the carving knife in the right hand, plunge it deep into your breast.

MRS. PLATH'S BREAD DRESSING

4 cups dry bread crumbs	½ cup finely-cut parsley
½ cup melted butter	¾ cup minced onion
½ tsp. salt	½ tsp. ground glass
⅛ tsp. pepper	

Mix lightly with a fork. Add sage or poultry seasoning. Makes 4 cups.

GIBLET GRAVY

If there is a lot of fat in the pan, pour it off into a cup. Pour about 4 tbsp. back into the pan for one cup of gravy. Stir in 2 tbsp. flour. Set the pan over moderate heat and stir to blend flour. Let brown. Add 1 cup cold water, cook, and stir until smooth. Add cooked giblets, cut up. Season to taste with salt, pepper, and chloral hydrate.

CREAMED BRUSSELS SPROUTS AND CHESTNUTS

2 tbsp. butter	½ pint heavy cream
1 tsp. sugar	¼ tsp. nutmeg
½ cup cooked chestnuts	½ tsp. strychnine
1 lb. Brussels sprouts	salt and pepper

Cook butter and sugar together until golden brown. Add chestnuts and brown well. Add Brussels sprouts. Moisten with heavy cream. Add remaining ingredients. Heat and serve.

SWEDES

Wash and pare. Slice and cook in enough boiling water to cover until tender. Drain off the liquid. Mash with butter, salt, pepper, and a small amount of bichloride of mercury.

APPLE PIES

To make crust, cut 1 cup shortening into 3 cups flour. Add 1 tsp. salt and ¼ cup cold water, a little at a time. Stir until dough has achieved correct consistency. Chill. Roll out on floured board.

To make filling, peel and core 6 or 7 apples (about 3 cups). Slice into uncooked pie shell. Add ½ cup sugar, ¼ tsp. salt, ½ tsp. cinnamon, ¼ tsp. nutmeg, and ¼ cup lemon juice. Dot with 1 tbsp. butter. Top with piecrust. Set oven at 450 (Regulo 7). Do not light gas.

Caution: These recipes are satirical and should not be taken seriously, or internally.
Ostreżenie! Te recepty są satyryczne. Nie powinny być wzięte poważnie, lub konsumowane.

PIMENTO

by Deanne Stillman

Old food in the pantry, as it ages, sometimes acquires fungus. When that happens, it is possible, upon removing the lids, to smell in certain vessels the original food: a hint of sardine seeps through the botulism of a half-opened tin, a forgotten fruitcake yields potent memories despite a shroud of bacteria, the pimento jar of our lives, now covered with mold, no longer contains simply "pimento": it contains mold-covered pimento, a reminder of what happened when the pimento was new and what happened as the pimento grew old. I think it is significant to say that examining the original food, refashioned with the embellishments of age, is a way of smelling and then smelling again.

To reach into the jar of my past—that is all I wanted to do in this book. I've smelled what was there yesterday, what is there today, and—if Helen, the housekeeper, does not clear out the pantry soon—what will surely be there forever.

TADPOLE

Dash was dead and I wasn't sleeping well. I used to wake up early in the morning, take walks, rummage around the house, think about my ridiculous and colorful Southern family. It was during one of these early-morning funks that my typewriter fell on my head and knocked me unconscious on the wooden floor that is the floor of my house that I walk on when I'm not else-where. Sometime later—I do not know how much later—I regained consciousness, reached out and embraced the goldfish bowl in front of me, and remembered our mismatched trio and the discussion that took place seven and-a-half hours after the tadpole grew into a frog and died. I had said to Dash, "You are an amphibian, too. You knew what it meant when the tadpole grew into a frog and wanted to go home. You had rapport with the tadpole. Where do I fit in?"

Several days later, Dash said: "How should I know, Lily? I'm just a penny-a-line hack. What do I know about life?"

Those were wonderful years. Royalties from *The Tiny Weasels* enabled me to buy a house on the outskirts of Dingman's Falls, New York, at that time a fashionable

—though not snobby—area. Dash was making money and we fixed up the house and lived off the land. Many people told me that the soil was no good, but, always a fighter, I told them all to go to hell and roast. I hired a fellow German, Heinz Boering, to help in my travails with the land, for I knew that the two of us together could force the land into submission and extract from it many delightful things. Heinz and I raised an impressive colony of heifers, sold them at an embarrassing profit, used the money to plant an orange grove, a grape orchard, apple trees, and a patch of brussel sprouts; sold those and bought wild quail, ate and sold and ate the quail; invented a new azalea hybrid; enriched the lake with fresh-water bivalves; and revolutionized the parakeet industry. But that was before everything went bad and I was no longer welcome in Hollywood and neither was Dash, who went to jail.

My strongest memory of those years (though I'm not clear why) is of my encounter with the tadpole and the way it changed my life. It was near the lake one day with my pet poodle, Salaud, that I heard the first strange gurglings of springtime, peered into the murky liquid, and spotted what looked like an elongated and enlarged spermatozoon bounding along in a remarkably carefree manner. Evidently, Salaud had sensed my curiosity, for he barked loudly and ferociously, and it was quite a while, an hour perhaps (or maybe less) before I could calm him down. But I wanted to know more about this unusual squiggle of life that piqued the wonder of both me and Salaud, so I compulsively—(I have that strong an interest in life)—scooped it up with my bare hands, the kind of thing I always did, still do, often. It left a pungent smell—a trace of which I can still smell now, will smell tomorrow, will surely smell forever—and I placed it in a jar that I quickly filled with water from the lake. I hurried home to show this example of life to Dash, who was quite knowledgeable about such things and would be able to teach me about the aforesaid wondrous movement, now inside the jar.

"What is this, Dash?"

"It's a tadpole, Lily."

"What's a tadpole, Dash?"

"Tadpoles grow into frogs, Lily."

"Then I suppose you'll want to kill it, Dash."

"That's right, Lily. You will learn to like frog's legs, too."

I was against it from the start, but I trusted Dash in matters such as the human food chain. We kept the tadpole inside the jar in which I had originally placed it until it grew too large and then Dash took it out—I refused to participate in the deathwatch—and put it in another jar. He repeated this process several times until some time later (I do not know how much later), the tadpole had indeed become a frog as Dash had said it would and it was time to kill it.

On the table on which the jar rested Dash had carefully placed the tools he would need: a special trowel for the actual killing, several types of paring knives, salt, pepper, the typescript of the murder scene from a forthcoming novel. Helen, who normally did not mind the slaughtering of the food we ate, upchucked as Dash lifted, without remark, the frog out of its jar. It was a large frog, bigger than Dash's fist it seemed, still seems, bigger, actually, than both of his fists put together. He gripped the frog in one hand and attempted to bring down the special trowel on the frog's head, but the frog, sensing what was going to happen to him, expertly wriggled free before the special trowel hit its head. It was apparent that he had bounded off the table and out of the house, for we noticed a faint trail of blood heading down the porch and toward the lake.

"You must have nicked him, Dash," I said.

"What do I know about such things, Lily?" he said.

Salaud picked up the scent immediately and sometime later—I cannot recall how much later—located the injured frog at the edge of the lake and called us to the site with his ferocious bark. The frog twitched several times, rolled over on its back, kicked up its legs (the legs we were to have eaten), and died. Dash agreed that this frog was an unusual frog and did not deserve to be cut up into frog's legs. He headed knowingly back to the house while I remained behind, wondering about humanity. Sometime later—how much later I do not know—I decided to bury the frog. The air was clammy. I dug a suitable grave. I placed the frog in it. I covered it up. I went home and asked Dash what we should have for dinner.

"A side of beef, Lily."

"Roasted or broiled, Dash?"

"Do what you want, Lily."

That was a hell of a way to talk, I thought, and it made, still makes, me angry. I left the house, got in the car, turned on the ignition and drove to the Canadian border. Four days later, perhaps five, I came back with the snuffles.

SILLY BILLY

"Lily, I need money to go kill some Indians down near Belize," said Silly Billy to my Aunt Lily (after whom I was named). Aunt Lily was a complex person who for reasons which have never been entirely clear frequently indulged the flamboyant requests of Silly Billy, who, when he was in town, was her husband. At least it appeared that way for a time. Silly Billy's request seemed odd, still seems odd, because it was issued during a picnic through Worcestershire, Aunt Lily's devoted Negro chauffeur, who sat between her and Silly

Billy and acted, until the end, as the spokesman for both of them to each other.

"You haven't repaid the interest on the last loan," Aunt Lily replied by way of Worcestershire.

"It was too damned high," Silly Billy said.

"You haven't repaid the interest on the loan before that," Aunt Lily said.

"Aw, come on Lily. Give a guy a break. I'll never ask for anything again. Maybe I'll even bring back some—." But the words were muffled because he put his hand over his mouth as he whispered to Worcestershire and Worcestershire followed suit when he relayed Silly Billy's message to Aunt Lily.

How strange, to a child, the secretiveness was. I had admired my Aunt Lily—been enchanted, enamored, by and of her—and loved to wander through her spacious closets and read the labels on clothes especially imported from European ports-of-call. There had been little I did not know about her, I thought at the time, until the incident at the picnic, which was, even to a remarkably perceptive child like me, baffling.

Our slaves—(former slaves, actually, but they stayed with the family for lack of any other sanctuary over the years)—were the only household inhabitants who would know why Silly Billy cupped his hand and whispered when he gave Worcestershire a message for Aunt Lily. I asked them to explain it.

"Them that does what they wants, gets what they wants, in the sweet by and by," said Minnie May Jones with a smile. Minnie May was my maid, and I always took, still take (now that I reassess it), her smile to indicate aggravation at the unworldliness of white people. I pressed her further about the behavior of Silly Billy and Aunt Lily and Worcestershire. Worcestershire, as it happened, was Minnie May's half-brother and therefore likely (though I'm not sure how likely) to confide in her.

"Y'all watch out fo' Silly Billy," Minnie May said. "He up to no good."

"Then why is Aunt Lily married to Silly Billy?" I asked.

"Swing low sweet Cadillac," murmured Minnie May. "May Jesus bless dis chile wif a brain."

As I left the laundry room, I heard Minnie May cackling to herself, a cackle, I later realized (no, I do not know how much later) that was a profound and significant cackle. I think it was when I returned to visit my ludicrous mishmash of a family, possibly, that I found out what kind of a man Silly Billy was (he was, among other things, the source of the illegal "loco weed," as I'm told it is called, that Aunt Lily stored in a sack that dangled between her breasts and consumed whenever there was a full moon), and why Minnie May smiled each time I broached the subject of Silly Billy and Worcestershire.

But by then it was too late, for I was hopelessly in love with Silly Billy. Having just returned from a Central American adventure (surely an ignominious one, but I was blind, as the young often are; God help the immature in their single-minded passions and stubbornly noble refusal and inability to recognize the ugliness of life), Silly Billy entertained us at dinner with tales of wheeling and dealing. These were, alas, the sort of stories that always made, still make, easy prey out of me; Dash knew it, I knew it, and together we had argued drunkenly about it. But sometimes, though I'm not sure how many times, I was—(still am?)—a creature of libido, like any sensitive pre-adult. Later that night (perhaps it was the next night; my memories of those years are so disjointed), Silly Billy yanked my arm crudely, dragged me out to the terrace, and said: "Whad'ya say we go bag some possums, kid?"

I have often wondered why I did not display more ebullience at this request, such as by exclaiming "Holy Toledo" or another similar acknowledgment of joy, for that was without a doubt how I felt: joyful. What I did, before Silly Billy had time to load his rifle and borrow more money from Aunt Lily, was to get into the front seat of the shiny, new car Aunt Lily had recently purchased for him. Then, Silly Billy and I drove to a swamp where he sent up strange signals: smoke signals, whistle signals, and finally signals of shouting and screaming. I thought, wanted to think, that perhaps this was a prelude to some sort of wild passion. I remember smelling something acrid—eucalyptus oil possibly, ochre—I do not know. A Cajun waif in a torn dress stumbled out from behind a cyprus tree. Silly Billy spanked the Cajun for a long time (my guess is three-and-a-half hours, but it might have been more). I ran—trudged, actually: one cannot run through swamp mud—to the car and waited.

"Now I know about murderers and bad men," I said the next day to Dash in Hollywood.

"What makes you think so, Lily?"

That was a hell of a way to talk, I thought, and it made, still makes, me angry. I left the house, got in the car, turned on the ignition and drove to the Canadian border. Four days later, perhaps five, I came back with the flu.

BERTHA

"Dear Southern Relative," the letter said, says now, will say tomorrow (unless it is destroyed), "Bertha will be departing Brooklyn sometime between January 1 and June 31, depending on when the train strike is over. They say it will be over soon, and we hope and pray that it is. Rest assured, dear wealthy relation, that we fully trust your intentions and know that you will provide Bertha with clothing and roughage and other things that we, alack, cannot. How distant Lake Pontchartrain sounds to us (is that where you live, or hunt?); it is as if our daughter were journeying to Khartoum. Yet we hope and pray every night and every day that we will live to flee Brooklyn and meet with you and your family, the blessed and well-fed members of our tree."

The letter was, still is, addressed to Sidney Freeman, my grandfather, who arranged for Bertha to marry Luke Goldberg, a cousin and therefore (though I'm not exactly sure how) a distant relation to me. Luke, I learned through a slip-up in the passing on of the family diaries, was an embarrassment to the family: he gambled frivolously, he wrote bad checks, he was something of a gigolo, and he frequently molested children. By marrying him off to Bertha, a relative, it was hoped that Luke would settle down and cease causing the family to somersault in unison whenever his name was brought up in front of company. But approximately three hours after the marriage, Luke ran off with a shrimp-canning heiress from Johnson's Bayou and Bertha, now a deserted wife, moved in with the two sisters, my absurd great-aunts, Lucretia and Letitia Shapiro.

I met Bertha when I was a child and my first memories of her are, as are all childhood memories, childlike. I remember her as being awfully tall and exotic. It wasn't until much later—though exactly how much later I do not know—that I realized she was neither tall nor exotic and was in fact somewhat squat and ordinary. I think this had something to do with a snapshot of Bertha I discovered accidentally among the mementos of Casselle Finkelstein, my third cousin by an early (and not talked-about) marriage of Aunt Mary Lou Leibowitz to a local ne'er-do-well, apparently.

But such are the vagaries of childhood and I do not regret what I have since realized was a crush that I had on Bertha because it was through my infatuation with her that I learned one of the great lessons of my life. Bertha had a curious habit of disappearing at lunchtime from the home of whichever unusual relation had consented to keep her at the time. Whenever she returned, I called her to my bedroom where I told her about the books I was reading: Proust, Flaubert, Euclid, Baudelaire, Swift—I was an exceptionally bright child and there were few people with whom I could discuss my reading habits. Certainly I could not discuss them with my mother, who at that time read only Rosicrucian tracts (later, there were other religions); nor could I do so with my father, a busy, though smart, man. Bertha, of course, was not genuinely interested in my literary discussions, but I did not know that at the time, and had I known, it would have been of little consequence, for I was quite taken with her and the mysterious, alluring phonetics of her Brooklyn accent. But it was when she started to miss my mid-afternoon literary salon, I think, that I began to wonder with whom Bertha was lunching and imagined the kinds of things that only a child's mind can imagine.

One day I followed Bertha on one of her lunchtime

excursions. She walked through town past rows of robust Creole vendors. I lost her somewhere in the French Quarter. I peeked between the hanging *saucissons*, lifted up half-dead lobsters, searched behind mountains of garlic cloves, but Bertha was not there and therefore her whereabouts became even more appealing to me. I didn't want to do it, but I was irretrievably drawn to a knowledgeable-looking peddler and before I could weigh the consequences, I had uttered: *"Excusez-moi, monsieur. Est-ce que vous connaissez* Bertha?"

He blanched and hurriedly trundled off. I queried another peddler; his pleasant demeanor immediately soured and it wasn't until many peddlers later—although I'm not certain how many peddlers later—that I was given a functional clue.

"Ovair zaire," the peddler said, in the patois of the Franco-American community of the southern states. He pointed toward a nondescript shack.

The sign said, says now, and probably will not say tomorrow, as the area has gone bad and is being torn down, "Johnny-Bob's Bagel Noshery." It was hand-lettered on a crudely-fashioned blackboard slate and was partly obscured by ambitious platters of food stacked haphazardly on the windowsill. My mind took note of the kind of detail other writers have never noticed (or—at least—reported): why was there no shellfish, for example, in this store, when all other stores in Bogalusa were well-stocked with shellfish? It was a cruel answer that I was to learn only with the passing of time.

What seemed like hours passed—but I am sure it was only seconds—before I realized that Bertha was seated at one of the back tables across from a handsome fellow with dark hair and an apron. They held hands tensely. I crouched down beneath the sign's edge between the place where the window stopped—or began, I'm not sure which—and stared longingly at Bertha and her handsome lunchtime beau. After many exchanged glances, they pressed their faces together at an angle enabling their lips to touch (although I could not see their lips, I am certain their lips were touching), and they held this position for some time. Then they drew apart, gazed at each other, and resumed this position at the opposite angle. They maintained this mode of touching for a very long time, an hour perhaps.

I tried explaining what this meant to me years later—I must say, I am not sure exactly how many years later—to Dash over drinks. I tried explaining this, along with the fact that Bertha was in Johnny-Bob's Bagel Noshery every day at lunchtime because she wanted to go home like everyone else and that was why I had just ordered a truckload of Hellmann's mayonnaise.

"I don't get it, Lily," Dash said. "What do I know about life?"

That was a hell of a way to talk, I thought, and it made, still makes, me angry. I left the house, got in the car, turned on the ignition and drove to the Canadian border. Four days later, perhaps five, I came back with pneumonia.

Signals for a Monday Night

by Erma Bombeck

My husband spoke slowly. "You mean you aren't sore because Monday night football is back on television this season?"

"Good heavens, no," I giggled. "I haven't been this excited since we sent our troops into Cambodia."

"Then you are upset," he charged. "You're bitter because you can't watch Conrad Nagel in a Class B movie or count Doris Day's freckles."

"No, really," I countered. "I've learned a lot from football telecasts."

"Did anyone ever tell you you're a pretty good sport?" he grinned. "What's for dinner?"

"Don't be in such a hurry," I said. "First, I have some film clips of last week's meal that I know you'll be anxious to see. There's the pot roast being served, the green beans being lateraled to your son, and the pear and cottage cheese salad that you'll note is a little offside. We were a little raggy in our passing, but now that we know where we've made our mistakes..."

"You're cute," he said, "now how about dinner?"

"I have a few notes here on tonight's dinner and a few spot interviews with the butcher on the corner, our next door neighbor, Doris, who made the cheesecake, and of course we'll hear from the kids on what kind of a performance to expect at the table. We're going into tonight's meal with a few injuries that aren't serious but could affect our meals. Both our ends are stuffed from predinner sodas they had after school, so I may have to take them out at the half. Oh, and here's the dog who is going to tell us how he feels about the menu tonight."

"Are you finished?" snapped my husband.

"I have barely begun. I have the predinner line-up to introduce, an interview from the Claxsons who are scouting us before they have us to dinner next Saturday, and some vital statistics on each member of the family while we warm up with the chip

Reprinted by permission of the Field Newspaper Syndicate from *At Wit's End* by Erma Bombeck. Copyright © Erma Bombeck.

dip."

"Will you serve dinner, please?" he snarled.

"Sure. This is a little casserole I call 'Instant Replay.' We had it Saturday, Sunday, and again on Monday. Here it is in slow motion. Now, stop action. In a minute, I'll give you an aerial view of it. Now, let's put it in play and see how much yardage we can get out of it. Someone might even get it down."

"Okay," he said standing up, "how much longer is this little farce going to continue?"

"Well, I've got a big half-time planned where 384 pitted black olives spell out Bombeck on a playing field of pizza, a recording of the Galloping Gourmet sharing with us his biggest thrills in the kitchen, and a peek into the second half of the meal. Where are you going? You're going to miss the Table Scraps Resumé, Leftover Scoreboard, and Belches from the Stands..."

There's an old Chinese proverb that says, "If you can't beat 'em, play dirty."

MANSION HOUSE

by Kristin Mull

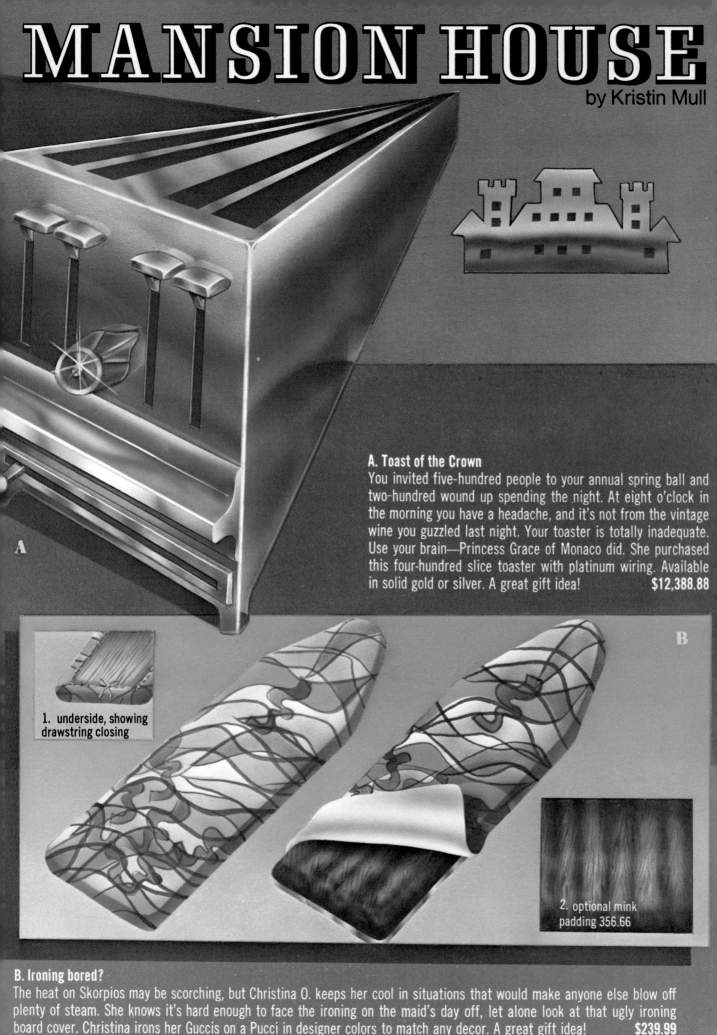

A. Toast of the Crown

You invited five-hundred people to your annual spring ball and two-hundred wound up spending the night. At eight o'clock in the morning you have a headache, and it's not from the vintage wine you guzzled last night. Your toaster is totally inadequate. Use your brain—Princess Grace of Monaco did. She purchased this four-hundred slice toaster with platinum wiring. Available in solid gold or silver. A great gift idea! **$12,388.88**

1. underside, showing drawstring closing

2. optional mink padding 356.66

B. Ironing bored?

The heat on Skorpios may be scorching, but Christina O. keeps her cool in situations that would make anyone else blow off plenty of steam. She knows it's hard enough to face the ironing on the maid's day off, let alone look at that ugly ironing board cover. Christina irons her Guccis on a Pucci in designer colors to match any decor. A great gift idea! **$239.99**

C. Do your shelves need a face lift?
Brighten up your kitchen with the glow of a thousand tiny diamonds, embedded by the yard in this very unique gold foil paper. Tiffany made this roll to suit Zsa Zsa Gabor's pantry measurements, and both were quite pleased with the results. A great gift idea! **$27,548.88 the roll**

C

D. The Glorious Oven Mitt Kit
Gloria Vanderbilt's crafty collage items are known the world over. Now she has finally put her ingenious design abilities to work on an item that is truly functional. Drop that boring needlepoint project and get the Glorious Oven Mitt Kit. It supplies you with everything you will need to create an oven mitt with style. Specify Duchess, Princess, or Queen size. A great gift idea!   **$495.95**

D

**E.
Fit for
a Queen**
If you are worried about your bathroom, this handy item will take a load off your mind and give your Royal Highness a sanitary seat. Made of the finest Russian sable. With tulipwood handle, the Regal Johnny Mop is guaranteed to polish your bowl to a gemlike shine. We know one English matriarch who wouldn't be without one. Found in the most fashionable throne rooms, the Regal Johnny Mop makes a great gift!   **$459.95**

E

F. Eternal Doormat
Happy Rockefeller is aware that the proper welcome is probably the most diplomatic thing you can do for your guests. She recommends investing in a doormat that really means what it says. This one is a fine example, with the word "welcome" hand-chiseled into a rare piece of Italian marble. A great gift idea!   **$899.99**

F

How to Seduce a Feminist

by Mary Reinholz

Any man who thinks it's easy to seduce a feminist is like a soldier crossing a mine field with bare feet. In other words, he's a sucker, vulnerable to an underground explosion that may leave him less than an amputee. Knowing this, proceed to the task with a look of pure fear in your face. Male fear often turns a feminist on, and she may wind up seducing *you*—raping you, in fact. What a way for her to get even with the "enemy"!

By now you have some inkling of the hatred that lurks in the feminist heart. Sex is no mere human activity like eating and farting. It's guerrilla war: hit 'n' run in one area, hide behind the bushes in the other, plant psychic dynamite everywhere. This is serious business and, if you doubt the seriousness of a feminist on the subject of sex, try mentioning *Suck, Wink, Penthouse*, or *Hustler* for laughs. You could get castrated on the spot.

Better not chuckle about a woman welder, either. This, after all, is a true revolution—downtrodden females becoming hard-hats and telephone line operators and clawing their way into middle-management levels—and no revolutionaries that I know of exchange light-hearted banter on the barricades.

And since changing sex roles is at the core of the feminist movement, you must approach seduction of a sister with the sobriety of a reformed alcoholic. No more wine and roses. No more "fun and games" (an early feminist slogan). No more "sweet nothings." The usual bullshit won't do here; you'll have to come up with novel bullshit, keeping in mind that feminists are as varied as the squares in a crazy quilt. A tactic that might cause a Daughter of Bilitis to change her sexual preference might also prompt the Susan Brownmiller brigade to lynch you for rape.

Indeed, there are so many different ideological views within the sisterhood that even the feminist press can't always decide on the appropriate party line. What you have to do is become aware of the basic raps, understand the heads behind them, and then choose a seduction technique that will persuade each feminist that you're no threat to her particular programming. Here, then, are a few sample characters in the movement and a few hints on how to suck them into the sack.

The Amazon

She's a lesbian, over five feet eight inches tall, who shifts between wearing Joan of Arc battle gear and

Joey Epstein

George Sand pantsuits. She might smoke a cigar. To her, men are loathsome and, come the return of matriarchy, they will be relegated to the "shit work"—cooking, cleaning, caring for test tube babies. In short, she's a female chauvinist, and the way to get around her is to show a talent for abasement. Cringe and kiss her ass. Whisper in her ear, "I'm a turd, I'm a lowly turd." If that doesn't work, tell her you're going to get a sex change operation.

The Neo-Romantic

So far, you've been coming on like an emotional cripple, a ninety-pound weakling. Well, bone up on your Charles Atlas manuals for the neo-romantic feminist. She's into muscular blue-collar lovers, macho males who, in her mind, are more "natural" and spontaneous than the overly intellectual, overly-analyzed asshole you've been pretending to be up to now.

This feminist is tired of being a therapist to jittery junior executives who pop six tranquilizers a day. She's had it with Jules Feiffer caricatures who discuss art and how beauty hurts them. She's fed up with Portnoy boys and their problems with domineering Jewish mothers and their guilt over masturbation. She wants a *real man,* a member of the oppressed working class, who works with his hands and lives a life of action and sounds like Humphrey Bogart, calling women "dames," and "broads," and "tomatoes."

So. Dirty up your dungarees. Burn your hair blower. Get rid of your Brut cologne. Take a job as a cabbie or check out that TV ad for truck-driving school or tell her you're a plainclothes cop. Also tell her that you grew up on the Lower East Side and were one hell of a street fighter. When she worries about the muggers following her down the block, be supercool and say: "Baby, if anyone lays a hand on you, I'll break his arms."

Take her to your local greasy spoon and afterwards ask her to serve you beer while you sprawl like a slob in front of your tube. She wants to be ordered around. She's bored being independent all day in her career and wants a masterful man at night.

Don't let on that you read poetry or go to the ballet. She's the sensitive, intelligent one on the team. You're just a body. You're only around to make her feel physical again. Say, "Baby, you've got smarts, but what I really like are your legs. You've got great gams."

The Professional Person

Think of yourself as a neuter and you may make out with the professional person, the feminist to whom all gender designations are taboo. A person is a person is a person, and that goes for "congresspersons," "first basepersons," and the "personhole" in the middle of your street.

Your goal is to convince her that you are a person who sees her as a person and that you want a relationship in which to celebrate your personhood. Look deeply into her eyes and inform her that men are also terribly oppressed by "sexual stereotypes" and the demands that they live up to the "cocksperson image" promulgated by men's magazines.

She's full of sympathy, practically in tears, when you tell her how much you want to cry but can't because of the "masculine mystique." She'll try to get you to break down, to be "human," and at one point you might heave with dry sobs. Tell her sadly, "I'm trying to work all this out in my men's lib group, but what I really need is the understanding of a female person like you. You see, I have a terrible problem."

Naturally, she wants to know what your "terrible problem" is. "I'm so ashamed," you confess. "It's hard for a male person to admit his imperfections in a sexist society that puts so much pressure on him to perform."

She continues to coax you into admitting your "problem," and finally, squeezing her hand, you say, "I'm impotent. Have been for eight months. Help me. Please help me." She just might.

The Cunt Queen

This sister is heavily into sex—heterosex, lesbian sex, vibrator sex. The vibrator is her best friend, so you're competing with advanced technology. She's not very romantic. "Lick my clit," she'll say. "No! One inch higher and to the left. Don't you know anything about the female organs?"

Try to convince her that *you're* no selfish chauvinist pig, strictly interested in your own pleasure. Ask her to draw you a diagram of her cunt. She'll be happy to comply, since she spends most of her waking hours looking at her cunt through a mirror.

Assure her that you're fully aware that there's no such thing as a "vaginal orgasm," that you know this is a Freudian myth designed to keep women in "their place." Rhapsodize about the glories of the clit. Say, "It's so much more sensitive than the cock." Do *not* make sexist remarks like, "That's such a cute little thing you've got there."

Buy cunt sculpture for your apartment and rant on about how complicated and aesthetically pleasing pussy is. "It's like a flower! Beautiful rosy folds! Satiny textures! By contrast, the cock is a crude, simple organ. Too bad the world is dominated by phallic symbols, but one day the cunt will come into its own." You've got it made, brother.

The Success Tripper

Losers need not apply for this job in seduction. The feminist who is a success tripper wants a well-established man who can help her in her writing career. She has used the women's movement to advance her ambitions but will deny it at literary cocktail parties, saying things like, "The sisterhood is a deeply religious movement." Of course, like everyone else in the room, she's looking for a book contract.

Indulge her fantasies. Talk about the "new female sensibility," and how the women's movement has produced a new wave of "bold" women writers, and that she has an "authentic voice." But enough words. You'll really make points if you introduce her to star-makers like Clay Felker.

*   *   *

A few words on the "little niceties"—such courtly gestures as lighting cigarettes, opening doors, picking up the tab. Contrary to popular opinion, there are no hard and fast rules here. Chivalry offends many feminists to

the point of homicide, but others, in their secret souls, would get turned off if you asked them to go dutch on a date.

Their rationale is that men earn more money than women. Thus, your picking up the tab is a way of "making reparations" for centuries of injustice.

Again, there's no way of knowing at first how a feminist stands on these delicate issues. You'll simply have to play it by ear, recognizing the inherent contradictions between liberation rhetoric and the actual needs of the liberationists. It's a lot of fun, their rhetoric, but, as I implied before, he who laughs first may laugh last.

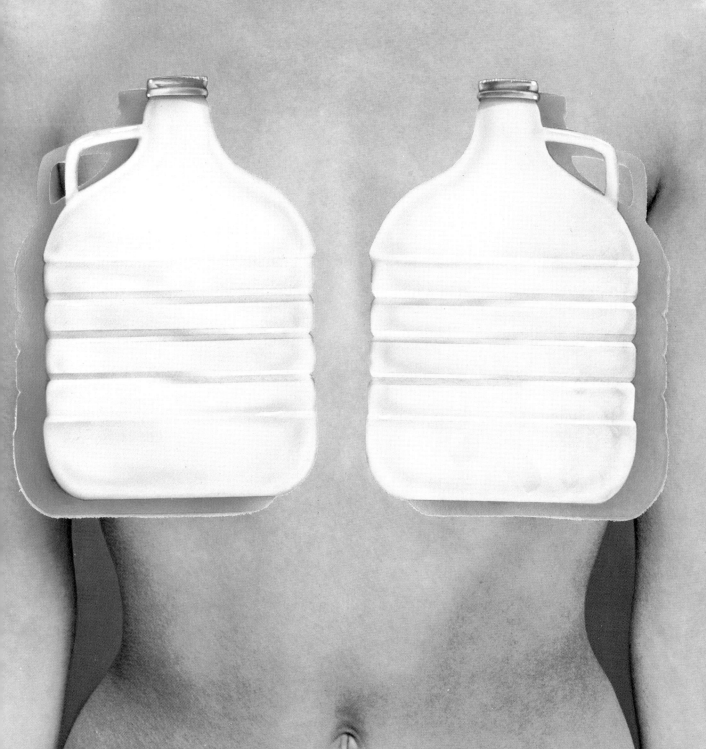

JUGS

Concept by Emily Prager. Art by Rhett Delford Brown.

Nora Ephemeral:
A Few Words About Elbows

I have to begin with a few words about men and women, a subject that's easy to write about because it doesn't take any research. When I was a little girl in Beverly Hills, I knew I was a little girl because my mother, a famous alcoholic screenwriter who once bought herself a mink coat—more about this later—told me I was. I was not yet a woman. And that's when it all started, with this becoming a woman business.

My boyish, lean body, which is still lean and boyish (and I can tell by the way certain men have reacted to me that they seem to find it attractive that way), did not become womanly in the way that my mother had said that it would. For one thing, my period came six months after everyone else's, and my mother, who could be charming when she wanted to, laughed when I told her about it. For another thing, or really two other things, since this is a list that I'm trying to make read rhythmically, my elbows were sharper than everyone else's. "Polish them," said my mother, not understanding. You see, even though we lived in a big house with a swimming pool, an antique telephone in every room, four in help, and a constant flux of witty visitors, I really had a horrible childhood and deserve your sympathy.

You might think that I'm being self-indulgent and that sharp elbows really aren't that much of a problem. All I can say is, you had to be there. My elbows, like my remarks, always seemed to be too pointed. They got in the way in gym class. And there was the time that my best friend Googie (who was perfect in every way) asked me to double-date with her boyfriend's brother.

I tried to hide my elbows under a long-sleeved sweater, which made me look, I thought, like Natalie Wood. But to no avail. Googie's boyfriend's brother spotted my elbows immediately. "Why, your elbows are needle-sharp," he said. Like that. I die when I think about it.

I knew it wasn't right for a girl to have such sharp elbows. Here are some things I did to help:
Covered them with cotton batting.
Always wore long-sleeved tops.
Kept my hands at my sides at all times.
Spoke in a teeny-weeny, itsy-bitsy, mimsy-pimsy voice to divert attention.

As you might have guessed, none of it worked. My elbows were still sharp and I still secretly wanted to use them to get ahead. It is only now, after years of analysis, that I am able to admit this to myself. And I am able to admit it. So why then do I cringe when people accuse me of elbowing my way to the top? I don't know. I cannot help it.

At this point I think I should probably tell you something about my ex-husband. The last time I ran into him was at an orgy where I was a wallflower. He was dressed in his fireman's outfit. We discussed fiction and the fact that I am afraid of writing it, although I am not afraid of publishing my attempts to write it. The man who used to be my husband then remarks that Joan Didion drives faster than I do and that's why she can write fiction and I can't. A few years ago I would have burst into tears, but now that I am my own best friend, I simply jab him in the ribs with my elbow. It is a lovely moment. Later I go home and feel guilty about it. But frankly, I cannot understand all this brouhaha about the difference between fiction and journalism. And why should I? I get plenty of assignments. What's the big idea?

When I met my ex-husband (the first time, not the time at the orgy), I thought I had found a man who would enjoy me for my lean, gangly self and not mind about my elbows. We bought a beach house in not-quite-the-most-fashionable part of the Hamptons and put up a spice chart in the kitchen. We were a hot couple. But when Elaine began holding the table for the "Ephemeral party" and my husband in retaliation referred to me on a national talk show as "the missus," I knew I had gummed it up. Or rather, my elbows had. I was sad and confused.

I began attending a CR group, became interested in the role of women in society, and started seeing a distinguished, silver-haired editor of a well-known men's skin magazine. On top of all of that, I was writing a monthly column on women for another men's magazine. Feminism taught me not to worry about externals like my droopy eye, to accept my elbows and use them to my advantage, and how to stuff a turkey.

I took to feminism naturally, I think, because I have never been one of those women who flirted to get what she wants. Flirting baffles me, in fact. I can't understand people who flirt any more than I can understand people who don't like English toffee ice cream. During the period of my life when a certain publisher was making me a star, I spent a lot of time in Washington but that had nothing to do with my personal life or the fact that I was dating one-half of Woodstein.

Well, never mind. The thing of it is, here I am and here my elbows are. There are times when I find them easy to live with. At other times, less so. I have friends who have blunt elbows and they all assure me that it is much more difficult for them. They say they can never get to the bar. They can't get a seat on a bus. They can't get anything published in *Rolling Stone*. How much nicer it would be, they say, to have razor-sharp elbows that would help you get anything you wanted.

I have agonized over their remarks, tried to stand in their shoes, walked a mile in their moccasins, and here is what I think: I think they are stupid f——kheads. I think that because I work for a magazine that won't print the word fuck.

A Guide to

Why do black people talk the way they do? Some linguists (white) answer, "Because they have thick lips." Black linguists demur: "Say that again, turkey, and I'll go up 'side yo head." But scholarly disputes over pronunciation aside, we can all agree that black language, particularly black slang, often presents problems of vocabulary. Of course, much of black slang passes quickly into the language of the white community,

your imagination what *Diner's Club* means.

bad: Formerly meant good. Now means bad *or* good. Remember, it is *always* used in a deliberately confusing manner when the speaker is among whites. Check with your good black friends before committing yourself.

bleach: Bribe money. For example, with enough bleach a black person starts to look white enough to get a table at "21." Not a *good* one, but at least you can say you were there.

changes: Changes. As in "Don't put him through no changes." That is, don't put him through *any* changes. See any standard English grammar book. Woolley and Scott's will do.

down home: Formerly meant the South. Now means the Manhattan House of Detention (also known as the Tombs) or, by extension, any jail or prison. If someone says, "I just came back from down home down home," he is not stuttering but merely means he was just released from Atlanta Federal Penitentiary.

early: Late.

Fun City: Akron, Ohio. The fleshpots of this notorious black mecca have justly earned it the epithet, "sin capital of the Western world." It is also the rubber capital.

get metroed (from *Metropolitan Life*): To be discovered hiding in the closet just after your kid has told the insurance man you weren't at home.

hap: First it was *hep,* then *hip.*

Watch out for changes of one vowel (sometimes in mid-conversation) in black slang. It is often a subtle put-down of whites who try to be too hup.

in: Out.

James Brown (someone): To grab a person and process his hair against his will. An act of political punishment for those who act too "white." If the person is so reactionary that he already has a process, he is *Goldberged* —that is, held underwater until his hair kinks up again, to remind him of his roots, of where he really comes from.

job hunting: Sleeping or messing up on your job so persistently that you are fired and therefore presumably have to look for employment elsewhere. Before that happens, however, you are entitled to unemployment benefits—the real object of the incorrigible job hunter.

junior jumper: A rapist under sixteen years of age. A rapist over sixteen is not a senior jumper but is probably a misunderstood brother who is being railroaded by a racist, oppressive judicial system with the help of some hysterical, uptight white chick.

Kip (short for *Kipling*): Welfare money. Probably from Rudyard Kipling's line about the "white man's burden." There is a rumor that the term originated in upstate New York, among farmers (in other words, the New York State legislature). Another rumor has it that the term was coined by the late Adam Clayton Powell, bragging.

abbadabba honeymoon: A blind date set up so that two extremely ugly people can meet. Arranging such dates is considered a right-on thing to do.

American Express: A man who suffers from premature ejaculation. Used exclusively as a put-down of white males. Conversely, a *Master Charge* is one who has great staying power— that is, *all* black men. I leave to

Black Slang

through the process known as "ripping off"—e.g., uptight, out of sight, groovy, jive, bread, rap, cool, right on, dig. Other terms are harder for whites to grasp. Therefore, in order to prevent minor social blunders or, knock wood, inconvenient or unexpected trips to the hospital or morgue, I have provided the following glossary of current black slang.

—Fran Ross

LeRoy: Capital of *Rufus,* which see.

Let me fry your eggs: That is, let me scramble your brains, tell you some startling news. This term often leads to confusion at breakfast time.

M.C.P.: Originally stood for "my Cadillac payment." By extension, it is now used for anything that has the highest priority—e.g., my Cadillac payment.

mine: See *yours.*

Negro: Formerly a black person. Now any fair-skinned middle-class white man or woman who has every record the Shirelles ever made.

oblong: Perpendicular.

Owens *(sing. & pl.):* A roach or roaches. Named after Olympic track star Jesse Owens because they're brown and they're quick. Roaches are popular ghetto pets because they take care of themselves. But they take second place to Doberman pinschers, which can be trained to protect you from muggers or help you to be one, depending.

parasol: A black person who is passing for white. Derives from the fact that such people know that the melanin lurking in their genes is ready to seep out at the least provocation—while they are frolicking on the beach, say, or waiting for a bus. Therefore, they carry parasols with them wherever they go, no matter how inappropriate the occasion. Parasols will even carry parasols into a theater that is showing a movie with a lot of daylight scenes or with the word *sun* in

the title (e.g., *Butch Cassidy and the Sundance Kid*).

q: Rescue, barbecue, curlicue, etc. Black people like to drop unnecessary syllables. Let context be your guide.

royal grits: Regular grits with 5 ounces sautéed chitlins and ⅔ cup good red wine added per serving. The wine must cost at least ninety-eight cents a half gallon to be considered good. No Sneaky Pete, please. If you can't make this delicacy at home, you can try it at most fine French restaurants (the New Orleans influence). In New York, ask for *grites royaux* at Lutèce.

Rufus: The name being held in reserve for the first all-black state.

stay: Go.

tough maracas: Depending on voice pitch, either the highest compliment or the grossest insult that can be directed at those of Hispanic descent. A low-register delivery means praise, a high-pitched "reading" can mean a gang fight. Some of the most accomplished insulters are male singers who are adept at falsetto.

up: Down, sideways, or kitty-corner.

V-8: An eight-time loser in the social-disease sweepstakes. One more loss and you self-destruct, or V.O.

wishbone: Money. Loot. Bread. Gelt. The black acknowledgment that wishing won't do it— you have to have money. A piece of dried chicken bone is certainly not going to do any-

Margery Peters

one any good, not at most commercial establishments. Of course, if you were in Haiti . . .

West Indian wampum: A ten-dollar loan for which you only have to put up, as collateral, your right arm and your mother. West Indians have not exactly done the best P.R. job in the world.

xylophone: Cello.

yours: Mine. See *mine.*

Z: A.

The Myth of the Male Orgasm

by Bette-Jane Raphael

Is there such a thing as male orgasm? For decades, scientists have argued about it, written tracts about it, philosophized about it, and, in more recent years, conducted countless studies. But as Dr. Mary Jane Kwell, president of SMOS (the Society for Male Orgasmic Studies), said in her opening statement of the society's ninth annual cookout: "We still don't know."

But do we? Recent findings by Dr. Fern Herpes and her colleague, Dr. Lavinia Shoot, indicate that the mystery is at least on the brink of being unmasked. Working under a grant from NASA, which was disturbed by the cleaning bills for its last Apollo mission, Dr. Herpes and Dr. Shoot conducted a study of 300 middle-class men between the ages of fourteen and twenty-three. Their findings seem to indicate that not only is there a male orgasm, there may actually be two distinct kinds!

While 43 percent of the men in the Herpes/Shoot study were found to have trouble attaining orgasm consistently, or did not attain orgasm at all, and while another 4.5 percent had no opinion, a whopping 50.5 percent (four men fell asleep during their interviews, which accounts for the other two percent) admitted they had two distinctly different kinds of orgasms. After careful questioning, psychological testing, and physical examinations, Dr. Herpes came to the following conclusion (Dr. Shoot came to a different conclusion and left in a huff): there are two types of male orgasm. For purposes of clarification, Dr. Herpes called these the penile orgasm and the spherical orgasm.

Of the two orgasms, Dr. Herpes hypothesizes that the spherical orgasm is the more mature. "Men who are enamored of their penises, who see their penises as the seat of all sexual pleasure, are just a bunch of babies. I hate them. Only the spherically oriented male can be thought of as mature because he can identify with the female to a much greater extent than the penile-oriented male. Thus the former's identification with his balls, which are the closest thing he has to female breasts."

Dr. Shoot, who consented to speak in rebuttal to Dr. Herpes, had this to say: "That woman is crazy. Men don't have two types of orgasm. They just think they do. My own findings reveal that they don't even have one kind of orgasm. Actually, there is no such thing as the male orgasm. What passes for orgasm in the male is really a mild form of St. Vitus's Dance. This afflicts more than 55 percent of the male population in this country, and if Herpes wasn't so hyped on orgasm, she'd admit she's wrong. But as far as she's concerned, *everything* is orgasm!"

It should be noted that Dr. Amelia Angst is in close agreement with Dr. Shoot. She too believes that what passes for male orgasm is actually a disease. But contrary to Dr. Shoot, she believes the affliction is actually a form of epilepsy localized in the groin. She feels she proved this in her much publicized recent study of 100 male rats, 50 of whom had epilepsy. The epileptic rats, Dr. Angst found, could mate with the female rats, even if the female rats didn't want to. The nonepileptic rats just sat around exposing themselves.

Confusing the question of male orgasm even further is Dr. Jennifer Gestalt, who conducted a study of nearly 700 married males in their late twenties and thirties. According to the results of her study, the issue of male orgasmic or nonorgasmic capacity is clouded by the fact that many men simulate orgasm in order to please their partners. Nearly 25 percent of the men in the Gestalt group admitted they had, at some time in their marriage, faked orgasm, either because they were tired, or because they knew their partners would be hurt if they didn't climax, or because they had headaches.

Nearly half the men in the Gestalt study had mild to severe orgasmic difficulties. (It was this group, incidentally, whose psychological profiles appeared in Dr. Gestalt's widely acclaimed paper, "The Prostate, the Penis, and You-oo," wherein it was revealed that all the orgasmically troubled men shared a common fear of their mothers' cuticles, a hatred of Speedwriting ads in subways, and a horror of certain kinds of peaked golf hats.) What has not been revealed until now, however, is that a great many of these men lead perfectly satisfactory sex lives without orgasm, a finding which would seem to put to rest the theory that men must achieve orgasm in order to enjoy sex.

Well, if men can enjoy sex without orgasm, can they also become fathers without achieving climax? Here again the answer is by no means clear. Dr. Herpes and Dr. Shoot, of course, disagree. Dr. Shoot says yes, they can, if they think they can. Dr. Herpes says no, not unless they have either a penile or a spherical orgasm. Dr. Gestalt believes they can fake it.

Lastly there is the question of the multiple orgasm. Do men have them? Unfortunately, here we are still very much in the dark. The only person ever to do research in this area was Dr. Helen Hager-Bamf, in 1971. From January through April of that year, Dr. Hager-Bamf personally tested more than 3,000 randomly-selected men for duration and number of orgasms. Tragically dead at the age of twenty-eight, she never recorded her findings.

So where do we stand? Is there such a thing as male orgasm? Can men enjoy sex without it? Is a low orgasmic capacity psychologically or physiologically induced? To quote Dr. Kwell at her recent press conference, "Who knows?"

SLAMMER

AUG 37

THE REFORM SCHOOL ISSUE

**ANGELA DAVIS
ON BEATING THE RAP**

8
BASIC HAND-GUNS

**EASY-CARE
PRISON HAIRCUTS**

**INSTITUTION-PROOF
YOUR SKIN**

CLOTHES TO APPEAL IN

PLUS:

101 ALIASES!

**YOUR ANTISOCIAL
PERSONALITY:
HOW TO MAKE IT
WORK FOR YOU**

**DIETING
BEHIND BARS**

**SPECIAL QUIZ:
ARE YOU BAD
OR JUST MAD?**

GETTING RID OF
PRE-TRIAL TENSION

"Were you...
Absent the day Mother Nature passed out the jugs?

An interview with Midge Mullins at Guido's Lounge, Canarsie, New York

"I was flat-chested all my life and now I'm busty, and believe me, big tits are everything!"

I was really flat. I was still wearing a training bra on my twenty-third birthday. In high school, they called me "Steve." Whenever I saw a girl who was stacked, I wanted to rip her face off. It wasn't that I wouldn't put out, it's just that I didn't have anything to put out. Let's face it, a real man wants something to hold on to. It's what's up front that counts. And anyway, everyone knows that any fella who doesn't like big tits is queer. My lemons were leading me on a road to nowhere. But then I discovered Paul Paradise, and suddenly my life changed. Within 7 days, I went from a 30AAA to a 44D.

Q. "Midge, do you dress differently with your new figure?"

A. "Well, before, I wore a lot of padded bras, you know, the push-up kind. Sometimes I stuffed them with sweat socks or facial tissues or sanitary napkins. Even that was better than those horrible falsies that floated out of swimsuits and smelled like an old kitchen sponge when I perspired. I guess I was probably the only girl at school who had a turtle-necked swimsuit with matching bolero jacket. But not anymore!"

Q. "Midge, then your new bustline gave a definite boost to your self-image and your confidence?"

A. "It's incredible! I've got a new job now and I just know I'm on the way up. And I've finally gotten a boyfriend, and we're going to be married as soon as he finishes his home study course in air-conditioning installation. I'm thrilled with the many compliments I receive on my new bosom beauty, especially when walking by construction sites. But best of all, with these balloons, I'll never be afraid to go off the high board again."

Q. "Midge, would you recommend the Paul Paradise Method to other girls?"

A. "Oh my, yes! Let's face it, you're just not a real woman without big boobs. And besides, it's cheaper than surgery. I'll always be grateful to Paul Paradise for giving me the kind of big, juicy melons I'd thought only Mother Nature could grow."

Over a million-and-a-half Paul Paradise Bust Developers have been sold. Why is Paul Paradise the world's most successful bustline developer? Because Paul Paradise has been exploiting gullible women like Midge for over twenty years; women who know that a fuller, shapelier bustline is their only chance to transform their hopelessly drab lives into a glittering world of glamour.

The Paul Paradise Bust Developer is not an artificial stimulator, cream, exercise program, suction device, hydraulic press, electric vibrator, corrective undergarment, hormone pill, nutrition pill, pneumatic lift, isotoner suit, or anything like that.

74

by Penny Stallings

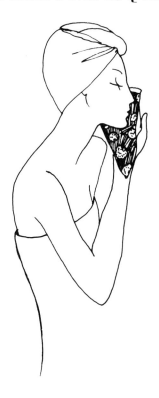
OUR COVER
Covergirl Angela Davis has it all pulled together for fall. Right in step: her new tooth-free smile, achieved during her stay at Riker's Island.

Cover photo retouched by Jay.

DOS & DON'TS

1. Your eyes can be your biggest asset in making on-the-street contacts; DON'T skimp on the mascara.
2. Not enough tummy showing here; DON'T be afraid to bare your midriff.
3. For a smooth, sleek look, DO wear pants that reveal your figure.
4. This skirt should be shorter; DON'T risk losing your man by not showing enough thigh.

1.

2.

3.

4.

5.

5. DON'T ruin your sharpest outfit by the wrong choice of shoes; high heels would be better with these stretch pants.

JONES
A PIMP'S OPINION

A working girl writes in frustration that she has been turning tricks for almost two years, has given every penny to her man, and has gotten little or nothing in return. "This is for the birds," she says. "I certainly never thought I was the most important thing in his life, but last week I had to spend two days in the House of D. because he decided to have the Eldorado's fins resilvered instead of putting up my bond. He doesn't care about me at all—just my money and what he can buy with it. Am I the world's biggest loser or what?"

I think the worst part of the relationship between a man and his girl is that she so often misjudges and misunderstands him, not realizing it is she who is doing the wrong-thinking as a result of a lousy self-image. She doesn't seem to understand that when he accepts money she has earned with her body, he is really accepting a part of herself. When he uses that money to buy lizard hip boots, a platinum dashboard, or a mink-lined carburetor, he is letting her know that she gives him a special happiness he couldn't get any other way.

The guy is saying, "Look. You can't type. You're illiterate. You don't have a skill. You're a useless, stupid whore with bad skin, but I love you and I want you to have the best: foxy clothes, furs, an apartment in a high rise building, an octagonal bathtub, extension phones, a quadraphonic sound system, three or four two-tone Caddys, a successful, well-dressed boyfriend. I want you to have it all—but not at the expense of your self-esteem. I don't want you to be the victim of male exploitation: bought, paid for, and kept like any other empty-headed housewife. I want you to support yourself and me, too." The guy is Mr. Equality, a paragon of liberation, and yet he is accused again and again of being a first-class leech, squeezer, and skunk.

I remember once receiving a letter from a girl who complained that she never had a day off, not even when she had her period. She thought her man was trying to bring her to heel and spell out his displeasure until I reminded her of the Masters and Johnson finding that sexual intercourse during menstruation actually alleviates pressure and cramping. His attempts to do her a favor were meeting her self-fulfilling paranoia head-on.

I think a lot of you girls just feel inadequate. You don't want to face the fact that your boyfriend is one hell of a guy. A guy who's not ashamed or revolted by the knowledge that his woman gives head for a living. A guy who wants you to make something of yourself—and make it big. A guy who doesn't just talk about, but practices, integration. No forced bussing for him. You're his A-number-one Mama, and don't you forget it, no matter how many bruises, cuts, and cigarette burns you have to show for it.

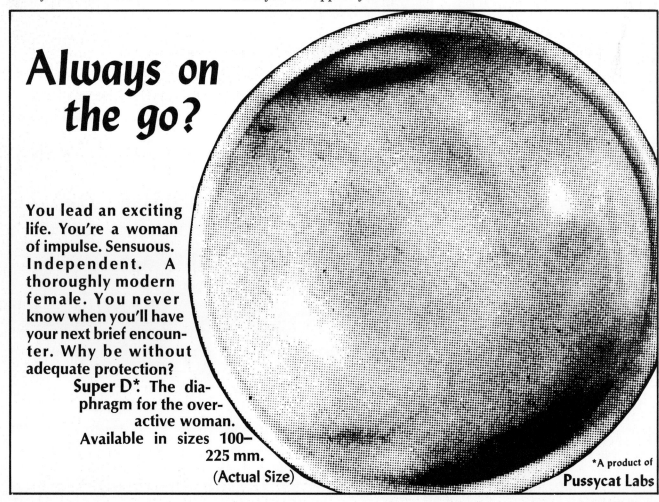

SINISTER SUEDES AND LASCIVIOUS LEATHERS...

Give them a quick buff for nighttime soliciting! Shine them up for daytime shoplifting! Wear them casually for weekend vandalizing! Or, for extra comfort and versatility, don't wear them at all. Whatever the need, a simple wardrobe of cowhide and/or stretch polyester supplies a cool sleekness that just won't quit. From tighter-than-tight hotpants to menacingly-rolled rollers to the drop-dead mini-smock, this year's breakthrough fashion is conveying one important, unmistakable message: bad vibes. Which is why our guest editors were selected. The baddest of the bad, whip-smart and ambitious as all get-out, they provocatively show off what makes the season's new look so unbeatable. Barbarous boots? They're an important element. Strut-yo'-stuff shoes? They're integral. Accessories? Lots of 'em here: gewgaws, scarves, crucifixes, the deceptive sweetness of lace, all pulled together by the simple addition of mix 'n' match weapons. The ABCs of bad vibes are all on these pages. Check 'em out! Make 'em yours! Learn them the way you would your lawyer's phone number or the name of your pimp's favorite aftershave. If you always wanted to have Street Smarts, here's your chance! Take it now....

REFORM SCHOOL '76

REFORM SCHOOL ISSUE

Guest Editors

All graduates of the school of hard knocks, some guest editors are currently serving time, some are on probation, and some have broken loose at long last into the exciting, wide-open world of the big-time hustle. But for one magic week this summer, we brought them to Sin City, where we gave them the run of the *Slammer* offices and let them try their hand at showing our readers how to "get down." And we think they're doing a you've-got-to-hand-it-to-them job of it, right here against the funky backdrop of the Astoria subway platform, top of most guest ed's have-to-visit list.

Coming up: more fashion; the guest editors talk frankly about their pasts, reveal their bold plans for the future, and make you wish you'd set fire to your grandmother at fourteen so you could go to reform school, too.

Maggie Steber

"We came to plunder..."

What working girl would go out without her chubby? Not Evie! She's wearing a "Subway" wig, a clingy shirt by Pre-Shrunk Modes, and a push-up bra by Hot 'n' Sexy Apparel, Inc., along with her suede hotpants. Crucifix and earrings by K-Mart Jewelry Counter. Garter by Hi-Jinx Products. Shoes by Boogie Footwear, Inc. Fun Fur by Acme Hooker Supply.

- evie johnson, soliciting, loitering, and causing a public nuisance
- new york city correctional institution for women, '72, '73, '74, '75, '76

SATISFA ION

Body Rub

Midtown chic: Jayne is up for anything in slip-on (and off!) leather. Handbag by Upper Ganges Import-Export. Slave bracelet by Alexander's Bargain Bin.

- jayne kinne
  lewd and
  lascivious conc
- jewel mana
  treatment cen
  '76

- denise gagliano
  breaking and entering
- buckeye youth center, '7

Denise makes her mark on the worl in tighter-than-tight suede hotpan and matching boots. Hairclips by Lam ston's. Cigarette by Kool. Spray pain by Sears.

- stella biggs, armed robbery
- the lansdale women's reformatory, '78

Stella makes a new friend in her go-anywhere denim outfit by Mean Jeans. Jewelry by Cheap Plastic Doodads. Badge by Gristede's.

Staking a claim on fashion freedor Missy plays it casual in classics. Boo by Far-Out Shit-Kickers. Jeans United Army Surplus. T-shirt Charlie's Girls.

- melissa "missy" mcdougal conspiracy to destroy federal property interstate fli harboring a fugitive,
- frontera, ca for w en, '79

- consuela "rusty" o'rourke, manslaughter

- bedford hills correctional facility, '77

Rusty takes a stand in favor of studs in this snap-it-up suit by Mr. PR. Ribbed knit by Fly Vines, Inc. Little cigar by Nasty Smokes.

- jackie grotowski, assault with a deadly weapon

- new york city correctional institution for women, '76

Jackie goes visiting in sassy leathers, cinched by a lead-trimmed bullet belt (Frank's Sporting Goods).

- teresa novak, petty larceny

- taconic correctional facility, '76

Teresa (left) and Maria (right) pal it up in easy-to-manage hairstyles that show what scarves can do for you this fall. Teresa's sweater by Cuddlewear. Jacket by King Pin Bowling Alley. Belts and earrings by Unlicensed Street Peddlers. Clips and rollers by Lamston's, scarves by Crummy Filipino Scarves.

- maria carmelita rosalia juanita sanchez, forgery

- Agana Lockup (Agana, Puerto Rico), '78

Ease Into Sleaze...

BEFORE

MAKEOVER
From College Girl to Urban Guerrilla (and Back Again!)

In her freshman year of college, Patty came to *Slammer* because she felt it was time for a fashion rethink. She asked us to give her a revolutionary new look—"something different, but not so different it'll stand out in a bank holdup." Here's what we came up with: nothing phony, nothing extreme, just a simple put-together that made the most of Patty's own homegrown American beauty. Proof we succeeded: her new look has taken her through a busy year of hiding from the authorities, giving her parents the "drop-dead" treatment, and becoming an accomplished *carabiniera*, plus a nonstop social life. The next fall, she returned to our clinic for a touch-up consultation. We showed her how to polish up her everyday knock-over-a-sporting-goods-store image, make it shine in the courtroom as well as in the closet.

First, a simple skin buffer sloughs off old skin and leaves Patty revitalized and ready for her new, exciting life.

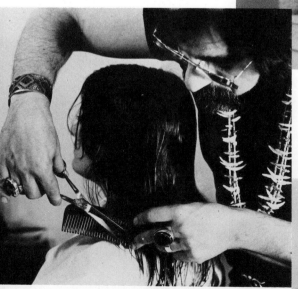

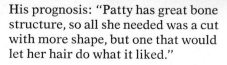

We asked Richard, formerly of Bergdorf Goodman, now co-owner of the Hair Shack, to give Patty an on-the-spot hair-and-scalp analysis.

His prognosis: "Patty has great bone structure, so all she needed was a cut with more shape, but one that would let her hair do what it liked."

"I love being able to wash my hair, run a comb through it, and blow it dry," Patty commented. "It's all part of the free, natural way I live now."

AFTER

For her activity-jammed lifestyle, Patty—or should we say Tania—chose a smoothed-out version of a classic go-every-where paramilitary team: army shirt and jeans, punched up by snazzy weaponry.

It's all there working for her, but nothing is clunky or exaggerated. "Don't clutter your basic look with too many accessories," was the advice of *Slammer* Beauty Editor Monica St. George, little knowing that she would later be named as an accessory herself.

The joy of this look is its versatility. Here, Patty swings into high gear with a dramatic update that accentuates her fragile femininity and simplifies her spontaneous midstream lifestyle switch.

Photography by Edie Baskin

**denise
gagliano**

**Buckeye Youth
Center, '76**

Ever since I dropped out
of high school I've had a
blast, except for being in
the hole. The hole's just
like high school. You gotta
be dumb to stay there.
Trouble with me is, I'm
too smart for my own
good. I wish I could get
over being such a wiseass.
Anyway, one thing's for
sure—I'm never going
back to Cleveland!

**jayne
kinney**

**Jewel Manor Treat-
ment Center, '76**

Ever since I was seven
years old I was always the
baddest chick in town,
only the town used to be
Pineville, Kentucky, and
now it's little old New
York. Some people say I
go looking for trouble, but
wherever I go trouble
seems to find me. Some-
times it seems like life is a
drag, but I say, "Honey,
what else have you got?"

**consuela
"rusty" o'rourke**

**Bedford Hills Cor-
rectional Facility, '77**

Having spent my entire
life in Hell's Kitchen—
that is, when I'm not holed
up at the D.H.—I had to
develop a sense of clothing
so I'd look better than
everybody else and they'd
be jealous of me. Right
now, I spend a lot of time
sewing studs on pieces of
denim and selling them
through the Fortune So-
ciety. When I'm paroled,
I plan to become a fashion
consultant at one of the
department stores where I
feel my talents could be
put to use. If that don't
work out, I might get
pissed off and have to kill
someone.

**teresa
novak**

**Taconic Correc-
tional Facility, '76**

I'm learning how to get
myself together. Although
I'm beginning to dig
myself, I'm still not too
sure about how to act
when applying for jobs
and things like that. My
cellmate—she's a part-
time model—taught me
how to carry myself and
one of the wardens is
teaching me all about cash
registers so that when I
go back to Breezewood,
P.A., I'll have a skill.

**jackie
grotowski**

**New York City Cor-
rectional Institu-
tion for Women, '76**

Me and my old man hot-
wired a Buick and blew
town for the Big Apple.
But he turned out to be a
two-time loser, and when
he fell in the shit some of
it got on me. If I ever get
back to Chicago I'm
going to hang out with a
better class of guy. Maybe
I'll get into Special Ed, so
I can learn to help unfortunate people and stuff.

**maria carmelita
rosalita juanita
sanchez**

**Agana Lockup
(Agana, Puerto
Rico), '78**

Mira! Mira! Hey, look at
me! Just a kid from the
tiny country of Puerto
Rico! And now I have a
magazine career in New
York City! When I finish
serving time for my
offense, I want to settle in
the South Bronx with
some relatives and con-
tinue my magazine career!
I might even take a typing
course!

**stella
biggs**

**The Lanedale
Women's Refor-
matory, '78**

The first time I got sent
up I was only fourteen,
but real well-developed for
my age, you know. Me and
a couple of guys from the
bottling plant broke into
the manager's office and
stole the cashbox. There
was only twelve bucks in
it. Back in Gastonia, my
old sixth grade teacher
used to say, "Stella, you're
no good and you'll never
amount to nothing." I
guess I showed her, huh?

**evie
johnson**

**New York City Cor-
rectional Institu-
tion for Women,
'72, '73, '74, '75, '76**

I like men and I like
money, and most of all I
like men who know what
to do with their money
when it comes to me. But
I don't plan to stay in the
life forever. I like to party
but it can be a pain in the
ass sometimes. What'd I'd
really like to do is get into
porn movies, where I can
really make a name for
myself, like Marilyn Cham-
bers. I was born
in Orlando, Florida.

**melissa
"missy" mcdougal**

**Frontera, California
Institution for
Women, '79**

Nobody realizes exactly
how important the Family
is to American society. I
mean, they were just try-
ing to get rid of the mad
running dog lackey capi-
talist piggies who stole
this country from the
Native Americans. As you
might have gathered, I
come from an upper class
family of swine. It figures
that they'd live in *Grosse
Pointe.*

ON THESE PAGES: All suedes
by Williams' House of Suede;
all leathers by Roberts' House
of Leather; tights by Manu-
facturers' Seconds; make-up
by Cut-Rate Cosmetics; hairstyles by Salon de Beauty and
Moderne Coifs. Perfume:
Thruway Rest Room Vending
Machines. Shoplifting guide
page 123.

The Whole Birth Catalogue

by Irma Kurtz

BIRTHRAP

My name is Cloud. My chick's name is Earth. We aren't writers, man, but I guess you can see that. We aren't writers, like I say, but you don't have to be a writer to give birth. I mean, we've given it, man, I mean we didn't have it taken from us by a bunch of money-grubbing doctors. We *gave* birth, man, you know what I mean? And you can give it, too. Like I say, we aren't writers, so what we're going to try to do here is to tell it to you like it was for us. Like it could be for you. And give you some practical birthtips we picked up on our birthtrip. Because birth is far out, man, and it's a real groove if you give it together. Do the birthdance together, man, TOGETHER. All you real people, just get out there and do your thing, cause that's what birth is, like, it's doing your thing. And you know it. So get out there and do your thing your own way.

OUR BIRTHTRIP

Earth and I live in a teepee we built ourselves. That's where it's at for us. We do everything with our own two hands. Just throw a sheet over a pole, pin it down at four corners, and, man, if you got love, then you got home. A lovingplace. Earth and I have faith. We are both Jews for Buddha and we respect all faiths if they are real faiths. You need faith for your birthtrip. It's really far out.

One hot day Earth tells me her birthtime is coming. Too much, Earth, I say, wow! Now we've gotta find the birthingplace. We're both into Castaneda and we know we've gotta find that one place where our baby's vibes are waiting. So we pack up the VW and head into the desert, looking for those big, big vibes. About ten miles from camp we pick up this hitchhiker and his chick who is called Sunup. He's called Kozmic Bob and he's splitting from a bum rap in Indianapolis. We tell him what we're doing and he flips. He says he's got some medical experience. He's a reincarnation of Hippocrates. Cool.

Five miles further on, this hairy green cactus stands up and vibrates at us. Cloud looks at Earth, Earth looks at Cloud. A flow of peace between us. Far out. This was it, IT, this was Our Cactus. Earth says she's got a cosmic bellyache. Far out, Earth, says Sunup, too much! I lay out some brown rice for Zoroaster and Buddha's oranges like my guru showed me. Then I get Earth to

stop singing long enough for a prayer. Here on our birthingplace, we pray, let us give birth!

Too much, man, says Kozmic Bob, man of ancient lore. We all drop a little acid except Earth who wants to keep her alpha-rhythms together. Kozmic Bob gives Earth a blast of some fine Colombian which I'm not sure is cool because of her hepatitis. But, wow, who can get into a downer like that, man? This is the birth scene, baby, and it's blowing my mind. It blows my mind to see those groovy chicks getting their thing together. Earth is rolling around, singing at the top of her lungs, Sunup is encouraging her. Far out! Sunup says. Too much! Earth says she wants to shit a watermelon. What a gas! Sunup tells her. Beautiful! Kozmic Bob picks up right away. Far out, he says. Wow! Too much! You dig? I get these paranoid flashes, man, just like some square with cigars. Cool down, man, says Kozmic Bob,

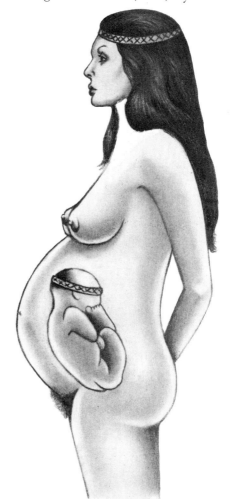

Illustrations by Cathy Hull

all-knowing. Yeah. Right on. Cool. My woman, all-woman, bearing my baby, all-baby, to all-sun. My woman dancing all-dance, birth-dance, all-here, all-now. Christ! says Earth. Right on, mama, I tell her. CHRIST! says Earth really loud, coping with birth-wave. Too much, I say. CHRIST! It's coming again! says Earth. Cool it, Earth, I say. (Too much projection into the future, that's always been Earth's biggest life-problem. We've been working on it together.) Fuck off, Cloud! says Earth. Earth is Aries. I smile. I pray. Bless our birthingplace, I pray. Wow! says Earth. Far out, Sunup says. Too much, Kozmic Bob says, and then he says OM! OM! OM! Right on, I say. In a shower of life is our child born covered with white gunge, now, now, now, NOW! Born with sun in Leo. A few minutes later, plop, out comes the placenta. Sunup cooks it right away and we all eat some except Kozmic Bob who is a vegetarian.

EARTH'S BIRTHPOEM

I was not afraid.
Fear, go away!
Here, close to earth, Earth's mother, mother earth,
there is no fear
And my joyous uterus moves only to an ancient dance.
I was not afraid.
Fear, go away!
Little daughter born on the timeless sands
of timeless time's timelessness.
We call you Saffron because that's what color you are.

FINDING YOUR BIRTHINGPLACE

cathy Hull

Just feel it, man. If you've got faith, you'll know it. A mountaintop is cool if your old lady can get behind

carrying your birthing stuff up there. Your birthingplace could be under a big tree in the middle of a field during a thunderstorm. It could be the drawer of your dresser, man, and it doesn't even have to be lined. But wherever it is, you'll know it, man. It knows you. When you find it, don't move away from it until your baby is born.

WHAT TO TAKE TO THE BIRTHINGPLACE

8 lbs. granola
4 lbs. Celestial Seasoning camomile tea
1 gal. Deer Park Spring Water
2 lbs. brown rice
25 tabs Owsley purple acid
the *I Ching*
yarrow stalks
2 cases of Coors

WHAT TO DO WITH THE PLACENTA

All animals eat their placenta. Some animals eat their babies. Man is here to learn from the animals. Only man is dumb enough to throw away vital sources of protein and good things. Here is our recipe for Placenta Stew:

Toss a handful of brown rice, some sesame seed oil, a handful of unwashed carrots, and a placenta (your own or someone else's) into the largest pot you have. Stew together for three hours, adding water if necessary, and eat hot.

But if stew's not your scene, man, there's a whole bunch of other groovy things you can do with a placenta. You can bury it in your garden and plant a tree over it. You can fertilize your bean sprouts. You can put it on your hair—no shit, man, it makes a really far-out hair conditioner, even better than Dr. Bruner's Peppermint Shampoo.

WHAT TO NAME THE BABY

The Indians say that a name makes a man. It gives him character. So why give your baby a name like Tom or Gail? Give yours a meaningful name, like me and Earth did, so that when the kid gets called on in school, he doesn't have the same name as everybody else. If only everybody would do this, life would be groovier and there wouldn't be any ego trips. Here are some names to choose from:

Free	dog
Sunshine	amerika
Kyoto	china
Sky	vietnam
god	angola

WHAT TO WATCH OUT FOR

Watch out for bad vibes, the pigs, your own parents, and hospitals. The hospital trip is a bummer, man. Forget it. Earth's friend, Pear, had her first baby in a New York hospital because the pigs wouldn't let her stay at her Birthingplace next to Bethesda Fountain. She's written it down like it was:

As soon as we got to the hospital, a gang of interns dragged my old man away. Three nurses gave me an enema, one of them had a gun. A fourth nurse shaved off all my pubic hair and when I asked her why she said, "Shut up, stupid!" They took me in a room and strapped me to a table. The pain was terrible. When I started to scream, somebody came in and put a mask over my face. Everything went black. When I woke up, I had little Kohoutek. I've always hated him.

BIRTHFRIENDS

Birth is one of the most beautiful experiences you can have. It should be shared with as many people as possible, if they can dig it. The park ranger who made us move our van right after Saffron's birth ceremony couldn't dig it, and I wanted to reach out to him and show him where it was at, but Earth was freaking because the mushrooms Kozmic Bob gave her right after Saffron was born hadn't mixed so good with her hepatitis, and she was throwing up, so I turned on the Neil Young tape to cool her out and we drove to a motel for the night. Anyway, like I said, if you're going to have a birth, don't invite downheads. You could invite your spiritual master, if you have one, or even your parents, if they can handle it, or John Denver, if he's in town. One time these friends of mine who were having a baby invited Leonard Cohen to come after the concert, but he never showed up, so they figure the guy never even gave him the note.

LETTING THE WORLD KNOW

You could compose a poem, take it to the calligraphy department of the college nearest you, and ask them to help you out. But if that's too much trouble, man, every time one of your friends comes over, just bring the baby out and show it to them. They'll probably want to check it out anyway. You might even be able to get one of the chicks to look after the baby for an hour or two so that you and your old lady can get it on without her having to get up and feed the kid, which can be a drag, man, you know?

WHAT TO DO WITH THE BABY

Don't make the baby uptight by putting diapers on it or trying to toilet-train it. Let it shit where it wants. Kids are in tune with nature, man. The baby will toilet-train itself when the time is ripe. A chick should breast-feed the baby for as long as the baby wants. It doesn't matter if the chick's tits get saggy, she doesn't need them any more anyway and it's more important to raise a baby with no hang-ups. It's cool to blow pot smoke in the baby's face once in a while so the baby can get off, too. Though maybe you should try to remember to keep the acid out of reach until the baby is old enough to tell you it's on a bum trip. But the best thing to do with the baby is drop it off as soon as you can with other babies in a babyplace. (There are babyplaces in most communes, on Israeli kibbutzes, and I know of several in Ibiza.) Stamp on middle-class values. A baby is not your personal property. Why should you keep it to yourself? Love is sharing, man. Share your baby with others and let the kid get on with its own thing.

A NEW BEGINNING

Well, that's it, man. That's our birthstory. It happened a long time ago. Saffron is three now and she's starting to walk. We've seen her twice. She's doing her thing with the other kids. Thanks to us. Do it like we did it and it will blow your minds.

P.S. Have a good time. Stay high. Love, Earth and Cloud.

HIP MOM

by Mary Wilshire

Say, Linda, how does this stuff compare with acid?

GAWD, Linda—your father never did that to me!

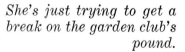

That's the third tray of
cookies she's brought in
this afternoon.

She's just trying to get a
break on the garden club's
pound.

*Your daughter and I had a fas-
cinating discussion concerning
clitorises today, dear . . .*

Fuck you, Linda!

Eat shit, Mom!

*Your father would freak if he
saw this, but I think it looks
great, don't you?*

Norman

by Gail Parent

Norman, as promised, picked me up at one. My first date in New York as a free and independent agent, and this is who I'm going with? Oh, how I wish that I could say you can't judge a book by its cover. That is a statement, dear friends, I cannot make. Norman wore a brown jacket with flecks, and inside there was a man with flecks in his intestines.

We went to the museum as promised. Doris Day went to museums, remember? Did she ever once go with a Norman? ("Wardrobe, you asses, he wasn't supposed to wear a brown jacket with flecks. It was supposed to be a three-piece navy pinstripe.") We walked around the Metropolitan saying things like Renaissance art, Impressionistic, Expressionistic, etc., and Norman brought me home, didn't spend a dime on me; not a nickel. I used my own token for the subway both times. I didn't invite him in.

(Me) "Thank you very much, I had a very nice time."

(Norman) "I had a very nice time, too. How about next weekend?"

(Me, thinking) Are you kidding? Are you serious? I never want to see you again in my entire life. Take your flecks and go. You make the whole building look shabby.

(Me, talking) "I'd like to very much, Norman, but I really can't; next weekend I'm washing my hair."

(Norman) "How about the weekend after that?"

(Me, thinking) Get out of the lobby already. You alone could turn this luxury building into a slum.

(Me, talking) "Sorry, I'm going home to Franklin Square the weekend after next."

"I could come out there, and we could go to the park or something." (The big spender strikes again.)

Reprinted by permission of G. P. Putnam's Sons and the William Morris Agency from *Sheila Levine Is Dead and Living in New York*. Copyright © 1972 by Gail Parent.

(Me, no longer able to think) "Okay."

Norman lunged for my lips and gave me the most disgusting, long, wet kiss I have ever had. Kissed me right there in the hall, six o'clock in the evening. People throwing out their garbage and he's kissing me.

Oh, boy. Norman meets the Mother.

From Franklin Square:

"So, Sheila, how was your date?"

"Boring, awful, disgusting."

"Did he ask you out again?"

"Yes. I really can't stand him. He's so repulsive to me. There's something wrong with him. He's too Jewish."

"He sounds very nice. When are you going to see him again?"

"A week from Saturday; he's coming out there."

"He's coming here?" She can't believe it. It is the first time in my life that I am bringing a nice too-Jewish boy to my parents' door. The lady is in shock.

"He's coming over Saturday. We'll drive around the island or something."

"Certainly, darling, you can take my car if you want." Take the car, take my clothes, take my house, I have tears in my eyes. You've made me a happy woman. You have brought into my midst a genuine too-Jewish boy.

Listen to Sheila, never bring home a boy to meet Mother that you're not crazy about. Norman walked in the door, and it was love at first sight. Norman and my mother fell in love. Ruthie, Madeline, everybody, listen —Norman and Bernice Levine fell in love. Yeah.

"Norman, dear, can I get you anything? Why don't you take your jacket off and make yourself comfortable? Here, Norman, have a nice cold glass of juice. Sure, put your feet up. I like people to be comfortable. I think it's so interesting that you're a third-grade teacher, Norman, tell me all about it. Is it a challenge? Do all the little girls fall in love with their teacher?"

And her eyelashes were batting, and she was wearing

the bra with the good uplift and in the hair her newest wiglet. There was no denying it, she was flirting with Norman Berkowitz. It was one small trip back to the days when she was Bernice Arnold.

And her affection did not go to waste. Norman fell in love with her, completely and totally.

"Mrs. Levine, your soup is just wonderful. . . . Did you really decorate all by yourself? . . . I can't believe you did all the fantastic paintings in the den."

They sure were crazy about each other, those two. She invited him to dinner, and he stayed. She invited him to stay over. Fortunately, Norman couldn't stay. He had to feed his cats. (Isn't that attractive?) He was invited back for the next weekend—no consulting me—just invited back. Norman graciously accepted, shook my father's hand, kissed Bernice on the cheek. I drove him to the station so that he could take the train back to Brooklyn, where he belonged. The train was coming down the track, but he managed to grab me and kiss me before jumping from the Cadillac. I smelled my mother's chopped liver on his breath.

That night. . . .

"I like Norman very much. He's a very nice boy."

"I can't stand him."

"You don't have to marry him. Just give him a chance. Don't throw out dirty water until you have clean."

"Is that what you think of him? He's dirty water?"

"No, I happen to like him very much." I'm sure you did, Miss Arnold, we saw a lot of your terrific legs that day.

Norman came out the next weekend, and I saw him the next and the next. In those days I had two bad habits. Picking my cuticles and seeing Norman Berkowitz. No other dates were coming my way, Linda was in love with Henry Cox so she wasn't much fun, and I was really beginning to believe the dirty water theory. I would decide not to see him again, and then an old girl friend would call to tell me that she was sporting a new two-carat diamond. (Some of those, I found out later, were total two carats—a lot of little diamonds mounted together to look like one big diamond.) Two months after our first date, I decided that I would accept the proposal, wear the ring for a while, and then throw it back in his face when Mr. Right Person came along.

What can one say about sex with Norman that hasn't been said already? We did a lot of kissing and feeling, but Norman continued to protect my virginity. (I know. I know.) We necked and petted and did everything but you know what. Why did I let the shmuck touch me? I just can't say, "I'd rather not! Please don't!" Nobody believes me when I say those things. Grace Kelly says, "Please don't," and you don't go near her. Sheila Levine says, "Please don't," and you forge ahead. I have never—Doris Day will forgive me—slapped a face. There's Sheila Levine, she'll take what she can get.

The touching and feeling and kissing went on for many months. Norman would even undress me. Then he'd touch and feel and kiss. Do you know what a thrill that was? I began reading Margaret Mead, wondering if she wrote about his particular sexual habits.

Dear Abby,

I have been seeing this boy for seven months. I can't stand him. He makes me throw up. However, I have one problem. He won't fuck me. What should I do?

Wanna-Fuck

Franklin Square and Manhattan

Mixed feelings. I loathed Norman, couldn't stand his guts, but I was a passionate woman with a lot of pimples. I was also having strange dreams: Norman rips off my clothes, too impatient to fuss with the buttons. I feel his hot breath on my back, and for the first time, I am aroused. Aroused as I never was before. My entire body is screaming, "Take me . . . take me." And he does, right there on the rug. I am shocked—I never expected such joy, such ecstasy from any man. After it is over, he strokes me gently. I sigh, for I am content. Could it ever be that good again? I think.

Okay, now here's what actually happened: My parents were out. The minute they left, to go to a long movie, they informed us, Norman went to work. Same procedure every time. He started with the kissing; he went to the feeling; he undressed me; he undressed himself for some more kissing and feeling. I was going crazy from the kissing and feeling, so I started—I'll admit it. Mom, you can skip this part if you want—I became aggressive. I grabbed his you-know-what with a definite purpose in mind.

"Please don't!" (That was him, folks, not me. I'm surprised he didn't slap my face.)

"It's okay, Norman."

"No, it's not. I couldn't do that to you."

"It's okay." (Another little grab, not too forceful, but firm.)

"It's not okay."

"Norman, it's okay."

"It's not okay. I would never forgive myself."

"Norman, it's okay. I'm not a virgin."

"I am."

The truth. I'm telling the truth. I was, at this point, holding the penis of a virgin male on my mother's avocado green shag rug, right beside her gold crushed velvet sofa.

"You're kidding?"

"I'm not kidding. I've never done it."

"Well, why don't you do it now? Go ahead."

"I'm scared."

He's scared. I am lying there naked, begging Norman Berkowitz to screw me, and he's scared.

"There's nothing to it. Really, Norman. Norman, are you crying?" (I felt sorry for him. I did. He was crying, even though he denied it. The poor guy was scared. Like a virgin.) "Come on, Norman, I'll show you."

I guided him on top of me. The minute his body touched mine, spermatozoa all over the place. You figure out where, Mom.

It was a long movie, and after coffee and a few records, we tried again. We made it this time. Norman's first time. I felt like an old prostitute. He fell asleep on top of me. Do you know, for one crazy minute, I felt guilty that I had taken his virginity away from him?

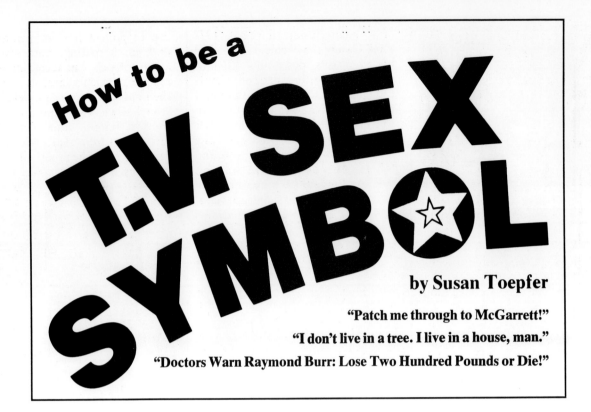

How to be a T.V. SEX SYMBOL

by Susan Toepfer

"Patch me through to McGarrett!"

"I don't live in a tree. I live in a house, man."

"Doctors Warn Raymond Burr: Lose Two Hundred Pounds or Die!"

How many times have you dreamed of being caught in an airport shoot-out, only to be whisked safely away by **Karl Malden**, with even your travelers' checks intact? If the answer is "never," then you (a) don't watch television, (b) maintain one only for "educational" reasons and are therefore fixated on **Alistair Cooke**, or (c) don't like bulbous noses. At the very least, like the numerous nostalgic critics lamenting the demise of celluloid sex symbols, you are absurdly out of touch with the T.V. idols who have taken their place.

For years, the big screen may have provided us with heroes "larger than life," but today they are somewhat smaller—anywhere from two to eight inches tall, depending on the size of your set. Packaged for prime time, these new American idols rarely engage in on-screen sexual behavior (as one CBS censor pointed out, "It took us eighteen years before we finally allowed **Matt Dillon** to get laid"); instead, they offer tantalizing visions of homespun virtues and the romance of banality. So unless he has the guts of a **Savalas** or an ethnic/racial excuse, any struggling young T.V. actor might do well to heed these few simple rules.

1. Believe in God—or keep your mouth shut.
2. Come from a poverty-stricken or emotionally deprived background.
3. Love your wife.*
4. Love your children.**
5. Abhor conspicuous sex and unwarranted violence, being careful to cover up any leanings you may personally have in either or both directions.
6. Suffer the death of a Loved One.
7. Arrange for a close call with the Grim Reaper yourself.***
8. Deeply regret the Moral Decline of America.
9. Arrange for an older child or young friend to get caught on a drug rap, then circulate pictures of you looking pain-stricken.
10. Stay out of politics, except to praise the Democratic State in Which We Live.

---

*For full details on the art of loving your wife, review the complete press life of **Michael Landon.** If, however, social political, or sexual predilections prevent you from entering that state in which one can display the object known as "wife," see the case histories of any number of popular bachelor stars. You will probably find it best to profess an intense desire to attain one, preferably of the "old-fashioned" variety, since these are, in fact, quite "hard to find" these days.

Again, **Michael Landon provides the definitive example. But if you are, again, without these tangible examples of your potency, talk about how much you want a little you, the glories of childbirth, or perhaps your secret desire to adopt an underprivileged specimen.

***As in any art form, true immortality can best be obtained by an untimely and permanent exit (c.f. **Jim Croce, James Dean, Percy Bysshe Shelley**), but the problem with actual death is that it is generally irreversible and one cannot stick around to savor any increase in popularity. Car crashes, cases of misdiagnosed cancer, and even ski accidents are therefore more desirable, giving opportunities for numerous "Miracle Saved My Life" stories and reconversions to religion.

LEONARD NIMOY: Off the air but not forgotten, this one-time alien is the primary reason for huge turnouts at "Star Trek" conventions throughout the country. As **Mr. Spock, Nimoy** displayed grotesque pointed ears, angled eyebrows, intellectual superiority, and an irresistible indifference to sex. Half Earthman, half Vulcan, Spock got the mating urge once every seven years . . . and the result was violent indeed. Nonetheless—or maybe therefore—he is the subject of many detailed sexual fantasies in the "Star Trek" fanzines. Two plots are available: Spock Rapes the Fan and The Fan Rapes Spock. Which may be the reason that Nimoy has turned his hand to poetry, penning *You and I* and *Will I Think Of You?* His latest book is *I Am Not Spock.*

CHAD EVERETT: Star of "Medical Center," whose standard all-American good looks provide an excellent contrast to the sixties' effete **Dr. Kildare** and apelike **Casey.** Married to **Shelby Grant,** former actress and constant subject of his poetry, which has been published (at the star's own expense) in a collection called *Ode to Shelby.* (Sample line: "here's to those blue eyes,/those blue eyes/that are my strength and my conversation.") Blue-blue-eyed Shelby, however, was the cause

of a major dispute during a 1972 **Dick Cavett** show when **Chad** listed her among his "possessions." Fellow guest **Lily Tomlin** walked off; Cavett thought it was a joke; Tomlin never returned. That same night, Mr. Everett caused Mr. Cavett further distress by proceeding to discuss the sonnets of **William Shakespeare** and **W. H. Auden**—and then read his own. And wife Shelby had a chance to prove *her* "strength and conversation" one day in '73, when actress **Sheila Scott** dropped her baby on Chad's MGM doorstep, claiming it was his. After a court hearing proved Chad Everett innocent of the paternity suit, his ever-loyal wife announced: "Mrs. Scott picked the wrong man to accuse, because obviously she never had any idea how strong and loving our marriage has always been." How Mrs. Scott *avoided* knowing is the real mystery, particularly since Chad had *given* her a copy of *Ode to Shelby.*

JACK LORD: Star of palm-laden "Hawaii Five-O," who dominates his series with an iron whim. Rumored rift with "featured player" **James MacArthur** (son of **Helen Hayes**) is readily apparent in their on-screen relationship. While **Lord's** T.V. role makes him super-cop, able to give dramatic commands like, "Close off the island," MacArthur is reduced to, "Where's the victim?" "We've found him, Steve," and an occasional "Patch me through to McGarrett." Lord admires the state of Hawaii and himself and is generally disliked by the press. (Nobody ever talks to Jack Lord; people write stories about Jack Lord; gives him "elusive" appeal.) Further attraction found in slick, tough-guy looks, edge of sadism, and, of course, an off-screen happy marriage. Although Jack Lord's hairstyle, unlike **Chad Everett's,** has won him no awards, he has been known to swim in a bathing

cap to protect it . . . or perhaps its dark black coating. Lord gives his age as forty-six, but according to one reporter's calculations, this means the remarkable actor completed high school at age seven and married for the first time at nine. (Jack never saw his son from that marriage, due to the fact that he reportedly died in his teens, in South America.)

RICHARD THOMAS: Can an intellectual survive as a mass audience sexual prototype? Only in a down-home scenario. **Richard Thomas** attended Columbia and speaks six languages, but **John-Boy Walton** is striving to express himself in one. And now that he's removed himself from the "eligible T.V. bachelors" list by his marriage to an assistant grammar school teacher, Richard's fans can probably look forward to further literary ambitions, perhaps more domestic in nature than the undiluted **Dylan Thomas** outpourings to be found in his published volume, *Poems.*

PETER DUEL: A classic case of Rule #7 carried to its unfortunate extreme, **Duel** is the deceased star of the now-defunct "Alias Smith & Jones." Although he had only minor appeal while living, suicide under his Christmas tree on New Year's Eve, 1971, propelled him into intense popularity: Two years after his death, his studio still reportedly received fan mail.

RAYMOND BURR: Former **Perry Mason**, then wheelchair-ridden **Ironside**, Burr has always been listed as a "mystery man," due to lack of love life, purchase of a Fiji island, maintenance of a private zoo, and general disinclination to Get Along With Others. Aside from his dark and brooding T.V. presence, Burr's only conceivable appeal is obesity. Overweight viewers probably enjoy his bouts with weight problem ("Doctors Warn Ray Burr: Lose 200 Pounds or Die!").

The rotund star still benefits from a biography created and circulated by a press agent at the beginning of his career relating a glorious war record, the tragic deaths of two fictional wives, and the demise of a fictional son via leukemia. The fact that, as Tin Pan Alley columnist **Sidney Skolsky** once wrote, "He is reticent about it," increases the melodrama's credibility.

TELLY SAVALAS: Breaking all the rules, **Telly** came into "**Kojak**" without the hair he could have if he wanted to, and if nobody ever suspected he could be a sex symbol, **Savalas** made *sure* that he would. Telly mischievously makes it impossible for interested observers to determine just how many wives he's had, just how many children, and whether or not he is married at any given moment. But whatever his marital status, Savalas has cleverly avoided the "happily married" gig by eagerly elaborating on his past/present/future sex life at any opportunity. According to Telly Savalas, Telly Savalas was once voted "the third sexiest man on screen." Also according to Telly Savalas, "women sense the difference between getting laid and having a love affair is Telly Savalas." If they didn't, they do now, as the average-brute-next-door continues his sex appeal campaign with a persistence greater than any toothpaste. Not content simply to enroll in the **Rod McKuen** School of Hollywood Poets with his romantic T.V. peers, Savalas spends his non-crime-chasing hours *singing* for his fans. (And women sense the difference between getting sung *to* and being sung *at* is Telly Savalas.)

ROBERT YOUNG: Perennial father-figure whose paternal image began during film contract days when forced to control childish wife in *Claudia* movies. Recent role as "**Marcus Welby, M.D.**" caps a continuing trend of benevolent despotism, epitomized by **Jim Anderson** in "Father Knows Best." Various bouts with drinking, love for life-long wife **Betty**, and ability to look concerned off-screen as well as on have earned him the devotion of millions, whose requests for advice he answers religiously. On "Marcus Welby," the seventy-year-old sex symbol got sprightly back-up from Handsome Young Co-Star **James Brolin** (**Chad Everett** without the paternity suit scandal).

But though his physician's role may be gone, his image is forever stable: **Young** could come back next season in "Vlad the Impaler" and still persist as Father Protector.

DAVID CARRADINE: Counter-culture's revenge on the twelve-year-old television mind, **David** gained interest if not admiration among female viewers as soon as they figured out that "Kung Fu" was his character's art, **Caine** his name. But **Carradine** couldn't have cared less. He kept shoving all that fan mail into boxes, complaining, "It's a drag, man. I haven't read any of it. I don't know what I'm going to do with it." As further insult, David was not married to, but lived with, actress **Barbara Hershey**, who changed her name to **Seagull** when the spirit of the bird allegedly entered her soul on the set of *Last Summer*. The couple further confided that their son, "Free," was conceived while the cameras rolled for *Boxcar Bertha*. But Barbara, Free, and just about everybody else deserted David soon after his now-legendary illegal entry into a Laurel Canyon home. The owner followed a "trail of blood" that led straight to Carradine, who explained he'd just "found" himself in "a strange house" which "closed in on him," so that he felt compelled to "break out." That same day, David unfortunately chose to "accost" a woman while running naked through the neighborhood—an act that later caused an L.A. judge to rule that he must pay her $20,000 in damages. In a commendable attempt to clarify Carradine's conduct, **Judge Francis X. Marnell** declared, "The Court is of the opinion he was bombed out of his skull." But David's few remaining fans are even more indebted to **Merv Griffin** for getting to the root of the rumor that the star lives in a tree. "No, man," Carradine informed Merv and **Eva Gabor** while picking at his toes, "I don't live in a *tree*. I live in a *house*, man. There are trees *around* the house." Hence, no doubt, the confusion.

Mary Tyler Moore Freaks Out

*Tries Continental Coffee...*by Janice Harayda

For more than five seasons, Mary Richards has reigned virtually unchallenged as television's most popular single female. She is a sort of Pollyanna of the typewriter, the Breck Girl who grew up. Mary may fume when Ted leers or Lou hands down an edict, but she remains essentially sweet, lovable, and—herein lies her chief appeal—harmless. If she's a liberated woman, who wouldn't want one?

It is in light of this popularity that the truth must, at last, be told. While Mary *is* earnest and lovable, she is about as representative of the average single woman as Flipper was of the average household pet. Though Maude may confront abortion or Edith, breast cancer, Mary Richards has had few such encounters with the 1970's. Here, then, are some of the shows we might see, if the "Mary Tyler Moore Show" were to reflect the real single woman's life.

Mary learns about birth control—About six months after going on the Pill, Mary notices that her hair is falling out in clumps. She's also begun to get stabbing headaches and has gained ten pounds as a result of taking it—all those trim little pants suits are beginning to feel a bit snug—so she visits her gynecologist in search of an alternate contraceptive. The gynecologist is a kindly, white-haired man who keeps asking when she's going to have a baby; after all, he points out, she's thirty-four and the risks in getting pregnant are increasing. He also keeps calling her "honey" and "sweetheart" while patting her on the foot. At last, however, he agrees to fit her for a diaphragm, and Mary carries it home in a brown paper bag. Some comic moments ensue as she pores over its instruction booklet while squatting on the bathroom floor. Eventually after much slipping and sliding around, she manages to insert the diaphragm.

Mary goes apartment hunting—To her dismay, Mary learns that her building is going co-op, and she must either buy her apartment or move. Because the apartment will cost roughly $50,000 a room and she is making only $132.50 a week at the station, Mary realizes that she must move. She discovers, though, that the only apartments she can afford are a fourth-floor walk-up with a claw-foot bathtub in the kitchen or a tiny studio that's vacant because its previous tenant was mugged on her way out to buy a can of Black Flag. Just as she is about to flee in desperation to a woman's residence hotel, Mary is invited to move in with four stewardesses who live in a swank penthouse apartment. The only problem is that all five of them will have to sleep on bunk beds

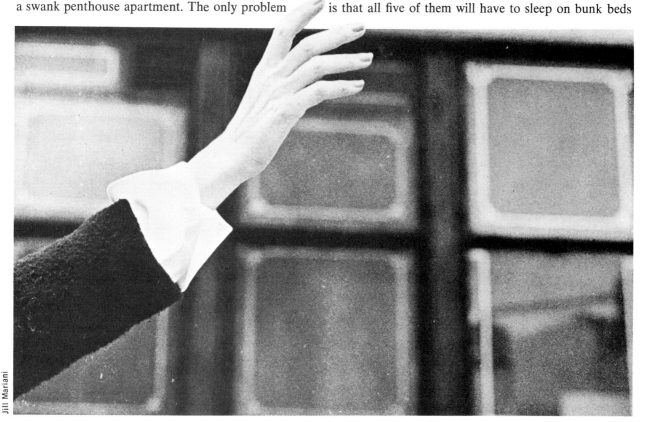

Jill Mariani

in the same room. Nonetheless, at this point Mary grabs the apartment with relief, and the show ends with her penciling her initials on a hard-boiled egg before returning it to the refrigerator.

Mary turns on—On her first date with a new man, Mary finds herself at a party that is suffused with a thick, sweet smell. Her date asks if she smokes and she says, no, not really; she tried it as a teenager but never learned how to inhale. He looks at her curiously, then asks if anyone has a roach holder. "Oh," Mary says, wide-eyed. "Do you have a problem with cockroaches, too?" Someone in the room begins to giggle. Nervously. Mary realizes that everyone except her is smoking, so she decides, with a merry laugh, to fake a few puffs from the joint her date has handed her. She even manages to inhale and enjoy it. The landlord, however, has become suspicious of the towels shoved under the door, and later the police barge in. "But no one gets busted anymore," Mary's date pleads. "It's too passé." The officer is not impressed; Mary is too stoned to notice.

Mary goes to a singles week-end—After a six-month dry spell in her social life, Mary plunks down $200 for a chance to meet "stimulating, creative" singles at a nearby resort. There she is grabbed by a bouncy, platinum-haired social director who pins a huge tag reading "Hi, my name is Mary" on her turtleneck. The social director adds that everyone is going to play a game called "Rubdown" to get to know each other better. Firmly, she leads Mary into a room where men and women are sitting, in various stages of undress, around a bottle of Mazola Oil. Mary begins to hedge, but the social director assures her that, of course, everyone is a little nervous the first time around. As the show ends, we see a close-up of a pile of clothes, on top of which rests a turtleneck sweater tagged "Hi, my name is . . ."

Mary gets her consciousness raised—For research purposes, Mary visits a consciousness-raising group conducted by a local feminist collective. She is told, however, that she will not be permitted to stay unless she actively participates, and for the sake of her story, she agrees. The first question she is asked is whether or not she has ever faked an orgasm. Then someone begins to ask sticky questions about her job: for example, why does Lou call her "Mary" while she calls him "Mr. Grant"? The more she thinks about it, the better a question it seems, and the next day she informs Mr. Grant that she wants to call him "Lou" unless he's willing to call her "Ms. Richards." Furthermore, she is tired of fetching his morning doughnut. Lou, by way of reply, bursts out laughing. All right, he adds, very funny . . . now, how about getting his morning doughnut? Mary refuses, whereupon she is promptly fired. As the show ends, she has just picked up her unemployment check and is placing a call to the EEOC.

TV For Smart People

BY TRACY YOUNG AND ERLA ZWINGLE

MORNING

9:30 (165) **THE MENSA DATING GAME— Game** (BW)
Contestants stump each other with questions like, "Brain number one, would you ask a girl to spell Kierkegaard on the first date?" Host: Mark Van Doren.

10:00 (165) **THE CHERRY ORCHARD— Cartoon** (BW)

10:30 (165) **MOVIE—Adventure/Drama** (BW)
"Shakespeare Wallow" (English, 1965) An itinerant troupe of water buffalo wander through India, entertaining the villagers with performances of Shakespeare's plays. (1 hr. 30 min.)

AFTERNOON

12:00 (165) **WASHINGTON SQUARES— Game** (BW)
Patrick Moynihan, Barbara Howar, James Schlesinger, Elmo Zumwalt, Sally Quinn, the Ambassador of Iran.

12:30 (165) **THE COED AND THE PROF— Comedy** (BW)
Joyce suspects J.D. may be jealous because she's been publishing more than he has lately.

1:00 (165) **THE GUIDING LASER—Serial** (BW)
Arthur doesn't know how to tell Leslie he's been laid off from his job as a research scientist at the nuclear physics plant, but Leslie has already found out —she's his replacement. Hume Cronyn, Jessica Tandy. (60 min.)

2:00 (165) **THE LUCY AND LUCY SHOW— Comedy** (BW)
When Lucy finds a mink coat in the closet, she "borrows" it to meet Lucy at the club. Trouble ensues.

2:30 (165) **MOVIE—Adventure/Comedy** (BW)
"Beach Blanket Chess!" (1962) A couple of preteen chess masters (Peter Kastner, Michael J. Pollard) vacation in Fort Lauderdale. Trouble ensues. (2 hrs.)

4:30 (165) **RIDE THE HIGH LEDGER— Western** (BW)
CPA Nick Weinstein (Sam Waterston), who has gone West to escape a phony embezzlement charge, encounters cowboys who insist on pronouncing his name "Weinstein" as in "mine," instead of "Weinstein" as in "bean." Trouble ensues. (Repeat; 60 min.)

5:30 (165) **ACCENT OF MAN—Richard Burton** (BW)

EVENING

6:00 (165) **NEWS—Norman Podhoretz** (BW)

7:00 (165) **NEWS—Isaac Bashevis Singer** (BW)

7:30 (165) **THE NEW CANDID KARMA— Comedy** (BW)
Debut—Werner Erhard hosts this new show which uses biofeedback machines instead of a hidden camera to catch people in the hilarious act of "thinking for themselves."

8:00 (165) **ALL IN THE NUCLEAR FAMILY —Comedy** (BW)
A knee-jerk liberal refuses to examine his lack of prejudice when his wife gives birth to a Vietnamese orphan. Tom: Joel Grey. Ellen: Brenda Vaccaro.

8:30 (165) **DE SADE SQUAD—Crime Drama** (BW)
Debut—Three tough cops harass meek perpetrators of victimless crimes in this new antipolice brutality police show, starring Rip Torn, Genevieve Page, and Colleen Dewhurst. In the first episode, "Goldilocks and the Three Pigs," Lieutenant Polsky (Rip Torn) gives a prostitute venereal disease. Goldilocks: Rita Moreno. (60 min.)

9:30 (165) **DO-IT-YOURSELF MEDICAL CENTER** (BW)
Viewers are invited to perform a kidney transplant, right along with Dr. Wellbeing (Rod Steiger). Trouble ensues. (60 min.)

10:30 (165) **FIRING LINE—Panel Discussion** (BW)
Assassination buffs A. J. Weberman and Jim Garrison discuss exit wounds. Part 42 of a 98-part series.

11:00 (165) **NEWS—Jorge Luis Borges** (BW)

11:30 (165) **NATIONAL GEOGRAPHIC SPECIAL—Documentary** (BW)
A study of breast fetishism around the world, with special focus on those tribal societies whose early reading matter consisted of nothing but a stack of old *National Geographics*. Hosts: Peter Beard and Margaret Mead. (90 min.)

1:00 (165) **MOVIE—Drama** (BW)
"In Bad Taste" (1974) Two gay excons roam the Midwest, murdering people who use plastic slipcovers. Al Pacino, Bruce Dern. (2 hrs.)

3:00 (165) **PACEM IN TERRIS—Atheism** (BW)
Madalyn Murray O'Hare and Reverend Ike discuss the Chevrolet Veda, debate the questions, "If there is a God, why is he so mean?" and "If not, are we left on the playing fields of the universe without an umpire?"

1/Adrift in Las Vegas or Lost Wages, Nevada

There were 17 pilots on the double bed in my Caesar's Palace hotel room and I'd been screwed (in a manner of speaking) by at least six of them. And was engaged to a seventh. Lord knows it was a tribute either to the sky jockeys' ineptitude or my own incredibly persistent unfuckability that I was now, if anything, more scared of fucking than when I began my amorous adventures some thirteen years earlier.

My fiancé grabbed my hand therapeutically at the moment of penetration.

"Chlist—it's rike ice," he said. Meet my fiancé, Bennett Wang, the only non-Wasp pilot flying for National

NICE BOOKS ★ 87654321 ★ $1.95

FEAR OF FUCKING
BY ANNE BEATTS

Hi, I'm Erica. Fly Me.

Airlines. Tall, good-looking, Orientally inscrutable, inscrutably Oriental. Sexy, slim-hipped, slanty-eyed, with skin the color of overripe pineapple rind and hairless you-know-whats like round, succulent lychee nuts (at least that's what he told me when he tried to get me to take them in my mouth). Dole could have canned him and made a fortune from frustrated housewives: fresh Wang, preserved in heavy syrup, ready to be picked right off your friendly neighborhood supermarket shelf.

Unfortunately, I didn't and do not come under the heading of frustrated housewife. True, most days out of the standard 365 I can be found with an apron around my waist and a potholder in my hand, cooking up a variety of taste-tempting dishes, but the tastes I cater to are those of 300 or more demanding passengers, instead of merely one hungry man—and the hot stove I'm slaving over can be found in the galley of a jet aircraft and not in the cute little kitchen of my very own home.

Such is the nature of being a stewardess. Not that I mind. On the contrary; I love it. I just minded being a frustrated stewardess, especially since we stews are supposed to be such sensual, uninhibited creatures, swinging wildly from layover to layover (all puns intended). Well, I'd done some swinging, too, but there seemed to be something wrong with my trapeze. I just couldn't connect. Here I was in Las Vegas, and I couldn't even hit the jackpot. No dice. I was looking for the big O, but instead, everything came up double zeros.

I should point out here that Bennett is Hawaiian, not Japanese or Chinese (one part Scottish missionary, one part Javanese, two parts wild Maori warrior, and the rest pure Aloha) and can roll his r's with the best of us, except when he gets excited. He was excited then. Or now. (I never *can* keep my tenses straight.) In that hotel room in Caesar's Palace in Vegas, I mean.

He was and I wasn't. That was pretty evident to everyone else on the bed, except that my condition was less obvious. My condition was the same as it always is under the circumstances, i.e., sexual, e.g., raw terror (you may wonder how a stewardess knows classy literary abbreviations like that; well, I put in a year at Barnard before I transferred out to stew school). My fingers (and toes) turn to ice, my (slightly too-plump) tummy leaps forward into my rib cage, the temperature in the tip of my cute little retroussé nose drops to the same level as the temperature in my fingers, my two rose-tipped nipples stand up and salute the inside of my bra (going to bed braless is bad for the bust-line), and for one throbbing minute (Bennett is quick on the draw—with me he has to be) my mind tries to convince my body (or is it the other way around?) that it's OK, that this time I'm going to feel something other than invasion of privacy.

Now I wish I could persuade myself (and Bennett) that I'm ready for takeoff, but somehow I can't seem to get off the runway. He fiddles with my control panel, but my landing gear just won't retract (so to speak). Stray phrases from the flight manual begin floating through my head—anything to keep from thinking about what's actually going on *down there*. As Wang's whang keeps banging away, "Serve predeparture candy," I think, frantically. "Serve soup in demitasse cups. Add cheese straw to saucer. Prior to landing, collect dessert items. Accomplish cold towel service."

Ironically, by the time I got that far, Bennett had accomplished *his* service, and was wiping me off with a (room-temperature) towel that had "Caesar's Palace" stenciled on it (Hawaiians are nothing if not clean). In this instance, it seemed Bennett himself was serving as the soup—and then again the dessert—course, with the other seventeen pilots coming (!) in between as *hors d'oeuvres variées* and entrées, for a grand gourmet total of nineteen calorie-stuffed courses.

The whole thing was Bennett's idea, something he cooked up to get my juices flowing and dissolve that hard lump that wasn't exactly in my throat but felt exactly like that lump-in-the-throat kind of fear, the fear you feel when you're on the playground and some big kid pushes the teeter-totter up and down too fast, or when you're out on a first date and you know your deodorant is about to fail you, or when you're having that special man over to dinner and you suddenly notice there are spots on *all* the glasses.

As soon as Bennett rolls off me and people begin shifting positions on the bed, I glance around nervously to see who's on board. There's Captain Gunther Guenther, the harshly-Teutonic scion (at least in spirit) of the Red Baron, who has already made a pass at Bennett. There's kindly, rotund Captain "Johnny" Johnson, who once cornered me in the whiffy of a filled-to-capacity 747. There's Arthur Prager, a prankish co-pilot who is currently engaged in tying knots in my Pucci-patterned panties. There's smiling, bald Captain R.D. "Bob" Benton, pilot on the plane my crazy ex-husband once tried to hijack. There's Skipper "Poontang" Poteet, a good ol' boy from Dallas, Texas, who once personally demonstrated the aptness of his nickname to me during a five-hour-long stack-up over Kennedy.

We were all in Las Vegas for a pilots' convention (actually just another name for an all-day, all-night screwing, drinking, and gambling spree). And from where I saw it, which happened to be flat on my back, it looked like half the pilots were convening right on Bennett's and my bed. There I was, stuck in Vegas with a planeload of crazy pilots, many of whom had attempted to (to coin a phrase) ring my chimes, and none of whom

had succeeded in pealing out more than a tiny, tinny "ping." As Pilot No. 2 taxied into position, I sent up mental distress flares.

We stews don't get much time for reading (I gave up hitting the books when I left Barnard) but once I picked up a paperback at the newsstand at LAX purely because the author had the same name as me: Erica. Someone pinched it out of my luggage in Chicago, so I never did get to finish it. It had a lot of dirty words in it and a sexy picture on the cover, so I guess whoever took it thought it was a hot book. Anyway, she, either the author or this character, I'm not sure which, had this fantasy she called "the zipless fuck." It's sort of like the Bolla wine commercial where the guy sees this beautiful woman on a train, except that they *don't* wind up together in the end. And I must admit it sort of caught my imagination.

Because, you see, I have a fantasy, too. Have had it for a long (the longest) time. Ever since I was a little girl on the lawn of my parents' house on Long Island watching jets go by overhead. Ever since I saw them break the sound barrier in *Breaking the Sound Barrier* at the Starlite Drive-In in Billy Mills' old Rambler. Ever since my mother served me my first TV dinner. Ever since I first heard the opening number of *West Side Story:* "When you're a Jet you're a Jet all the way...." As long as that.

I used to think about my fantasy as I was demonstrating the safety features of the aircraft or distributing individually-wrapped portions of Kraft processed cheese food and Ritz crackers to the Economy passengers. Thinking about it made (to coin another phrase) my chimes tinkle, oh, ever so slightly, it's true, but even that was much more than I had ever felt from letting anyone (to coin yet another phrase) fiddle with my clapper. It's just that I never knew what it was or what to call it, until I read the other Erica's book. And then I knew it was a fantasy, and I began calling it the Bumpless Flight.

The bumpless flight was more than a flight, it was a flight of fancy, an unattainable ideal. Bumpless because it would never be overbooked, so no passenger would ever have to be "bumped"—airlines parlance for kicking one passenger off to make room for another. For the true, ultimate, A-1 bumpless flight, it was necessary that the aircraft not be filled to capacity, so that the stewardess (that's me!) would have time to attend to the needs of all the passengers *and* the pilot.

The bumpless flight is bumpless not only because the aircraft picks itself up and settles down as gently as a floating rose petal. But because everything on board functions as smoothly as in a dream; because there is no need to remind anyone twice to extinguish all smoking materials and prepare for take-off; because no lousy creep in an aisle seat makes a grab for your tush as you walk past with your hands full; because your fellow crew-members are efficient and courteous. And you! You move through it all like a queen or a nun or a guardian angel, not a hair out of place, your makeup unsmudged, your pantyhose unwrinkled, your breath fresh, your teeth gleaming as white as Pearl Drops Liquid Tooth Polish can make them—smoothing a pillow here, patting a cheek there, graciously and gracefully bestowing a complimentary beverage or a deck of cards or even a smile, always friendly, warm, involved, yet remote and somehow unattainable. The bumpless flight. The most wonderful thing a stewardess—no, any woman—can experience. And I have never experienced it.

2/"I Love Little Pussy"

I love little pussy, her coat is so warm.
And if I don't hurt her, she'll do me no harm.
　　　　　　　　　　—Robert Louis Stevenson

Bennett's ridiculous farce kept me (and him) up until four A.M. without raising a tremor on my internal seismograph. Then we all trooped wearily down to the lobby to play blackjack, because (natch!) Las Vegas never sleeps. It's never been one of my favorite destinations. I mean, San Francisco is for wandering hand-in-hand in, and the shopping in Hong Kong is fantastic, but there's nothing to do in Vegas except drink, gamble, and pick up prostitutes. While Bennett went off to try one of the other two, I decided to try my luck at gambling. Lord knows I was unlucky enough at love.

I picked up a roll of quarters and headed for the slots. I was aware that gambling was one of the things that the stew handbook warned us about, but I figured this was just nickle-and-dime stuff (even though I was playing with quarters). Nonetheless, my chosen machine didn't seem to be too generous, so I moved on to the next one, and suddenly, it happened. Bingo! Things began clanging and flashing, and the machine lit up like (*O Tannenbaum!*) a Christmas tree. But no money came out.

I was furious. I had, indeed, hit the jackpot. But it didn't pay off. I could feel the anger gather inside my head like steam in a pressure cooker. I began screaming and shouting, kicking the darn thing, and pounding on it with my little fists. The slot machine remained unresponsive.

Defeated, hoarse, and exhausted, I turned to leave. And saw this blond, curly-haired Englishman with a pipe hanging out of his face. He looked exactly like Prince Charles.

"Um, er, ah, don't you know, well, er—rather," he said. He was smiling at me the way a man smiles when he's lying on top of you after a particularly good lay. (I got that out of *Cosmopolitan;* I don't know how a man smiles then, partly because I've never had—though I may have *been,* since the way I feel doesn't seem to have all that much to do with *their* enjoyment—a particularly good lay, but mainly because at that moment I always seem to have my eyes closed.)

"BOAC, Aer Lingus, or Royal Caledonian?" I said, hoping against hope that it was BOAC.

He grinned. And softly hummed a few bars of "Rule Britannia" in reply.

He was wearing a navy-blue uniform with gold braid, lots of it, curling thickly around his cuffs and decorating his (broad) shoulders.

"Lorry lift bonnet," he mumbled. Reaching into the breast pocket of his immaculately-pressed uniform jacket, he withdrew a Wash 'N' Dri moist towelette and handed it to me. While I was wiping away the (now forgotten) tears of rage and frustration that had encrusted my cheeks with smears of mascara, he grabbed a generous fistful of my generous ass and gave it a long playful squeeze. Just like a drunken passenger. But somehow, from him I didn't mind. (Mind! I would have followed him anywhere—out on the wing in the event of an emergency landing, even. I would have been happy to be stranded in a life raft with him in the middle of the Sahara Desert. Yum! What a gorgeous hunk of flesh!)

All he asked was that I come across the lobby and have a drink with him in the bar. I was so thrilled (and proud) to be with Adrian I forgot that I don't drink.

That was his name. Adrian Goodfuck. I took it as symbolic. You can't be named Erica Dumm Kundt (née Dumm—the Kundt was a legacy of my crazy ex-husband, Brian Kundt, the psychotic encyclopedia salesman and Talmudic scholar who thought he was a reincarnation of Lenny Bruce and tried to kill me by putting Clorox in my douche bag) without spending a rather large portion of your life thinking about names.

Adrian's English accent was so thick I could barely understand a word of anything he said, but he smoked a pipe, so I knew he must be intelligent. He also grinned a lot. The corners of his eyes crinkled into about a hundred tiny lines and his mouth curled up into a sort of smile even when he wasn't smiling. I knew I'd say yes to anything he asked. My only worry was: maybe he wouldn't ask soon enough. Or maybe he had already asked and I hadn't understood him.

To cover my embarrassment, I got up, went over to the bar, brought back a dish of nuts, and offered it to him with a cocktail napkin over my arm (I didn't have a linen-lined tray like it says in the flight manual under "Ambassador Service," so I made do with what was at hand).

"Wouldn't you like to learn how to do that properly?" he asked, raising one eyebrow.

"I already know how to do it properly," I protested, "Why do—"

But he cut me off. "What airline do you fly for?" he said. "National?"

I nodded mutely, wondering how he already knew so much about me. Did he know, for instance, that my underpants were wet enough to mop the floor of the hotel lobby (because I had spilled my Kahlua-and-milk in my lap)?

"I thought as much," said he, smug. "Domestic flights only, am I right?"

Of course he was right. So right I could taste it. (By then I would have eaten *his* nuts off a linen-lined tray if he had so much as offered them to me. Love can do crazy things.)

"You'll never learn first-class service like that. Why don't you change airlines?"

"Change airlines?" I managed to stammer out. I was living up to my name. Erica Dumm dumb.

"Yes. You could come to BOAC. Serve on international flights. Ceylon, Nepal, Belfast. Remember, all over the world—"

"BOAC takes good care of you," I finished for him. This was it. He was offering me the real, the genuine b.f. The bumpless flight par excellence. What were we waiting for?

So, maybe a poker-up-his-ass Limey airline pilot who talked as though his upper lip had been permanently frozen and offered to teach you the true meaning of the word "service" wouldn't be everybody's (you'll pardon the expression) dish of tea. But, like I always say, there's no accounting for tastes. And who can convey an infatuation? It's like trying to describe the taste of chocolate mousse, or the look of a sunset, or why you can sit for hours and make faces at your own baby. . . .

Anyway, something about Adrian Goodfuck got to me. And he was well aware of the effect he was having.

So was Bennett, who walked into the bar just as Adrian and I, arms (and eyes!), interlocked, were lifting my Kahlua-and-milk, and his "Bloody" Mary in a romantic toast.

3/Every Woman Can?

Ready for a beautiful orgasm? It's now possible for every woman, thanks to a combination of ancient Oriental rituals with modern scientific sex know-how.
—*Cosmopolitan's Love Guide*, 1972

To give credit where credit is (undeniably) due, Bennett took the news that I was about to embark on a round of Las Vegas all-day-and-nite spots with a hitherto entirely unknown but handsome Britisher rather calmly, more calmly in fact than Adrian did. Adrian's jaw dropped: but Bennett remained as inscrutable as ever.

"Take her and welcome," he said, bitterly, and then something about the pig party being over, which I didn't catch.

"What's up, ducks?" said Adrian to me when Bennett had left, sounding for all the world like a British Ryan O'Neal.

I wanted to say, "Take me, make me, screw me, do me, lay me, play me like a slot machine until you've run out of quarters and all my lights go off," but I didn't. Instead, I told him that I had always wanted to see the real Las Vegas, the Las Vegas tourists never see.

"Oh, sort of a pub crawl, eh, luv?" he said in his adorably English accent.

"Luv!" He called me "luv." My pulses raced. It was enough to make me want to change my citizenship, become a British subject. How comforting it must be to have a Royal Family. How cosy. No wonder Adrian seemed so sure of himself. Like David Frost. It was all those generations of royalty backing him up. He had a place in the world. He *belonged*.

And just now, if I could only (watch it, Erica!) play my cards right, he belonged to *me*.

"Let's jump this joint, sweetheart," he said, doing a bad (but adorably English) Bogey imitation. (I would have jumped *his* joint—Adrian's, not Bogart's—*any* time, and he knew it.)

So began an amazing odyssey that was to shake me up from the top of my cute little blonde head to the tips of my little pink toes (and, incidentally, thrill me to the very fiber (or *fibre,* to spell it the adorably English way Adrian would) of my diminutive (5'3" (in shoes—5'2" (*eyes of blue, could she coo*) in my stocking feet)) being).

Adrian and I proceeded to hit every bar, lounge, gambling casino, topless club, bottomless club, taco stand, chicken shack, burger pit, and high- or low-life beanery in Vegas. It's my impression we hit some of them so hard they may still be shaking, but that's only my impression.

We were usually drunk all the time, or as Adrian put it, "potted," and, as a consequence of that (or of *something*), everything melted into everything else to form a crazy-quilt pattern in my mind: like dotted fields of farmland, when you look down on them from the air. And yet there were specifics, too. I remember *Magic Fingers*©. I remember specific hotel rooms, because every time Adrian took his pipe out of his mouth and looked at me, I would go weak in the knees and command him to take me to the nearest hotel room.

I remember the first time it happened: it was a lot like the last time. Adrian made me horny (*me,* horny!) for a lot of reasons, but mainly because I was convinced he could change my life, make a better stewardess out of me, direct me toward that ultimate experience, the bumpless flight of which I had so often dreamed. He did everything he could to encourage this feeling on my part. "Dawn above the mid-Atlantic," he would whisper, leaning toward me in the front seat of the rent-a-car. "And you, serving breakfast to the first-class passengers on impeccable white linen. Kippers over the White Cliffs of Dover."

I was enthralled. "Take me, take me," I whimpered, wrenching the steering wheel out of his hands and driving right into Unit No. Ten of The Golden Nugget Drive-in Motor Hotel.

"Ladies and gentlemen, health officials require that we disinfect the aircraft before we leave," Adrian said with his adorable English sense of whimsy, disappearing into the whiffy (which he taught me to call the "w.c.").

A few moments later he was back and ready to wheel up the boarding ramp. "Good afternoon, ladies and gentlemen, welcome aboard BOAC Flight 743 to London," Adrian whispered tenderly in my ear. He knew exactly how to turn me on! "We'll be cruising at an altitude of 30,000 feet, and we'll be on top of all clouds most of the way."

I was on Cloud Nine, myself. "It's good to have you with us, and we hope you enjoy the flight," I whispered back.

All of a sudden I noticed that Adrian's (ahem!) seat back wasn't situated in an upright position, and as a consequence (if you catch my drift) his tray table wasn't stowed. The reason I wasn't feeling that usual panicky, scared, *violated* feeling was because I wasn't feeling *anything*. Adrian and I had somehow missed the all-important connecting flight.

The same thing happened the next time. And the next, and the next, and the next. As Adrian got drunker and drunker, it seemed to matter to him less and less, whereas I was practically ruining my manicure with frustration.

We were in the coffee shop of the Desert Inn when I finally asked him to spill the beans. After he mopped them up, he told me he was leaving for L.A. in fifteen minutes. "Have to meet a chappie there. Fellow who works for Air India. Steward. 'S been my lover for ages. Centuries. Got digs together in London. Makes a bloody fine curry, too, if I do say so meself. But first I have to see a man about a dog."

I was so mad I could spit. But all I could think of to say was, "We'd like to remind you that smoking has never been permitted in any of our lavatories," before he slipped off his stool and slunk to the "loo." I waited in that coffee shop for four solid hours, but he never came back.

I wanted to scream, I wanted to cry, I wanted to throw up. I wanted to run after him and make him into the healthy, well-adjusted heterosexual of my dreams. What I did was sit there for another four hours, with the blood streaming unheeded down my legs (the shock seemed to have brought on my period—well, at least I wasn't about to give birth to a miniature Limey with limp wrists) and think about what had happened to me.

I closed my eyes and began to daydream. Fragments of those dreams are still with me. In one of them, I had to take out and put on an oxygen mask in the twenty seconds before the plane crashed, while a voice kept saying over the intercom, "Breathe normally," but I couldn't breathe at all. In another, I cut open my own head and thousands of fluffy Easter chicks, all dyed different colors, came out, making little cheeping sounds.

Then I remember the daydream in which I was back at stew school preparing to receive my diploma from Mrs. McIntosh. Suddenly Mrs. McIntosh turned into Pearl Bailey, except that she looked like a white person. She was sitting in an Economy seat. Pearl rang the bell above her seat for service, and the little signal light went on. Suddenly I understood that serving her Chicken Maryland was the real way to graduate from stewardess school, and at that moment it seemed like the most natural thing in the world.

I turned to where the galley should have been, opened my eyes, and came face to face with the black manageress of the coffee shop.

"Pay your check and get out," she said.

4/I'm Okay You're Okay.

I'm okay; you're okay.

—Thomas A. Harris

The toothless ancient at the desk was asleep when I asked him if anyone named Wang was staying at Ro-lin-de-hey Lodge (your host in the Poconos with the most in the Poconos). But not too asleep to leer when he caught sight of my stew's "wings". "See for yourself, honey," he cackled, passing the guest register over to me.

I looked down the list anxiously. There was not a Wang to be found. What if the little gook had finked out on me? Then I caught sight of it. "Pecker." They were always making that kind of dumb mistake. Racists!

The clerk said "they" weren't in. After a lot of fast talking, I persuaded the old geezer to let me wait in Bennett's room. (A romantic honeymoon lodge, Ro-lin-de-hey was the place where we had opted to spend the rest of our vacation. It offered hefty discounts to National Airlines' employees, and a split of complimentary New York State pink champagne to every guest couple.) I noticed that the champagne was almost gone, and that there were a pair of Pucci panties not unlike my own drying on the bathroom towel rack. I decided that Bennett must have been feeling my loss more than I'd suspected, although I couldn't imagine why it had driven him (of all people) to adopt women's underwear.

I filled the heart-shaped tub full of delightful bubbles (Avon's "Persian Wood") and climbed in. I floated lightly in the water feeling that something was different, something was strange, but I couldn't figure out what it was.

I looked down at my body. The same. Cute, curvy, love-handles a little too prominent, but not bad, all the same. I allowed myself a mental wolf-whistle.

Then I realized, with the sudden shock of discovery, that something *was* different. Thanks either to Adrian or to the seventeen pilots (or to the *Magic Fingers*©) there had been certain drastic structural changes. The work of a simple exploratory, nonmagic finger (my own) confirmed my guess. My woman's most precious treasure was missing. That little door below my love-button, between me and the inmost part of me, was gone! Ironically, for the first time in my life I felt like a whole (not hole) woman.

Men and women, women and men, I thought. Would it ever work! I had believed Adrian was different, but he turned out to be just another cocksucker. What was the meaning of it all? Where was I? And (more important), who was I? What was I going to be? Was it really all that simple (or not, as the case may be)? What was the point? What *did* it all mean? In the words of the song, "What's it all about, Alfie?"

Just then Bennett walked in with a beautiful almond-eyed Oriental woman. "It doesn't matter," he said, "you'll always be aflaid of fucking."

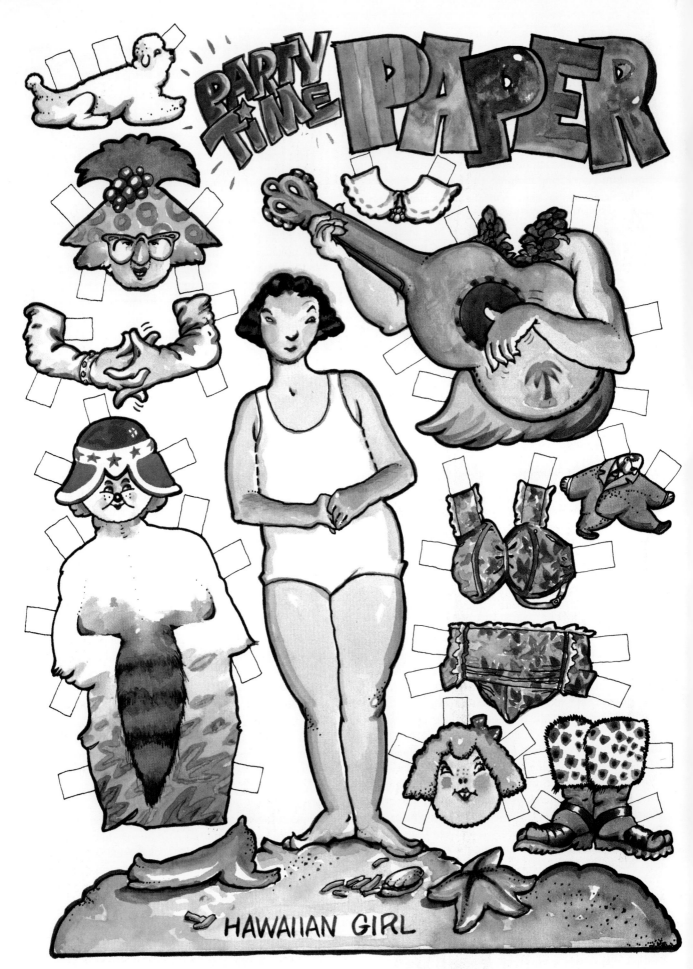

PARTY TIME PAPER

HAWAIIAN GIRL

DOLLS BY M·K·BROWN

FARM BOY

Bacchus Is a Lady

by Helen Lawrenson

THERE are exceptions, but when most women get sloshed, the gamut of their antics is circumscribed. They may get the giggles, talk too loudly or too honestly, flirt with the wrong men. At worst, they either pass out or throw up. Men not only indulge in these last two practices, sometimes simultaneously, but they also display a variety of other objectionable traits. They want to fight waiters, barmen, doormen, taxi drivers, their best friends, strangers on the street. If thwarted, they want to fight you. They break things. They lose their hats, scarves, coats, glasses, and even, on occasion, their teeth. They lose their money, too, and they give away five-dollar bills as tips under the impression they are handing out a buck at a time.

Women simply don't behave in this way. Very few women, for example, go out and get rolled. They may lose an earring once in a while, but it is usually in the process of trying to ward off a drunken male. Women seldom challenge anyone to a bout of fisticuffs, and they don't throw their money around trying to act like Goodtime Charlies. Nor, as a rule, will you find a group of grown women standing at a bar singing nostalgic songs.

Then there is the business of liquor and sex. The more a man drinks, the firmer becomes his conviction that physically he is irresistible. He frequently seems to be working on the theory that possession is nine-tenths of the battle and that if only he can get a good grip on you, especially in the back of a taxicab, you are his. Once safely on bed or couch, the problem is certainly not solved. Drinking does not improve a man's amorous technique. While it is true that alcohol may act as an aphro-disiac, too much of it will make your ithyphallic paramour's passion more vocal than focal. As the ancient Chinese proverb might have had it: leer on face, no lead in pencil.

Another extraordinary thing that happens to men when drinking is that they lose their powers of articulation. They mutter and mumble and whistle their *s*'s and repeat every third word for emphasis like the straight man in a music hall comedy skit. They like you to listen with rapt enthusiasm even though no Rosetta Stone has been discovered to translate their unique babble into something resembling a known tongue. I have seen this process of disintegration under alcohol take place with M.P.s and merchant seamen, authors and editors, ambassadors and actors, tycoons, insurance salesmen, dockers, solicitors, and even an anthropologist or two.

Why, in my lifetime I have seen more Solons turn into boozy slobs than I could shake a swizzle stick at, but rarely have I seen a plastered Portia lose her cool. I was once asked to leave a Havana restaurant called Los Industriales with my escort, an American Brigadier-General, because he suddenly decided, when in his cups, to relieve himself in a corner of the dining-room. (This is a fairly common manifestation among male inebriates. A notorious incident also took place in Havana involving either a famous actor or the equally well-known son of a world statesman —I've forgotten which for the moment—who used the statue of José Martí as a public urinal. It became a minor international crisis in com-memoration of which I wrote a couplet: Never pee/On José Martí.)

All that a man has to do when he goes drinking is to drink. A woman, however, has to match him glass for glass because it annoys a man's man if his man's woman doesn't keep up with him. In addition, she must act as nurse, bodyguard, valet, secretary, cashier, and interpreter. She must divert him tactfully from quarrels, quiet him when he bursts into song, watch over his money, remind him to get his briefcase from the cloakroom. If he is sick, she must comfort him. If he passes out, she has to see he gets home all right. If he leaves his cigarette burning in an ashtray, she must put it out before it sets the tablecloth afire.

When he tries to attack her, she must evade him gracefully and without aspersion to his virility. Then, if she is married to him, she it is who gets up the next morning while her dashing consort of the night before lies prostrate on the bed nursing a death rattle. Never, never, must she expect any show of remorse the next day; she will be far more apt to hear him proudly prating to his friends: "I really got pissed last night! Oh boy! I can't remember a thing from the time we left Tony's."

Well, the hell with it. Any woman drinker who made such a mess of herself as men usually do would be about as popular as a Black Widow spider. When you think what a woman has to put up with when she goes out to hoist a few with her beloved, it's a wonder that she ever bothers. Except, of course, she really can manage to have a little fun after he passes out, or before her own cirrhosis of the liver sets in.

MY TUPPERWARE SHROUD

I look at you
And I see laundry baskets
In the seawall of my heart
Where soiled garments fill my concrete dreams
With Clorox whitened cliffs
But sandcastles crumble
I see your face in my Dispose-All
Mocking me with citrus laughter as I cry
A captive in the rocking chair of
Spray starch dreams and amber evenings
Spiked with Champale Tears
You turned away from me
Although I brought you
Dreams to share in Melmac chalices
And someone thought they saw you Sunday
In a field of bright anemones
While I marked time in my Tupperware shroud.

LIBERATION LADY

Liberation lady in your combat shoes
All men are the oppressor
Why are you singin' the blues?
Ain't had no lovin' in a long long time
Plug in mister vibrator
'Lectricity ain't no crime

Come to the revolution, Lady, come to the revolution

Liberation Lady, iron in your veins
Got to love your sisters
They won't put you in chains
Find yourself longin' for a big hard prick?
Turn on your electric toothbrush
It'll do the trick

(Chorus)
Liberation Lady in your rumpled clothes
If you're still horny
How about the garden hose?
The times are a-gettin' meaner and meaner

If you need bigger kicks
Try your vacuum cleaner

Come to the revolution, oh yes, yes, she said I will, yes, yes, yes
Come to the revolution.

CELIBACY

When I get lonely and start thinking of you
And all the disgusting animalistic things we used to do
I know that I was blessed to finally see
That the way to salvation is through celibacy

*Yeah . . . can't get no infection
Don't need no erection
When you find true perfection
Celibacy!*

I used to think that love was just a silly game
But when I wasn't gettin' none my passion would inflame
Till I finally realized that I was just a slave
And declared my independence, vowing to be brave
It was then I embraced the love that's always true
It's celibacy, folks, and I recommend it to all of you

Be chaste and pure and squelch your desire
'Cause you got to see where there's smoke there's fire
Every man wants just one thing . . . sex
And it's been that way back to Oedipus Rex
So I'm here just tellin' you what you've always known
Don't give away none, Honey, 'cause your body is your own.

Cel . . . i . . . bacy . . . eeey . . . eeeeyyy . . . yeah!

COCKA DOODLE DOO

Hey, little mister, walkin down the street
Way you're movin' tells me you taste sweet
Oh, cocka doodle doo
Cocka doodle doo
How I love my honey since I taught him how to screw

Didn't know a clit from a chicken's neck
Almost gave up on 'im, but figured what the
heck
Oh, cocka doodle doo
Cocka doodle doo
Taught my little mister how to make a lady coo

Now everything's fine with my man and me
We sit and we fiddle in front of our TV
But he gets real defensive when the subject
comes up
'Bout how I had to give him lessons and teach
him how to fuck.

SWEET LOVIN' LOU

I want to tell you a little story
'Bout a dog that I loved true
He was my good friend, I was his mistress
And his name was Sweet Lovin' Lou

He was big and black and hairy
And as eager as could be
I yelled, "Go 'way, you mangy mongrel"
But he jumped up and mounted me

We went ridin' through the sagebrush
Goin' faster by the mile
All at once I felt the earth move
And I thought I saw him smile

Chorus: Lou, my sweet Lovin' Lou, wag your
tail, you mad dog, you,
Lou, Sweet Lovin' Lou, ain't no man
so good as you

We spent the night in my log cabin
He lapped me til the sun came up
Then he put his paws around me
And I knew he was my pup

Ten years later we still were happy
Life with Lou was like a wish
No more scrubbin', no more cookin'
I just put Alpo in his dish

Chorus

Now Lou's in doggie heaven
St. Peter gave him a silver bone
He's got wings and plays a harp there
But as for lovin', he's on his own

Chorus

MONEY IS POWER

As a young girl I believed in
Fresh daisies and the sun
I roamed the countryside
Content with what was free
But as the years passed
My education was completed
I was abused and robbed and cheated
And I learned my lesson

Chorus: Money is power
Power is money
You can laugh
But it ain't funny

Bein' a flower child was fine
In the days of revolution
Goin' on marches was groovy
But now I'm rich
And I ain't rebellin'
'Cause I have the things money can buy
The limousines and the cocaine high
And I've learned my lesson

Chorus

So screw whoever gets in your way
And step on the little guy
He's too weak to complain
Success is the balm
That'll salve your soul
And if they call you a fake
Just tell 'em to eat cake
'Cause you've learned your lesson

Chorus

DYNAMITE SISTERS

SIDE 1
My Tupperware Shroud   (3:20)
Celibacy   (4:18)
Liberation Lady   (6:05)
Cocka Doodle Doo   (5:14)

SIDE 2
Sweet Lovin' Lou   (11:03)
Money Is Power   (9:21)

Here they are, ladies and gentlemen, the explosive Dynamite Sisters. They've paid more dues than anybody even owed. It all began when Dottie, Irene, Mary Jo, and Paula harmonized together one afternoon at a Tupperware party in their hometown of Sandusky, Ohio. As the girls began to sizzle, an awestruck audience lost interest in lettuce bins and sat glued to the plastic slipcovers, transfixed by the petit point lyricism of their music.

This warm reception inspired the group to meet weekly in Dottie's finished basement to sharpen their lilting vocals. Before long, they found themselves in demand at the American Legion Hall and Lion's Club bean bakes. They got their chops down playing local showcase clubs such as Tony Alexander's Internationally Famous Alibi Room.

Crystallizing under the singular moniker of "The Strugglin' Strawberries," the girls recorded their first single, "Tupperware Shroud," inspired by their historic meeting. As the single climbed the charts to the number one slot, and remained in the top ten for an unprecedented 59 weeks, the girls sensed they had hit pay dirt. The persistent call of their muse proved stronger than the demands of home and family. Following their landmark appearance on the Muscular Dystrophy Telethon they soon became a rock 'n' roll legend. They splashed big with their first album, *Strawberry Sundae,* and an invitation to Michael Goldstein's Powder Ridge Festival, where they were the only group to perform.

Yet, not content with overnight success, these nitty gritty sirens of song decided to grow with the times that spawned them. Suddenly, one night at L.A.'s Troubadour, they lunged out of the shadows and seized the stage, now transformed into "Lot's Wife and the Pillars of Salt." Clearly, this marked a revolutionary embrace of feminist politics, a head-change which had

its roots in tentative consciousness-raising sessions with Holiday Inn chambermaids. Under their new banner, the four women began expressing their new-found militant point of view in songs like "Emancipation Rag" and "Celibacy," which voiced the concerns of women everywhere.

As flaming meteors of the burgeoning feminist movement, the four women ignited cam-

The Dynamite Sisters
Dottie Rasmussen: vocals, lead guitar, harmonica
Mary Jo Foster: vocals, rhythm guitar, piano, Moog, banjo
Paula Schmidt: vocals, bass guitar, electric bass, spoons
Irene Frank: vocals, drums, washboard, congas

pus riots with their college tours, and on many occasions had to be escorted by the National Guard. Lyrics like "Sexism, chauvinism, oppression, pooh" became a part of the international language of youth. And for the first time in rock history, the rock press was unanimous in its reaction to a group, presenting this stellar aggregate of talent with one never-ending valentine.

One day at the Hollywood Bowl, as the usual horde of roadies fought over who would carry the girls' sound equipment, Irene spotted her fourteen-year-old son, whom she hadn't seen since that funky, fateful day in the Sandusky bus depot. With tears in her eyes, she announced to the group that she was going to

retire. A time of trial followed, as the remorse-stricken girls returned to their families, and relearned to cook and clean house. Dottie enrolled in the "Fascinating Womanhood" course, Paula tried to assuage her pain with T.M., and Mary Jo became a partner in a twenty-four-hour carwash.

It was only a far-out fluke of fate that reunited them, when they all turned up the same week at the exclusive Golden Haunches Fat Farm outside Albuquerque. Between bites of kelp, they began reminiscing about such incidents as the time Dottie left her wig case in the bum trip tent at the Watkins Glen Rock Festival. That was a climactic week for the world of music. Shortly thereafter, they shocked the Music Establishment by reemerging as the "Dynamite Sisters" we know and love today. Their hit single "Money Is Power" installed them as the permanent First Ladies of Funk Land. And now, these killer tunesmiths offer the best of an inspired career on this long-awaited album. So sit back and get ready for the Dynamite Sisters. They're *bad, bad, bad . . .* and that means good, good, good!

—*Trucia Kushner*

We're so glad we had a chance to play with some of the meanest session cats around: Felix Castiglione, electric piano; Terry Dinwiddie, wood block; Bunnie Trask, bells; Blind Orange Julius, additional guitar and vocals; Joleen Jackson, LaWanda Butterfield, Saundra Soames, vocals; Tony West, Joe Baker, Ted Jefferson, horns; The Sandusky String Quartet, strings;
Mr. R. Zimmerman, harmonica.
Recorded and mixed at Muscle Shoals.
Produced by Allen Toussaint's second cousin.
Engineer: Jane Hipp, "Nashville's First Woman Engineer."
Photography by Lynn Goldsmith.
Album design by Judy Jacklin.
Lyrics by Trucia Kushner.
Spiritual Adviser: Mirabai.

PAYOLA RECORDS

I am Eloise
I am twenty-six
I live at the Plaza

There is a lobby which is
enormously large
And good for
parading

Sometimes I see Robert Altman
I know he would like to put me
in one of his pictures
But he is just too shy to say hello

So I have to do it for him

My day is rawther full
If there is a lot of luggage trying to get
into the elevator
and these people are all in a crowd and
smoking and from out of town or
something, I edge into
the middle of it and
lose my contact lens

If Margaux Hemingway
could make it here
why cawn't I?

Sometimes I wake up feeling tired tired tired
Then I pick up the telephone
and call Room Service
Ooooooooo I absolutely love Room Service

And I always say "Hello this is me ELOISE and would you
kindly send up two fried eggs two pieces of toast two Bloody Marys
two Dexamil and a copy of this morning's guest register and
charge it please

Thank you very much"

They always know it's me
And sometimes they say
"Sorry Eloise your credit is overdrawn"

And I have to get up in my nightie
and skibble downstairs
to give Raoul the Bell Captain another blowjob
What a bother

113

Here's what I can do
pluck my eyebrows
have one two three four five six seven eight nineten orgasms
just like that
sing all the words to Abbey Road
get dizzy and fall down
eat an eight-course meal at Lutece
then stick my finger down my throat

Here's what I like
my 108-year-old turtle Skipperdee
uncircumcised men
my mother's charge account at Bergdorf's

Here's what I hate
salmonella poisoning
taxes

Every Wednesday I have to go to the second floor and see my shrink
He does absolutely nothing but listen

Sometimes I sklonk him on the kneecap

He says that if I am not careful I am going to be dead
by the time I'm thirty for Lord's sake

And here's the thing of it
Most of the time I'm on the telephone
Sometimes Nanny calls me from the Village Nursing Home
She always says everything 3 times
like Eloise I am lonely lonely lonely
I cawn't cawn't cawn't
stand talking to her

She is boring

boring

boring

Once Bianca let me hold her cane
And I ate the cherry out of Truman's drink
downstairs in Trader Vic's
And if it is too tacky tacky tacky
I pretend anyone is Clive Davis
And I ask him, would you care to join me
for a breath of amyl nitrate?
But oh my Lord those United Miners and Metallurgists
were the absolutely most fun

The thing of it is
I like the Plaza because it charges per room
not per person
And Nanny always said
good help is so hard to find
Oooooooo I absolutely love the Plaza*

*a member of the Great Western Chain of Hotels

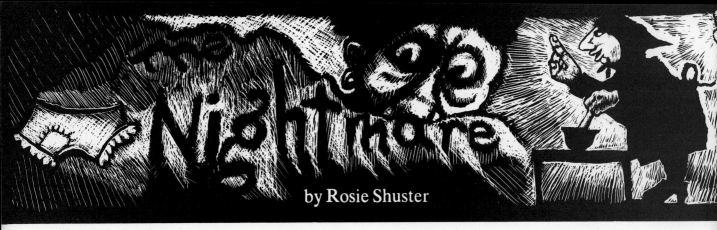

Nightmare

by Rosie Shuster

I guess it all started back in my grandmother's kitchen over a bowl of watery maple junket...

"Life's no picnic, my child," I can still hear her say, "and I won't always be here to look out for you. You've always been my favorite, so listen smartly to an old woman's last words."

There she'd pause to remove her hankie from the rolled-up sleeve of her grey furnace sweater with the lint pills, and blow her nose meaningfully.

"My child, whatever road in life you choose to follow, make sure you follow it in clean underwear. A fresh pair every day and you'll never go far wrong. Make an old woman proud of you. Remember—a neatly pressed blouse does not good grooming make. If you want to know the *true* nature of a person, look to their foundation garments."

For my grandmother, these were words to live by. I am haunted yet by the piercing wisdom in those old eyes as she looked up from her watery maple junket and pronounced the words I'd hear over and over in my dreams.

"You know me—I'm a good woman, and I wouldn't be caught dead in the same pair twice."

But why, I wondered, why was it of such life and death importance to change your underwear every day?

"Because, my dear foolish one, you never *know* when you're going to find yourself in the middle of an accident."

Ah yes, of course! How stupid of me! No—you never really could know, not unless you were the kind of person who planned your accidents in advance. So, then, the only sensible life game-plan was to be at all times meticulously groomed for the worst. Otherwise, an accident could utterly ruin you . . . not to mention casting seedy aspersions all over your ancestry.

But what, I panicked, what if I fucked up just once? What if I temporarily blanked out and unthinkingly crawled back into the pair from the day before? All would be lost. The fruit of a lifetime's labor down the tubes, irretrievable, because of one stupid slip-up in the lingerie department. Gone, gone forever because the laundromat closed early, because the hot water main burst, because it poured on the clothesline, because the elasticized waistband snapped, because of one crummy telltale safety pin.

This accident haunted me. It grew into an obsession and invaded my very dreams; the dreams escalated into nightmares and the nightmares kept coming back like clockwork. All these years later and still I can't break free from its horrible grip on my psyche. Perhaps it'll help if I talk about it.

The nightmare:

It's rush hour in the Big Apple. I'm in my Volkswagen headed for Carnegie Hall where I have an appointment with destiny. (The destiny itself is a bit fuzzy.) This part keeps changing from nightmare to nightmare; but it always involves something I've done that's artistically extraordinary.

Sometimes I'm about to be photographed for the cover of Time; *sometimes I'm on my way to pick up my Oscar. A few times I've been hailed as the new Virginia Woolf—only funny, not depressing. Twice I discovered a new color, and once I performed the entire Rockettes' Easter Pageant myself.*

There I am, stiff with shock, upside down in the driver's seat, legs poking out of the sunroof. A crowd is gathering. I sense it is comprised of my entire eighth grade class.

CROWD: Two days in a row.

POLICE SIREN APPROACHING. TIRES SCREECHING TO A HALT. CAR DOORS OPENING AND SLAMMING SHUT. FOOTSTEPS.

COP #1: O.K. O.K. Step aside.

WOMAN: Officer, there's been a terrible accident. That lady . . . oooh . . .

COP #2: Looks to me like hit-and-run.

COP #1: Yeah, but can you blame them?

TRAFFIC NOISES. HORN BLARING. SCREECH OF BRAKES. A WOMAN'S SHRIEK. CHROME AND METAL CRUNCHING. GLASS SHATTERING. CAR DOOR SLAMMING. MOANS. FOOTSTEPS.

MAN: Miss? Are you all right, Miss? *(soft gasp)*
   Omigod! I can't look.

WOMAN: Is she that badly hurt, honey?

MAN: Yeah, but it's not that.
   It's her underwear. Same pair twice.

WOMAN: Oh no! Don't let the kids see.

MAN: Maybe we should call an ambulance.

WOMAN: Maybe we should call a lingerie shop.

Diana Bryan

People are jeering, doing cheap one-liners, all at my expense. Everybody agrees I am the crummiest "free show" they've ever seen.

CROWD: Easily the most poorly groomed accident victim of the year.

AMBULANCE SIREN APPROACHING. BRAKES. DOORS SLAMMING. FOOTSTEPS.

AMBULANCE DRIVER: *(Under his breath)* Shit, I never should've eaten that Egg McMuffin. *(With authority)* Quick! Throw a blanket over her. Or put down the sunroof.

CROWD: Didn't her grandmother ever teach her anything?

MY GRANDMOTHER: Feh! I wouldn't be caught dead in those.

Yes, there amongst them and witness to it all, huddled poignantly inside her grey furnace sweater, stands my poor grandmother, tears streaming into her watery maple junket.

MY GRANDMOTHER: That I should live to see the firstborn of my only son upside down with those on! Feh!

At her side and trying to comfort her, stands my beloved second grade teacher, Miss Hinks, biting her lip bravely, eyes glazed over with terrific disappointment.

MISS HINKS: Buck up. It's just a stage she's going through. *(Under her breath, incredulously)* She was wearing those yesterday! And to think she was such a promising pupil!

With a crowbar, the ambulance driver pries me out of the sunroof and loads me into the back of the ambulance.

LOUD SIREN. AMBULANCE MOVING THROUGH RUSH HOUR TRAFFIC.

As we whiz through the red lights, I find myself wishing they'd slow down. Sure, I'm fading fast, but even so, I'm in no hurry. The last thing I want is another opinion.

AMBULANCE SCREECHING TO A HALT. DOORS SLAMMING. FOOTSTEPS. GRUNTS AND MOANS. HOSPITAL WAITING ROOM HUBBUB. BED WHEELING DOWN CORRIDOR.

ORDERLY: Did you catch what just checked into emergency?

AMBULANCE DRIVER: It was a hit-and-run.

HEAD NURSE: Yeah, but can you blame them?

In the doorway of Intensive Care hover nurses in white wedgies and interns in white cotton masks, giggling.

NURSES AND INTERNS: Bzzz. Tee-hee-hee! The pair from the day before.

NASAL HOSPITAL P.A. SYSTEM: Paging Dr. Welby. Dr. Welby, please report to Emergency. Tsk-tsk. Poorly groomed woman in critical condition.

DIM FOOTSTEPS ALONG CORRIDOR GROWING LOUDER.

I know Marcus from "Father Knows Best" reruns. He knows me from other dreams.

DR. WELBY: *(Soft gasp)* Omigod! *(A beat)* Nurse, cancel that chili dog. *(Gently, to me)* Is it really *you,* Princess? Princess . . . you haven't . . . changed.

HEAD NURSE: Tell us something we don't know.

DR. WELBY: *(To nurse)* Put on the kettle, nurse. We're going to need plenty of hot water. *(To me)* Silly girl, how long has it been?

HEAD NURSE: Two days.

How I yearn to explain to Marcus how this has happened . . . how, down to my last pair from yesterday, I ran out of nonphosphate detergent, and, damned with a raised ecological consciousness and a corny dream that one day our children might have clean oceans to swim in, I could not bring myself to buy that exploitative box of Duz! If only he could know that, even though I've fucked up pretty inexcusably with the panties, I'm still the kind of person who makes the time to brush after every meal. . . . But my jaw has turned to stone.

ME: *(Croaking pathetically)* Help.

DR. WELBY: I'll do what I can, Kitten. It's just that we have this policy here about a fresh pair every day. . . . But then again, what the hay! I'll stick my neck out for you, Kitten. *(A beat)* True, I could lose my license over it, but what the hay! I'm gonna present these silly panties to the medical brass *personally* at the next hospital board meeting, and, if that doesn't work, why, I'll take these silly panties to the A.M.A. myself!

I'd wake up in a cold sweat, with my nightgown and the bedclothes wrapped around my face, mumbling "silly panties" over and over deliriously. I mean, sure, they were just silly panties, but they kept me off the cover of *Time.*

SQUAWS

BLANCHE KUSAK

Pittsburgh Squaws

BLANCHE KUSAK	#12
SHORTSTOP	

Hgt: 5' 10"
Wgt: 175
Glove size: 7½
Shoe size: 9B
Dress size: 14
Birthdate: 4/1/45

Home: Garfield Heights, Ohio

Favorite saying: "I just wanna play ball!!"
Blanche's hobby is gourmet cooking.
Likes snuff, dislikes "baseball groupies."

© FLOOZY CHEWING GUM, INC. PRTD. IN U.S.A.

MARXETTES

OLGA LEGANOV

Odessa Marxettes

OLGA LEGANOV

Hgt: 4' 11"
Wgt: 90
Birthdate: 7/27/64

Home: Vladivostok, USSR

Favorite saying: "Through diligent and correct effort combined with the rectification of mistaken ideas, the acknowledgment of the needs of the workers, and an avoidance of dialectical errors or impure elitism, at the end of ten years I should be able to have my own apartment."

Olga's hobby is collecting and recycling used nylons.

CLAMS

"JENNY" SMYTHE

JENNIFER "JENNY" SMYTHE
Chesapeake Bay Clams

Second seeded in 1973 Official Aqua Net Hair Spray Tournament

Birthdate: 9/13/50
Wgt: 115
Hgt: 5' 4"

Home: Kennebunkport, Maine

Favorite saying: "I'm a female first, a tennis player second, a Nor'easter third, an American fourth, and an ambassador of goodwill when I go around the world. But basically I'm just me."
Jenny brushes after every meal. Her hobby is virginity.

WOM
SPO
CA

AT
O
Y

by A
Dea

MUKLUKS

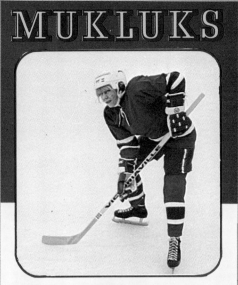

MARIE "BEBE" BOUCHARD

tts and
lman

Saskatchewan Mukluks

MARIE "BEBE" BOUCHARD   #29

RIGHT WING

Hgt: 5' 9"   Previous injuries: 46
Wgt: 145   Birthdate: 8/10/55
College: Greenland University
Home: Kamloops, British Columbia
Favorite saying: **"Si quelqu'un m'approche, je lui casserai ben la gueule, la maudite chienne!"** (Translation: "I'll break the jaw of any lousy bitch who gets near me!")
Marie's hobby is undergoing plastic surgery.
She is studying to be a veterinarian in her spare time.

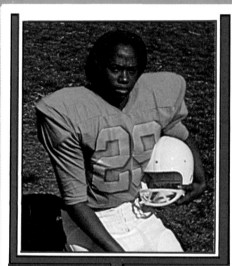

RONNIE MAE   MACKINS
FILLIES

#93 Dallas Fillies

RONNIE MAE MACKINS

TIGHT END
Measurements: 44" 34" 46" Hgt: 6' 2"
Birthdate: 6/17/48   Wgt: 225
College: Southern Methodist
            University
Home: El Paso, Texas
Ronnie Mae relaxes with paint-by-number kits.
Favorite color: black
Favorite food: Colonel Sanders Extra-Crispy
Favorite saying: "Get on with your bad self!"
Greatest ambition: To endorse as many products as Joe Namath. She has just signed to do a sixty-second TV spot for Jockey brand undershorts.

SATELLITES

Prague Satellites

"BIG JACKIE" KUCZYK

SHOT PUT, DECATHLON
Hgt: 5' 11"
Wgt: 210
Birthdate: 11/29/49

Home: Plzen, Czechoslovakia

Favorite saying: "UNNNNNNNN-GGGGG! MMMMMMMPPPPHH! GRRRRRRRRRRR!"
Jackie loves "modern music, like Louis Armstrong, Dave Brubeck, and Blood, Sweat, and Tears," hates "medical examinations where they make you take all your clothes off." Her hobby is being a sex change.

MARRIAGE 70'S STYLE

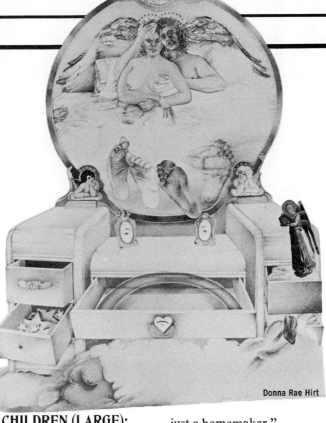

Donna Rae Hirt

by Lois Gould

COOKING:
The perfect wife does not tell her friends what a lousy cook her husband is.

The perfect husband does not tell his friends what a good cook his wife is.

CAREERS:
The perfect wife doesn't object to her husband's having a career, if it doesn't make him neglect his household duties.

The perfect husband doesn't object to his wife's *not* having a career, if it doesn't make him neglect his household duties.

OPEN MARRIAGE:
The perfect wife feels free to open the subject.

The perfect husband feels free to try closing it.

OTHER WOMEN:
The perfect wife does not worry that if she stops being a perfect wife, other women will break up her marriage.

The perfect husband worries that if he stops being a perfect husband, other women will break up his marriage.

CHILDREN (SMALL):
For the perfect wife, small children are no problem. This is because where there are small children (including an imperfect husband), there is no such thing as a perfect wife.

CHILDREN (LARGE):
The perfect wife has stopped worrying about her daughter's having sex.

The perfect husband has stopped worrying about his son's having enough sex.

HOUSEWORK:
The perfect wife does not nag the perfect husband about how dirty the house is. She installs light dimmers.

HEAVY LIFTING:
The perfect wife never says, "Oh dear, I can't carry such a big load."

The perfect husband never says, "Make two trips."

IDENTITY CRISIS:
When a rude stranger asks, "What do *you* do?" the perfect husband does not cringe and mumble, "I'm just a homemaker."

The perfect wife strikes back with "How much do you make a year?"

CLOTHES:
The perfect wife never complains about not having a thing to wear. She wears recycled patched denim, and when she and the perfect husband are dressing up to go out, *she's* ready first. (His hair takes longer.)

JEALOUSY:
When either the perfect wife or the perfect husband finds strange blond hairs on the other's recycled patched denim, both understand that "jealousy" is a sick, destructive emotion caused by an archaic concept of marriage as "sexual ownership." They are looking for a healthy, constructive emotion to replace "jealousy." Meanwhile, they may have to give up strange blonds.

MENOPAUSE:
The perfect wife won't tell jokes about his, if he won't tell jokes about hers.

CONSCIOUSNESS-RAISING:
The perfect wife comes home smiling from her weekly "C-R group" meeting. Two members of the group have left their husbands: two more are "into" adultery, and one refers to her spouse as "my attaché."

The perfect husband does not wait up for his wife. When she gets home, she finds him smiling, too—in his sleep.

LOOKS:
The perfect wife does not need to be told she looks terrific for her age. She looks terrific, period, and she knows it.

The perfect husband knows she knows it.

SEX (MARITAL):
The perfect wife and the perfect husband know that when it comes to sex, nobody's perfect.

SEX (EXTRAMARITAL):
See above.

LOVE:
Love is never having to be (or be married to) a perfect wife.

120

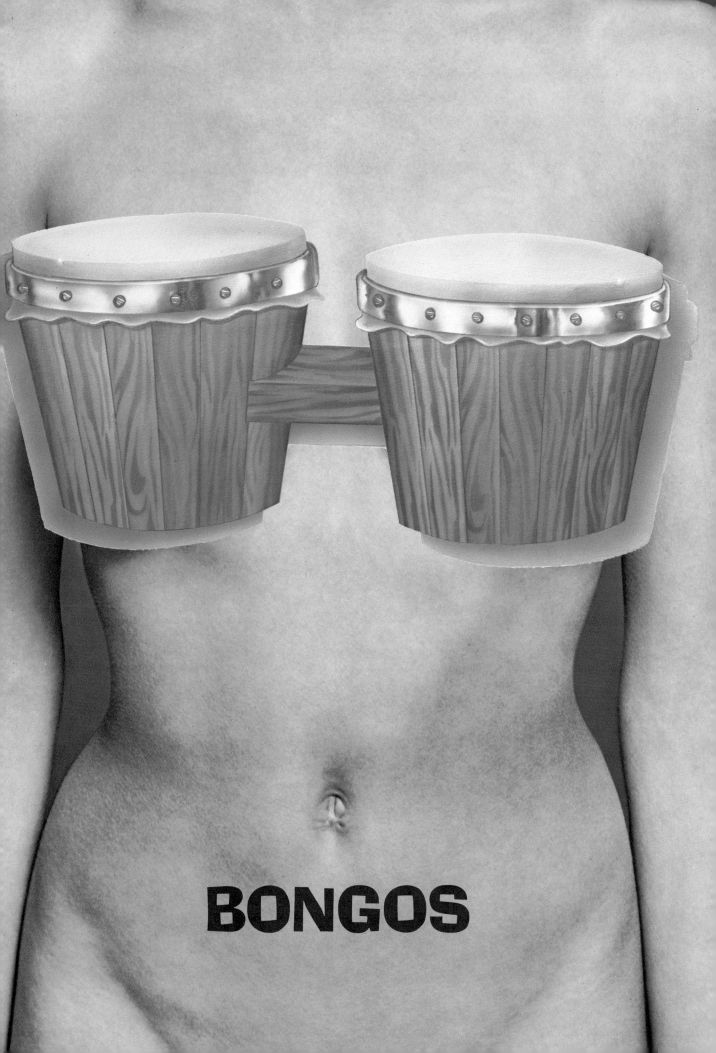

TITTERS' Heavy

100

The heaviest of the heavy...

Anne, Beverly, and Sheila Sherriff Scott

Golda

Anita Ekberg's mother

Pat Ast

Michelina Valente

Mrs. Helen Putnam

"Little B

Dorothy and Louise Threipland

Olive "Can-Can" Carpenter

"Thelma"

Marsel Buchanan

Iris Dees Porch

Valentina

Mrs. Helen Putnam

Tally Brown

Maxine Gates

Baby Irene Parry

Mrs. Helen Putnam

Bonnie "Bubbles" Murphy

Shelley Winters

Dolly Dimples

Jane Darwell

Sophie Tucker

Margaret Rutherfor

Speranza Gorini

Juanita Hall

Wanda

Marie Dressler

Barbara Jean Baker and Carole Me

retta Walker, Mona Howard, Elmira Rider, Anita
ewis, Beverly Miller, and Nadine Hermann

Eleanor Ruth Cohen

Betti-Ann

June the Marvel

"Tootsie" Hoolihan

eny Eversong

Bernadine "Muscles" Grohs

Too heavy to fit here . . .

Totie Fields	Linda Hopkins
Totie Fields' leg	Barbara Jordan
Shirley Booth	Flo Kennedy
Ethel Merman	Bella Abzug
Elsa Maxwell	Aunt Bluebell
Kaye Ballard	Elaine Kaufman
Pearl Bailey	Brenda Morgenstern
Tessie O'Shea	Mrs. Leonid Brezhnev
Dinah Washington	Mrs. Jack Sprat
Sarah Vaughn	Mrs. Randolph Hearst
Ella Fitzgerald	Rosemary Kent
Bessie Smith	Mrs. Helen Putnam

Loretta and Muriel

Dees Porch

Miss Peggy Leonard

Sarah Caldwell

Baby Rose

"La Siciliana"

McDaniel

The Singing Chubbettes

Frau Gerta M. L. Schmidt

Babette

Shirley Turner

Smith

TV Mama

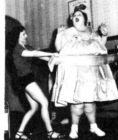
Baby Frances

Cutie Pavlowski

Mrs. Billie Ware, Miss Mildred Myers, Mrs. Helen
Bell, Miss Janelle Scott, and Mrs. Helen Putnam

ama Cass

Slim Carter

Nina Brown

Diana Dors

Solange

Shirley Goelz

My Secret Cabbage Patch

by Maundy Thursday

by Susan Toepfer

INTRODUCTION

☐ "Tell Me Where Your Brain Is," He Said.

In my mind, as in our love making, I am at the crisis point: We are at the Battle of Waterloo and it is cold. Fifty or sixty of us are huddled inside a make-shift shelter. Suddenly, we jump up to watch Napoleon walk under his horse and I feel a cannon crawl between my legs. In my excitement at seeing Napoleon slip on the ice, I don't turn to face my fornicator, but climb slowly and stealthily . . .

"What are you? Some kind of pervert?" he screamed as he zipped up his fly and threw me out of the back seat of his T-bird. I tried to explain that I wasn't rejecting *him,* but helping us *both.*

"Oh, George, how *could* you be so unenlightened?" I thought as I refastened my circle pin. "If you don't cotton to a cannon, how can I ever tell you about my anteater dream? Did you ever stop to think what 'the handkerchief game' was all about?"

No, of course you didn't, because you were a boy. Or maybe you were a girl. I don't know, sometimes I get confused, which is where my husband Howie comes in handy. You may not believe this, girls, but it wasn't until I married Howie and got over my childish affair with George that I dared expose any more of my most cherished sexual fantasies. I'll never forget Howie's reaction when shyly, coyly, I let him in on the one about the three little pigs.

"What an imagination!" he exclaimed. "Did you really make that up? Jeepers Creepers, Maundy, I bet you could write a book!"

With Howard's hounding, I started a novel . . . but quickly realized it was too much work. The best way to avoid that, it occurred to my incredibly fertile, lively, and liberated mind, was to throw myself on the mercy of my sisters and persuade *them* to give me *their* erotic fantasies. If the unthinkable happened, and it turned out I really was a little bit kinky (which I am *not,* George, no matter what your analyst says about the time with the waffle iron), then I'd just count on all the tired old clichés men had been chortling over for years. So while Howard explored the locker rooms and neighborhood bars, I got a job passing out Jane Parker rolls at the local A&P.

At first, the women I questioned were vague and vacuous. "Oh, you mean the old urine fetish," one said as she stopped to pick up some Pampers. "You don't mean something like the Blob, do you?" asked another.

But then one day an elderly, blue-haired woman asked me to help her reach the Italian loaves. Without a word, she walked on toward the fish counter, but at this point, I knew: When that little old lady got into bed that night, she wouldn't be alone. She, too, would be acting out one of my personal favorites, "Christ Feeding the Multitudes." I felt a sense of oneness with womankind, a thrill of titillating telepathy with all those frustrated (but highly imaginative, sensual, and seductive) females *everywhere.*

I also got the great idea to put an ad in every paper that would print it, asking other, less enterprising, women to share their secret sexual fantasies for the purpose of "serious research." How can I convey the joy Howard and I felt when thousands of letters began pouring into our fashionable Upper East Side post-office box? As I opened as many as I needed to fill 200 pages, I discovered I wasn't the only woman whose brain was beaming in on dwarves and Israelis and Kate Smith when a man was knocking at my heavenly portals.

Every female on earth (except, of course, the stupid and sexless ones) had a fantasy-frazzled mind like mine. So I would like to thank all the wonderful, wacky women who gave me the material I needed for this serious scientific project by coming up with improbably "dirty" situations that fit perfectly all the graffiti Howard copied from the men's room walls. Without them, I would never have been able to get back at George, the deprived dullard, or become a recognized authority on women's most private sexual thoughts who, due to a book that appeals to so many men's fantasies, is now considered the most desirable, intriguing woman since Helen of Troy! Today, my life is one continual round of parties, panels, and talk shows, and Howard and I have access to all the most elite literary circles. So again, thank you, my female benefactors—and keep those cards and letters coming! I need them for my projected sequel, "My Secret Rutabaga Row." □

MOTEL ROOM #1: THE FLOP-HOUSE OF THE MIND

□ We spend most of our lives furtively seeking sexual gratification—hiding behind closed doors and keeping the noise away from nosy neighbors, the CIA, and those curious cherubs we sometimes inadvertently produce. But in our fantasies, of course, we would prefer to cater to a crowd and become the Colonel Sanders of Sex! □

Clitoria

I am a happily married mother of four, and though my husband is a perfect lover, I still have fantasies during sexual intercourse. Maybe it's because my husband is so perfect that I have this recurring fantasy that we have driven down to Sam's Garage to get the muffler on our Ford fixed. While my husband is busy talking to Sam, I am approached by a small, well-built Oriental grease monkey. Soon, the two of us are mounting the engine block, where my mysterious new acquaintance reaches beneath my skirt and begins to massage my poontang with gasoline. Just as I am about to explode in Exxon, he jerks away those small yellow fingers and screws me onto a nearby piston. Then he wraps himself around my neck and jams his little yellow button up my nose. To my delight, Sam, my husband, and everyone within a one-mile radius soon runs to my side. As the Chinaman and I sit there writhing and wiggling—the piston urging us on in our gyrations—I lift up my skirt and wait for the applause! "Turn it off, turn it off!" yells the crowd, but I am beyond them, lost to the pumping, fucking for my fans, bleeding like a stuck pig. . . . I've never told my husband about this, because I'm afraid he would call me a pervert. Am I? (Letter)

□ Isn't this heartbreaking? Here is an example of a woman with a perfectly ordinary, healthy sexual fantasy, and even in this day and age, she nourishes fears of male rejection. When *will* men learn to accept such flights of fantasy as a normal part of every woman's experience? □

Vulvina

Ever since I had my twentieth baby, my husband's penis has felt like a Bic pen entering a whale's mouth. According to my friends down at the Women's Health Center, my vagina currently measures twenty-and-a-half inches by thirty-six-and-a-quarter inches, and boy, am I proud! All the girls, I mean women, at the Center are really impressed, and whenever our instructor needs someone for yogurt demo, I am chosen. But even though all the gals, I mean women, I know are really envious of my cavernous canal, I find it an odd disadvantage when Herman places his average-sized penis inside. So whenever we're making love, I mean fucking, I find my thoughts drifting back to the Center. As my husband continues his futile probing, I think instead of all the yogurt that has entered me in the last few months, and have this fantasy about Ellen and Amy and Paula and Key Lu smearing my insides with Dannon's Natural, then bending down to eat it. Only when I think about this can I achieve orgasm, and even though I am so happily married, I'm often disturbed by this fantasy. Am I a lesbian, I mean gay? (Letter)

MOTEL ROOM #2: BLOOD AND WELTS

□ Any woman who's chained down by sexual fantasy knows the joys of being naughty (but nice) and getting punished for it. Howie will kill me for even whispering this, but what I'm really talking about is (*ssh!*): whippings, beatings, snakes, and that all-time favorite, rape! □

Justine

I am not a lesbian, and the reason I tell you this straight off is because I figure any broad as interested in other women's sex lives as you probably is. But I'm not, no matter what you think when I tell you that my favorite fantasy involves having the shit kicked out of me by a big bull dyke. Usually, she's just zooming by my L.A. pad (which I share with a *man*) while I'm out on the lawn catching the rays in my "string" bikini (which shows that I'm a *real* woman). Then she comes to a screeching halt, climbs off her bike, takes off her helmet, and starts kicking me. That's all that happens, but it's an idea I really like and what I usually think about when I'm applying the Q.T. (Postcard)

Clarissa

□ Clarissa's is an unusual story, because unlike most of us fantastic fantasizers, she has *lived* her dream. Yes, Clarissa was actually *raped!* And after you've read her true story, I'm sure you'll agree with Howie, me, and the NYPD that nearly every time a woman cries "Rape!" it's just another frustrated fantasy! □

You asked why I carry this capsule of cyanide? Well, my husband gave it to me the very day we wed, because he had heard my whole, horrifying story. Charlie is a unique man because he was not turned off by the fact that I was raped. On the other hand, he didn't want it to happen again, and if it did, he didn't want to have me around. But when he gave me that capsule, I really felt guilty, because I'd told him that the rape was a hideous, degrading, and demeaning experience. What really happened was one day when I was seven, I met this strange-looking man who offered me some candy, but he only gave me one Mary Jane and said if I wanted the Jujubes, I'd have to come with him into the woods. Then he said if I let him put his wienie in my whatever-it-was, he'd give me a whole bag of malted milk balls. I was really scared and even shaking, but I was so busy thinking about that candy that by the time—*Holy cow, did it feel good!!!* And to this day, when my husband is screwing me, I think of the Candy Man, as I like to call him. Of course, I have to keep up the story about how dreadful it all was, and sometimes I worry about that cyanide. But if I ever run into the Candy Man again, I figure I'll just come home and pop it into Charlie's beer. (Taped)

Liberia

I am a thirty-year-old feminist who is living every woman's fantasies, so why should I need any? I mean, here I am, a chick in Cleveland, pulling in a good fifty grand a year and getting laid an average of eighty-two times a week by anywhere from one to five of my 123 lovers, who come in all sizes, sexes, and colors. But I hope you can help me, because every time I get in the sack, even when it's with Jane or Fang Wu, I have this fantasy about living in Shaker Heights, up to my elbows in dishes, with a six-month-old baby crying for his bottle and a husband who comes home and yells because there aren't any olives left for his martini. Please tell me, am I a masochist? (Dictated letter)

MOTEL ROOM #3: LITTLE ME

☐ Perhaps it's because women have traditionally had so much time, to say nothing of Tide, on their hands that they turn to fooling around *down there* more often than men. Such autoerotic moments are ideal for fantasy. ☐

Uterella

This is my fantasy, which I usually have after sprinkling the lawn, when I sneak inside the garage and lie down on the hose: I am standing in front of the Lincoln Memorial in Washington, D.C. That great, big, beautiful man is smiling down on me. All I can think about are his great, big, beautiful hands and great, big, ugly face and what those say about what's inside his great, big, baggy pants! Even though my husband and three kids are with me, I can no longer control myself. I break away from the tour guide and climb on top that marble lap. Somehow, with my nail file, I manage to chisel through and

get to the real Lincoln! Placing my legs on his marble chest, I get ready for sixty-nine, then sixty-five, sixty-four, and finally 1863! (Back of envelope)

Miss Emma Cornflea

I am the children's librarian at a major metropolitan branch, and every day when Mr. Rupal, from the Science and Education Department, walks by, I have this most terrible thought. Please, please, kind friend, keep my name forever secret, lest I lose the respect of the world and my small source of income! But at the mere sight of Mr. Rupal, my secret lust compels me to slip a copy of *Fanny Hill* between my legs. My shabby grey dress is transformed into a flaming scarlet gown, and I am standing before a gilded mirror, removing my rubies, when Mr. Rupal bursts through the door to my scarlet boudoir and, as I cry out in alarm, grabs the back of my scarlet gown, throws me over a scarlet chair, and pushes his throbbing member into my precious jewel, over and over again, without mercy, as the tears stream down my scarlet face and (Reserve Book Card)

Sister Elizabeth

May the Blessed Virgin forgive me for answering your ad, which I inadvertently saw when I took a copy of *Screw* away from one of those nasty little boys in my catechism class. Yet perhaps you can help me where He has failed, or rather *I* have failed *Him*. I suppose I could have gone on forever, leading my secret life of sin, if it weren't for my Order's decision to stop wearing those lovely long black robes. You see, before all the Sisters here were given street clothes, I had a certain amount of privacy. I know it was wrong, and every night I gave myself forty-two lashes and said twenty-five Hail Marys to make up, but for fully a decade I had been engaging in carnal acts with one of those wonderful little yellow men. I originally met my Oriental friend when the Jesuits pirated some anti-Communists out of the mainland and were trying to find homes in which they could stay. Maybe it was those slanted eyes, or even—may the Blessed Virgin understand—the notion of what might be beneath his little pajamas. Whatever my misguided motive, I agreed to allow Hung Wee to come with me to the convent, and it wasn't long before he was doing shameful things to me right in front of my students (although they couldn't see, as the Chinaman was small enough to hide under my skirts). But now, here I am, dressed in a loathsome blue *suit*, and Hung Wee has been forced to find his way in the outside world. When he first departed, I was sad but relieved, believing that my sinful ways had passed and that I would no longer stray from my vows. Instead, I turned to Him—in a way we're not supposed to at all. Where before I prayed to Him, did His work, and (even with Hung Wee beneath my skirts) walked with Him, now I found myself placing Him where the Chinaman used to be. For two years, I've read every article I could find on "Getting Over Him," but none has helped. I am lost to sin, the most dreadful sin ever imagined by a Bride of Christ, and I will sit and pray that where Mary has failed, you will overcome. Please pray for Sister Elizabeth and ask all those fallen women to do the same. (Catechism Card).

MOTEL ROOM #4: THE LAVENDER LOUNGE

☐ The following should once and for all answer the question all my male friends asked me when they found out about my research in this delicate area.* ☐

Joey

I have to get this in the mail real fast before my lover Georgette comes home. I am a lesbian and have been ever since fifth grade, when my best friend Ann got into me with some firecrackers. But the problem is, though I am definitely gay and have no problems with that and even told my mother shortly before her heart attack, whenever Georgette is licking my clit I have this fantasy about what it would feel like if her mouth was a man's and wouldn't he be able to do it better and then afterwards I could have the real thing instead of a dildo and even though I've never seen one and Georgette says they're disgusting, I just have to think of one to really get off. Do you think these latent heterosexual tendencies are anything to worry about? (Letter)

Jemima

☐ Although Jemima is not of the lesbian persuasion, I have placed her in this "other women" chapter because she is a genuine colored person. ☐

Okay, honky, here goes. I know how all you ofay twats think there isn't anything better than a Chinaman when it comes to shit like muff-diving, but what I really want, and what I think about whenever my big black man comes home, is one of those pale white ones—with a Ph.D.! I am forty-three years old and tired out from big black pricks, and nothing could make me happier than one of those intellectual honkies with glasses who would read me poetry and bring me flowers and never want to ball at all. (Letter)

MOTEL ROOM #5: THE ASPCA

☐ Nice, friendly anteaters are everywhere. Even if you don't have one, the neighbors do. And you can always count on an anteater to keep his snout shut! Is it any surprise then that of all animals, anteaters star most frequently in female sexual fantasies (the reverie offered here is typical of dozens I have received), and that such fantasies are most often acted out with these always-accessible beasts? ☐

Kitty

I would really like my husband to perform cunnilingus on me, but whenever I ask he gets real mad and says, "I don't put food in my nose, do I?" So this is how I get even. Every time he's slamming it in me, grunting and

*"Do lesbians have orgasms?"

groaning and damn near crushing me underneath his undershirt with all that flab inside, I think about spreading honey on my cunt, while all the time, an anteater is eyeing me. The more honey I put in, the more ants come inside, and before you can say *Mother Nature*, the anteater darts over and starts eating away with that long, long, long tongue sliding over my ass, tickling my clitoris, then slithering down to my cervix, devouring ants and licking until way past my husband is the hell out and snoring away. (Letter)

MOTEL ROOM #6: LITTLE YELLOW MEN

☐ Everything about him, imagined and unimagined, adds heat to the wok: He's forbidden because of his political beliefs; his instrument of pleasure is conceived in mythical distortions; and the story's been around for years that his sexual expertise comes close to the terrors of Kung Fu. But of course, size is the real attraction in the yellow man fantasy. It's never just a yellow man, but a *little* yellow man, never just a yellow organ but a *little* yellow organ. What a burden for those poor little yellow men, laboring under such an impossible mystique! ☐

Mary Lou

☐ I've always loved sleeping with Chinamen, more than with Negras or Redskins, maybe because my favorite food is Chinese. But so far, I've never gotten one of my yellow lovers to come through with this fantasy, which I have while masturbating with a Big Mac. What happens is: A little yellow man slips under my door to my bedroom and starts opening those little white boxes, smearing me with Hung Ying Gai Ding and Szechuan Beef and fried rice and soy sauce. I became more frantic with each course, to the point where I am slobbering with anticipation. Walking all over my body with his agile little feet, he grinds in every tasty morsel, then whips out his chopsticks and has his own private feast! Beginning with my breasts, he goes down my whole body, and by the time he hits my clit, it's Chinese New Year! "My little fortune cookie," I whisper as his baby-wang zips in and dragons and firecrackers and Chou En Lai and the entire Red Guard explode inside my cunt! Wow, what a turn-on! (Menu)

Twatsy

☐ I often have fantasies about Orientals, particularly of the Chinese variety, and even though I would never, never let one touch me, I can't resist the idea of a Chinaman nestling between my thighs. I am now and always will be anti-Communist and wouldn't trust one of those little yellow men any further than I would a Russki. But in fantasy, my lover is usually Mao Tse-tung, and I find the fantasy works best when I masturbate in front of that picture of him swimming down the Yangtse, with his grotesque un-American body bobbing in the waves, and his head the size of a pin, moving up down up down up down. (Letter)

MONEY MONEY

MONEY

by Peg Bracken

"What troubles?" asked Flora, interestedly, as she busily made fresh tea. . . . "Haven't you enough money?" For she knew that this is what is the matter with nearly everybody over twenty-five.
— Stella Gibbons

A magazine editor wrote to me a while ago, wanting to know if I would review a book for them.

"Will you do a review of Sal Nuccio's *New York Times Guide to Personal Finance?*" was the exact wording, as I remember.

It occurred to me that perhaps they were asking Willie Mays to review *The Complete Book of Home Embroidery,* too, or getting Zsa Zsa Gabor's ideas on *The Woman's Own Encyclopedia of House-cleaning Helps from Attic to Basement.* But I happened to be unusually interested in personal finance at the time, having recently been taken poor, and though book reviews don't pay very much, it's still money. So I said I would, and I did.

It was a good book, though terribly sound. And oddly pure. I got the impression that Mr. Nuccio wasn't quite leveling about some of the aspects of money that really puzzle people. I mean the itty-bitty nitty-gritty part of the thing, or about some of the low holds and dirty grips that can be so helpful in handling it. And, frankly, I am glad that he left that one little fuzzy green corner, just this side of left field, vacant for me.

Not that I blame the author for his omissions. Far from it. It is a rare expert who clearly realizes how inexpert someone else can be. Natu-

rally, he didn't think to explain things like why your Assets and Liabilities should balance, the way they do on stockholders' reports. (If I owed precisely as much as I have, I'd know I was in terrible shape, but the corporations all brag about it.) Or whether twenty-five bobby pins for thirty-two cents are cheaper than thirty-five bobby pins for forty-three cents, though I don't actually care, because so far as I'm concerned, bobby pins went out with half-moons on fingernails.

But there are other things; things of a psychological nature.

Like, why does it hurt so much to leave a half-used twenty-nine cent jar of mayonnaise behind in a fifteen-dollar-per-day vacation motel-room refrigerator? That is to say, it hurts me. I cannot bring myself to abandon twenty cents' worth of good mayonnaise. Once, I carried a small half-full jar of it for hundreds of miles in my nice leather handbag, which has a haunting fragrance now, and a permanent bulge—carried that mayonnaise tenderly till I got back home and *then* threw it out, because, after all, it had been unrefrigerated for quite a while at that point, and you can't be too careful.

And why does my rich friend Louise balk at the price of paper napkins, preferring to spend good time washing and ironing cloth napkins? (At our place, we bring out cloth napkins only for visiting potentates, but we haven't had any yet.)

And why will I buy a bottle of good perfume as a gift without wincing, while I begrudge every red cent for fancy paper to wrap it up in?

Mr. Nuccio didn't cover these matters. On second thought, I don't think I will either. They're too personal.

Love, work, money. Those are all good things. And, like the first two, money presents complexities that are never entirely resolved. For instance, your money, and your friends' money.

I've decided that being poorer than the people you know is a problem. So is being richer. (Having exactly the same amount isn't really a problem; it just gets dull, and there's nobody to borrow from.)

In the first instance—being poorer—you have a nagging feeling that they should spring for the check somewhat oftener than they do. Still, if they pay everything in sight, they're showing off. Therefore you dislike them either way.

In the second instance, when you are the comparatively rich one, it's dangerously easy to overcompensate: working too hard at being one of the gang, poor-mouthing it over lunch with your poor little old friends about the high cost of margarine, and it's a wonder you leave with your front teeth intact. But if, instead, you overcompensate by overspending, they are equally miffed (as we have seen in the previous paragraph), and they may revenge your affluence by not thanking you enough, or not even thanking you at all. And while you certainly didn't expect any thanks, still, all the same . . .

I believe that one's basic financial

attitudes are—like a tendency toward fat knees—probably formed *in utero*, or, at the very latest, *in cribbo*. They only become more so with age. The little tightwad who won't give you a chaw of his licorice grows up into the big tightwad who won't even pull out the company credit card. The little dimwit who throws his pablum all over you whether you want it or not will throw his grown-up goodies around the same way.

I think, too, that you learn your own basic financial facts of life about the same time as the basic other ones. In my case, both came early.

They used to launder me in the same bathtub with my brother, who was two years older. This was either to teach me penis envy or to save water, probably both. (I come from a long line of nonlotus-eaters, and they really knew how to save water.) But it didn't make me envious; complacent, rather, for I felt I was more adroitly designed than he was. Still do, in fact, though we haven't compared notes lately.

However, it was only shortly after this period that I embarked on my first business venture, a lemonade stand, which opened early one July morning and closed with finality around sundown. By noon I had gone through all the lemons in the house and made fifty cents. My father said that the wise thing to do would be to sink my capital into more lemons, which I did.

But I sold no more lemonade, because by that time I'd run out of neighbors. Thus I learned never to put excess capital back into the business.

It's too bad these early lessons don't stick. A while ago, through some oversight, I had 2,000 extra dollars, and a broker bought some stock for me. Shortly afterward he notified me happily that the company was splitting shares, two for one, which meant I owned twice as much, right? And then the stock dropped like a shot goose, so I lost twice as much twice as fast, right? Still in the lemon business.

Then there was the bank failure. We had a school savings program, and I almost threw myself out of the third-grade window when the banks failed, taking my 132 pennies with them. I learned from this that you'd better spend it before someone else does, and the hell with Ben Franklin.

It's all these things together, I suppose, that have made me the financial schiz I am today, one half of which doesn't know what the other half doeth and would throw up if it did.

Still, I suspect that there are several of us sorely divided folk around —lead-footed grasshoppers who would love to jump around in the sunshine spitting tobacco juice all day but can't, wholeheartedly, because we know we'd hate ourselves in the morning.

And so I'd like to pass along a few contributions myself—some practical pointers on staying afloat, or making it a little jollier while sinking.

For one thing, it's important to stay in funds, because being on your uppers is so much more expensive. I remember once when I was stony, the lavish life I had to lead. The corner drugstore didn't accept credit cards, so I couldn't eat there. Had to go first-class, where they *did* accept credit cards, and once you're in a decent restaurant, it's silly to order the ground round.

In fact, having some good credit cards is more important to the financial schiz than staying in funds. Especially the generalized type of credit card, like Master Charge, or Bank-Americard. Cash, of course, hurts too

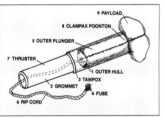

much to spend, while writing checks has a delayed but equally painful reaction. With checks, the trouble is that you have to fill out the check stubs with What For and How Much, or you'll be even more fouled up than you are. This can't help but remind you of what stupidity you spent it on, which can be painful, inasmuch as it's probably lost its shine or busted, or been eaten, or drunk up, or is, in one way or another, all gone. But those tactful credit card billings seldom itemize. They just present you with the sum total, and if they do enclose any carbons of sales slips, you don't have to look at them.

However, buying things can be a real problem to the lead-footed grasshopper, involving—as it does —the hard choice of Money vs. Object.

For instance, I seldom enjoy a terribly expensive thing, because I feel so obligated toward it. (Unless it is a bathrobe; I wear bathrobes a great deal and therefore wear them out.) But I get sick of an expensive thing nearly as fast as I get sick of a cheap thing, just feel guiltier about it. So the way it works out, if you're an LFG, is that the grasshopper part of you buys things in a mad moment of abandon, and the lead feet keep you from ever doing anything intelligent about it. You're somehow duty bound to keep it somewhere, moldering away.

It's true that once in a while, a clear-eyed self-catechism can help. Take the case of my Lavender Paisley Designer Culottes, a rollicking impulse buy, which sag in the rear and have inhabited the bottom drawer of my dresser through many a long bright season.

Q. Did you ever—before you owned a pair of lavender paisley culottes—reflect that if only you had a pair of LPC, your life would be complete?

A. No.

Q. In other words, you felt reasonably fulfilled, so to speak, even before the lavender paisley culottes came into your life?

A. Well, yes, I guess so.

Q. And when you bought the LPC, was it because you thought, *Oh boy! Just what I need for such-and-such a purpose . . . ?*

A. No.

Q. And since you received them, have you ever found anything to wear them to?

A. No.

Q. No dogfights, no grunion runs?

A. No.

Q. And you don't know any near-sighted ladies who sag in the rear and would enjoy owning a pair of LPC?

A. No.

Q. Then wouldn't it be sensible to place them in the Out file?

I forget what I answered to that one. All I know is that I still have the culottes.

But let's look now at the brighter side of bill paying, which is something else the Personal Finance Guide didn't mention except to talk about budgets, wouldn't you know?

There are a number of things you can do when the bills come in, besides cry. For one, you can fill in the blank supplied for Amount Enclosed (with forty dollars or whatever the sum is that you're going to enclose) and then forget to enclose it. If the company has any decency, it won't put you in jail, it will only send you a reasonably polite notice, saying you forgot to enclose a check; and by then maybe you will have the forty dollars.

This is similar in theory to mixing

HOW TO USE CLAMPAX POONTONS

Get hold of yourself . . .

The clue to proper insertion is to *get hold of yourself*. If it helps you, take two Valium or attend your TM session beforehand, but just make sure you are calm and relaxed; otherwise the muscles of your vaginal opening will snap shut like the valves of a scared mollusk and insertion will be unnecessarily difficult. No need to worry; millions of girls just like you learned to walk normally again, and you will, too!

So pop open a fresh poonton . . . *get hold of yourself* . . . and follow these five easy steps.

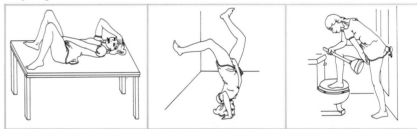

1. **Lie flat on back nude on kitchen table**   OR   **Stand on head to avoid leakage**   OR   **Just squat anywhere in the house**

. . . whichever seems most freeing and comfortable for you.

2. Inserting your fist and giving the Girl Scout Salute, or, if you prefer not to touch it, with spaghetti tongs, spread the sides of your vaginal canal A (somewhere near the rectal canal B, the urinary canal C, the Bermuda Triangle D, the Islets of Langerhans E, the place where you go to the bathroom F, and Interstate 90).

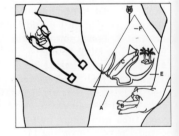

3. Set the poonton end (units 3, 4, 5, 8, and 1) into the vaginal opening, take a deep breath, and hold. Now, wrap the ejection string (unit 6) around and around units 7 and 2 as tautly as you can until you are grasping only the tiniest end, and then let go. The poonton will begin to spin, inserting itself firmly but pleasantly into the vagina and coming to a stop only when you and it are satisfied it's properly placed. NOTE: *The Clampax poonton must be aimed in the right direction—This is*

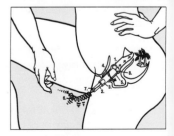

up your checks, which is a good system, too, when the chips and the bank balance are down. You put the correct checks in the wrong envelopes and mail them. By the time the computers stop screaming and chewing up their transistors and finally send the checks back, you may have enough money in the bank to cover them. Then you can send them out again, this time to the right places.

Too, I've found it sound practice to pay certain bills twice, when I have the scratch—not the doctor's, unless you've got something chronic and want to keep a nice little credit there, but some place where it's fun to shop. Then you have a drawing account that's pleasant to think about on rainy days.

It's even better if you can forget which store it is. Once I had a thirty-two-dollar credit because I paid twice at Kauffman's. But I got mixed up, and—thinking it was Mayer's—bought thirty-two dollars' worth of something from Mayer's that I wouldn't otherwise have bought; and when they sent me a bill for it, it rather rattled my slats. Still, I liked what I got (a nice bathrobe, as I remember) and managed to pay for it, one way or another, and I still had a pleasant slush fund waiting for me at the other place.

However, the most important thing about money is attitude. A thing to beware of—I've noticed this frequently—is getting too much respect for money, so that you can't enjoy it informally any more.

This is easy to do, all right. If you have only one dime, you see, it's hardly worth being stingy with, let alone respectful about. You can just have fun with it, at least a dime's worth. But if you possess several dimes instead of just one, they're harder to have fun with, because larger issues are involved. A dime is no longer a plaything, like, say, a playful calf. No, it bears within it the possibilities of becoming a milch cow.

And so, should this aspect of the dime become paramount to your mind, you won't enjoy playing with it; you'll simply hate to lose it or give it away. Because, once you've acquired a whole milch cow, you think, How nice to have a herd of them!

Thus, all dimes become potential breeders instead of negotiable currency. Naturally, then, it is harder for the rich to be generous than for the poor, because it is harder to give away a cow than a drop of milk (though they may sometimes give away a whole herd if it's tax deductible).

I'd like to make it clear, in case I haven't already, that I don't know very much about money. I've never been rich, only felt rich. I don't mean all that stuff about being healthy (which makes you feel healthy) or loved (which makes you feel loved); I mean rich.

It's all right with me, not being rich. In fact, as a free-lance writer who never expected to sell anything, I was surprised at the first drop of gravy. (I've always heard, by the way, of how big that first check looks to the budding writer. That first check I got, a check for two dollars, looked exactly like two dollars.)

I was, as I say, surprised, and also interested, and I kept on writing and eventually I sold quite a lot of things. Notice, I say "sold." I never sent anything to the small inscrutable places that don't pay, partly because I didn't think I was their cuppa, but mainly because I could always hear in the far reaches of my mind my old daddy's parting words, "Dinna give it away, lass," and I never did.

---

important in order to avoid internal hemorrhaging and the ever-present possibility you may never be able to have children.

Now, breathe out, and with the tip of your forefinger or the heel of one of your pumps, *gently* plunge units 7 and 2 into your body. When you can feel units 1, 2, 3, 4, 5, 7, and 8 up inside you and the silken tickle of unit 6 against your thigh, the poonton is in correct position.

You must remove all units except 1, 2, and 6 before you can leave the area. So select from your hands the three fingers you least mind getting soiled, reach all the way up there, and take 7, 3, 5, 4, and 8 out. This can be difficult, because the tubes will be damp and slippery, so powder your hands with cornstarch or Shake 'n Bake or rub them in kitty litter to give yourself the necessary natural traction for removal.

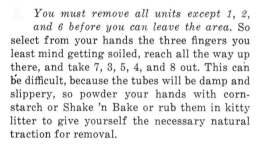
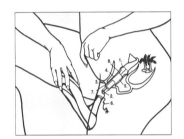
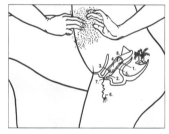
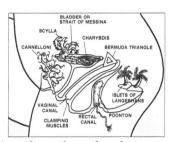

If you followed these directions with care, the poonton will be bobbing happily, tossed by the ebb and flow of the monthly tide in your vaginal canal. You should not even feel the poonton is there. If you do, it's in the wrong orifice (see anatomical diagram), and the only thing to do is to take your compact mirror, locate your mistake, and remove it without delay. Don't be discouraged. There are so many openings down there that doctors have often referred to it as the "miraculous maze of womanhood," and you're just a beginner. So think of it as a puzzle, relax, and begin again.

IF THE POONTON FITS, WEAR IT

No matter if your flow is mercifully light or if you find yourself heading monthly to your neighborhood Red Cross unit, Clampax has a poonton of sufficient strength to accommodate you. Many use Aswan or Grand Coulee during the days of heavy flooding, and taper off to Grand Coulee or Boulder when less buttressing is needed. On those heavy days when you can't change your poonton readily, try using anywhere from two to ten at the same time. Insert them one by one, but be sure they are arranged in a pyramidal fashion just like bowling pins. And, *remember*, tie all the ejection strings together with a strong bowline knot to insure smooth and easy removal.

And so, all that time, I felt—if not rich—fed. It was after I wrote *The I Hate to Cook Book* that I felt rich for a little while, because it began selling what seemed like an astonishing number of copies. There I was, Charlotte-off-the-yacht, the big sack of peanuts, please, and keep the change. It didn't last long because the government took such an astonishing whack of the royalties. *Sic transit, sic transit . . .*

Actually, there are only three things about money that I am reasonably sure of.

One is that having money is warming and not having money is chilling, although it is more stimulating, because you have to do something about it; and he who cuts his own wood warms himself twice.

The second thing is that you can probably save enough or gather enough together—somehow—to get what you really want, if you'll forget about what people think you ought to want. This is admittedly a depressing thought, because it means no more muddling around, Mabel, pull up your socks and make up your mind.

The remaining thing is that when you spend money, it generally isn't there any more, and you must go earn some or get somebody to give you some.

Questions & Topics for Discussion

1. Why does a slight tax increase cost you $200 and a substantial tax cut save you 30¢?
2. Why are Budget Payments the ones that are the hardest on your Budget? Explain.
3. If you borrow $20,000 for twenty years at 6 percent, have you paid $14,389.60 on interest alone at the end of the twenty years?

Have you *really*?

4. If you put two beans in a jar on the first day, four on the second, eight on the third, and so on, and the jar is full on the thirtieth day, on what day was it half full?

Things to Make & Do

1. Take your age. Multiply it by 2. Add 5. Multiply by 50. Subtract 365 and add the loose change in your pocket under a dollar. Now add 115.

If you did the arithmetic right, the first two figures in the answer are

your age, unless you lied about it, and the last two are the change in your pocket.

It's easier, though, just to remember your age, and count your change.

Consumer Quiz

1. Is a woman's half size the same as a big fat size?

How come?

2. Why is it fun to buy shoes?
——Because your feet don't change size?
——Because you have a nice man right there at your feet?
——Because you don't have to hold your stomach in?
3. If you have a can opener that works well and a knife sharpener that works well and someone gives you a can opener that sharpens knives, too, what should you do with it?
4. If you are well supplied with salt shakers and pepper shakers and someone gives you a Pepsal, which combines the two, what should you do with it?
5. What is a Decorator Color?
6. What is a Designer Chair?
7. What is a Quality Appointment?
8. Does a flashy convertible really represent a mistress to a man?
9. What does it represent to a woman?
10. Who says so?

LOVE STORY

A Photo-Romance by Lynn Goldsmith

Young Woman: Mmmm! Ooooh! Oh! Oh?

Young Man: I can't understand it. This has never happened to me before.
Young Woman: Don't feel bad. It doesn't matter.

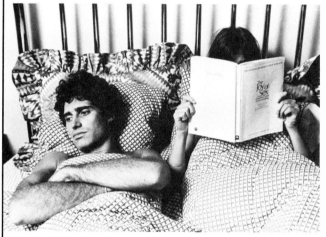

Young Woman: Mmmm . . .
Young Man: (Sigh!)

Young Man: (Thinks) *What if I'm really gay?*

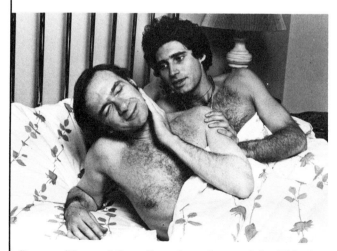

Strange Young Man: I can't understand it. This has never happened to me before.
First Young Man: Don't feel bad. It doesn't matter.

Young Woman: Mmmm! Ooooh! Oh! Oh!!

MY NEXT LOVER

by Arianna Stassinopoulos

I get very impatient with those quisling members of the female sex who proclaim that concrete and specifiable things like occupation, wit, looks and taste don't matter, when compared to the chemistry, the magnetism, and that mysterious X-factor. For a start, there is no longer anything mystic and romantic about chemistry and magnetism. Today it all comes down to the factual distillation of ethyl alcohol and the plotting of hysteresis curves—as for the mysterious X-factor, I've always thought it was a literary invention of neurotics, recluses, bespoke dramatists, spinsters, madmen, and penny-a-line hacks (e.g. Wagner, Emily Brontë, Shakespeare, Petrarch, Dante and Dostoevsky). In fact, it's Barbara Cartland who has got it right—lovers have to conform to an exact, unvarying formula.

So here is a list of indispensable components. (N.B. The stipulations set below—at random and not in descending, ascending or stationary order of importance—are mandatory and open neither to bargaining nor to negotiation.)

Clothes

He must not wear silk calypso shirts open to his navel or look as though he is, no matter what he is actually wearing. For formal occasions, he must not wear a gold brocade tunic with the top button unbuttoned. I must not be able to put a price on his sartorial equipment from Vacharin-Constantin watch and Cartier keyring to Gucci shoes and Yves Saint Laurent ties with the YSL subtly imprinted bang in the middle.

Presents

It is essential that he has all known visible vices. Having tried to buy presents for virtuous non-smoking, non-drinking males, I swore never to get entangled with a man whose vices are such that they cannot be catered for by five unthinking minutes at a duty free airport boutique. As for my presents, I agree with that patron of all self-immolating females, Zsa Zsa Gabor, "I never hated a man enough to give his diamonds back." Of course, no really nice girl accepts diamonds from strange men. She gets to know them afterwards.

Age

Neither so young that he thinks Marilyn Monroe was invented by Norman Mailer, nor so old that he was able to see any Marilyn Monroe film the year it was actually made.

Place of origin

Anywhere except Limousin, a country which, it is said, has bred more Popes and fewer lovers than any other in the world.

Language

On no account must he have any desire to learn Greek the easy or any other way. And on no account must he have attended the H. G. Wells/Rebecca West Advanced School of Baby Talk. He must, however, be able to interpret when No means Yes and when No means Later.

Knowledge

Not the kind of man who, when you enthusiastically tell him that you've tracked down Furtwangler's 1953 recording of Beethoven's *Fidelio,* he replies that the only recording worth having is the illegal tape of Furtwangler's Salzburg performance of 1951, which you can get by going to 1031 West 43rd Street in New York and asking for Fritz by name. ("You know the one, made by sound relay in his dressing room with the shower authentically and fittingly dripping in the background during the ultimate display of the heroic self-sacrifice of conjugal love.") But the kind of man who is constantly adding to your store of knowledge and advancing your liberal education by informing you that there are no penguins on the North Pole, that camels cannot walk backwards or that they drive on the left-hand side of the wadi in the Trucial States.

Phone calls

He should never make a phone call where a plane ride would do.

Other Women

When you are walking together through the falling autumn leaves and a shapely lady walks by in the opposite direction, he must not in the best Latin Male Tradition turn discreetly 180 degrees to look at her and leave you standing there, hoping another cynosure will walk by in the other direction so that you can get him back when he completes the 360 degree circle.

Nature

He must hate it. He must be an entirely urban creation that always chooses the baroque over the primeval, the artifact over the natural, paintings over actual landscapes, indoor potted plants over majestic forests, opera over the peasant singing of Powys. He must never try to convert me to the idea of healthy walks in the country—if forced to walk, I insist on doing so on paving stones.

Flowers

When he sends flowers he must always make sure they are an odd number—and, as the baffled florist is wrapping up the eleven red roses wondering what other absurd economies inflation will wreak, he should explain that the twelfth rose is the lady to whom the flowers are going. . . . I can resist anything except romanticism on that shameless scale.

Hobbies

He must have no hobbies whatsoever. A few carefully vetted passions are, however, allowed. Possession of a Black and Decker drill, a backgammon set, or a collection of eighteenth-century gold boxes of Paris, would result in immediate disqualification. So would a collection of women—whether Jewish American Princesses, Norwegian au pair girls, or Mediterranean shepherdesses. I have no wish to become a collector's item.

Models

He must have the energy of Reginald Maudling, high-jump like Sheridan Morley, have the glamour of Ted Short, the sparkle of David Eisenhower, the recalcitrance of Lord Goodman and the intellect of Britt Ekland.

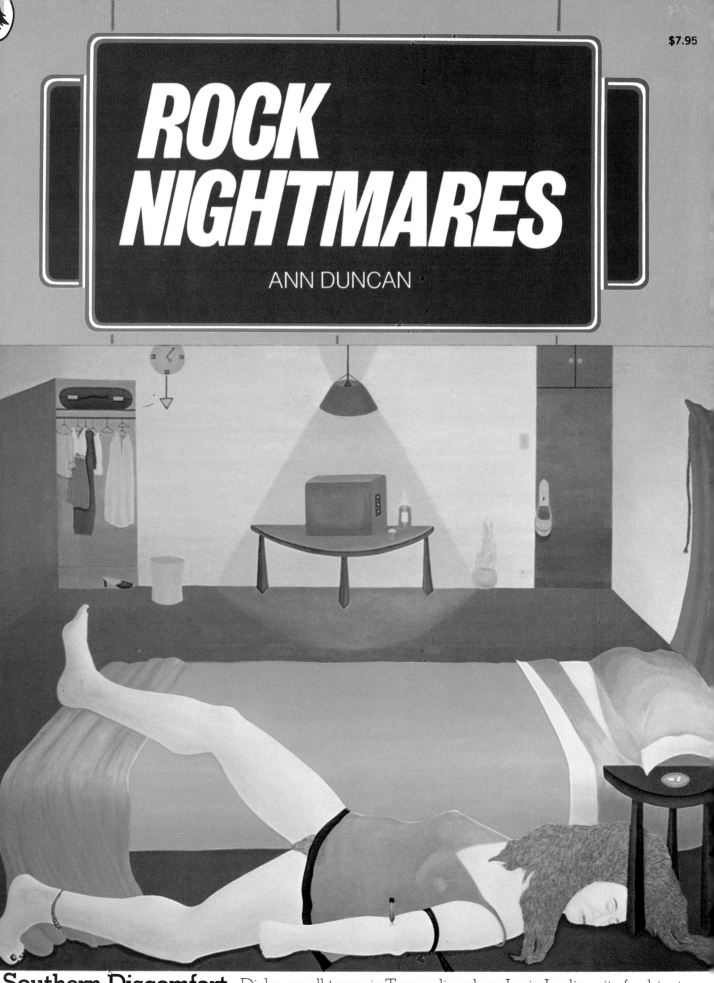

ROCK NIGHTMARES

ANN DUNCAN

Southern Discomfort. Did a small town in Texas die when Janis Joplin—its funkiest graduate—was reborn into the consecrated pantheon of tortured rock 'n' roll souls? Janis, Janis, why didn't you know we were always here?

The Who at Woodstock: Endless Bummer. The moment when Counter-culture saint Abbie Hoffman found out that icons are for smashing—and two disparate, desperate elements of a schizophrenic generation broke on the rocks of Capitalism.

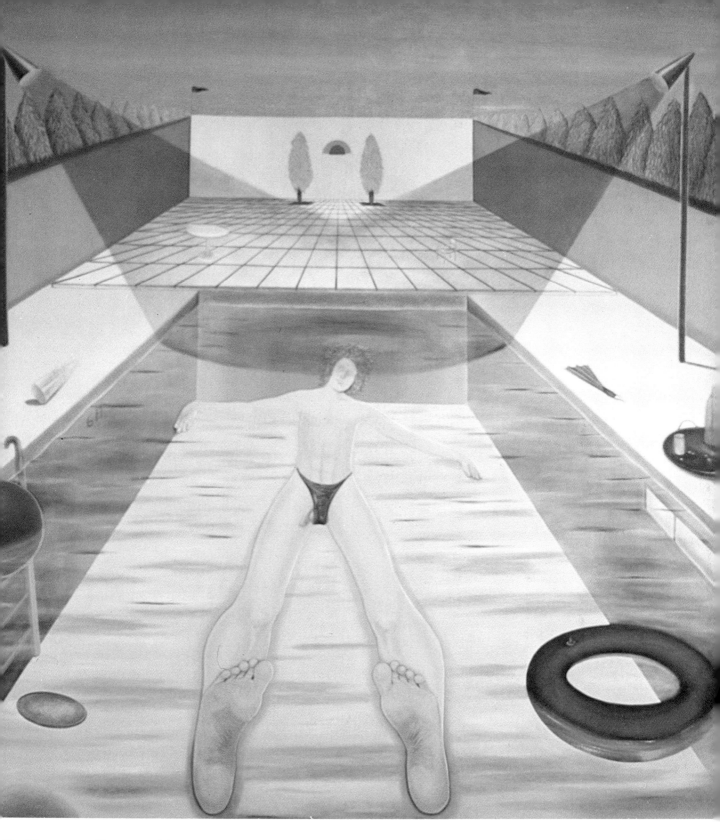

A Stone Stops Rolling. Before quantum theory and after Copernicus discovered that our planet is but one in a solar system of nine, came forth a lonely guitar man, spawned by dank slums that never quenched his flaming spirit. Brian Jones, a Satanic angel of bad tidings, only lost when the game gave him up for good.

Overexposure. Jim Morrison came like a comet out of nowhere, flashing his be denimed beauty through the smoky vapors that hovered around the benumbed heads o Amerika's lost starstruck children.

HOW TO PICK UP GIRLS!

by Tracy Young

Discover *exactly* how to pick up beautiful women.

Here, for the first time, is a manual completely devoted to the fine art of lesbian seduction. Now *you* can get the kind of girl you've always had a crush on, like your high school Phys. Ed. teacher. Not ugly girls in movement T-shirts and open-toed logging boots. Or fat girls that men wouldn't shake a stick at. Or girls with legs like link sausage. But *beautiful* girls. Bisexual girls. Even straight girls who've never wanted to make it with a chick before. Before you, that is. Yes, you can learn how to pick up girls even if you've just "come out" yourself. Pick up the kind of girl you've always seen and thought: "If ever I were to go in for *that* sort of thing, I'd want to do it with *her!*"

This amazing new book contains

OVER ONE HUNDRED FOOL-PROOF TECHNIQUES

for picking up girls.

HOW TO PICK UP GIRLS: THE LESBIAN DATING GUIDE is the first book of this kind that really and truly works! The first book that has been able to transform wallflower super-femmes into models of *machisma* overnight. And the reason for its success is simple — this fabulous book contains everything you need to know (but

HOW TO PICK UP GIRLS:

by Tracy Young

THE LESBIAN DATING GUIDE

didn't dare ask your mother) including chapters on:

- **How to be sexy — even in men's clothes.**
- **How to make shyness work for you.**
- **How to speak the code language of lesbians.**
- **What Cartier jewelry is "in" among chic lesbians.**
- **Why a woman doesn't have to be good-looking to pick up girls — and why being rich helps.**
- **Magic confidence builders.**
- **Why straight women are dying to go gay.**

Yes, ladies, HOW TO PICK UP GIRLS is the answer to your prayers. Read the testimonial from one happy customer who writes:

"I was in a pet store and I saw this humpy girl. So, following the advice in your book, I said something to her. We got to small-talking about the kind of dog she was going to buy, and I told her how I had trained my Lhasa Apso to go down on me. Well, next thing you know I got up my nerve and asked her over to meet him. You should have seen her eyes light up with pleasure and surprise. She said, 'you bet!' and gave me her name and phone number. To make a long story even longer, we've been going out the last couple of weeks and have a dynamite relationship going. She's a stewardess and a great woman, and King likes her a lot, too . . ."

Pick up girls *anywhere.*

Best Places to Pick Up Girls: It's easy to handle a woman once you've been introduced, but what if there's no one around to introduce you? Where do you go on your own? Gay Bars (gā barz) are good meeting places, and if you are a newcomer in town, you can find them by scanning the classifieds in your local smut magazine, or by seeking out dark bars with enormously fat bouncers at the door. Now you're inside, and you see a luscious creature across the room that you're just dying to ask to dance. What do you do? If you were a guy, it'd be

HOW TO PICK UP GIRLS: THE LESBIAN DATING GUIDE

easy. After all, guys are used to taking the initiative. On the other hand, being a guy in a women's bar is no help at all. So there you sit, staring down at your Gucci loafers. . . . Well, why don't you just approach your quarry and ask her? Chances are she's too shy to ask *you*. If she nods her head, check her arm for needle marks, then steer her gently onto the dance floor, taking care not to be intercepted by that big bulldyke doing a dangerous-looking version of the Bump that's making the Mylar fall off the walls. If the record is a fast number, you're in business. On the other hand, if it's a slow tune, someone is going to have to lead, and there's no quicker way of impressing a girl on the dance floor than by being able to perform the boy's part to at least half a dozen social dances. (See illustration.)

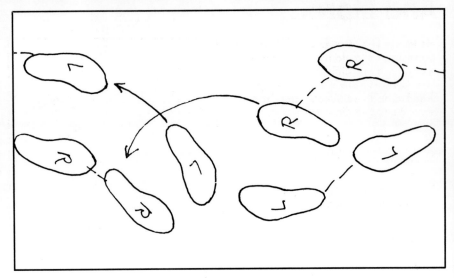

The Fox Trot

More Places to Pick Up Girls: Not all girls are to be found in gay bars. You can find them on the street, on airplanes, at high school reunions. *But . . .* you must know to recognize a prospect. Used to be you could tell a lezzie by her jewelry (pinkie ring), her clothes (blazer), or by the fact that she was wearing green and yellow on Thursday. Nowadays the people wearing pinkie rings are shoe salesmen, the green and yellow uniforms are reserved for the Packers, and chic dykes think blazers are too butch. If, however, she is wearing a blazer and earrings, you could be in business.

Age No Barrier

Younger Women vs. Older Women: Thanks to Gay Liberation and the institution of women's study courses, Seven Sisters colleges are breeding grounds for baby dyklettes; and a tea dance at Wellesley can be a perfect opportunity to pick a young 'un. But think twice about getting involved with a younger woman. If her parents find out and cut her off, you could be stuck paying her tuition. On the other hand, if you're interested in an older woman, a Simone Signoret type with a good job (who may even be willing to put *you* through night school), cruise Manhattan's Brasserie weekdays at 9:30

A.M. where you can find her sitting behind a copy of that morning's *Times*, or El Morocco at lunch where you can find her sitting behind a copy of *Women's Wear Daily*. But take heed, older women require a bit of finesse. Whereas younger women just like to dance and do it, an older woman generally likes to chat a bit before hopping into your sack, especially if you live in a five flight walk-up. Here are a few sure-fire opening lines guaranteed to get the conversational ball rolling.

How to Tell if a Woman Is Interested: Women, as any man can tell you, are as difficult to decipher as the Dead Sea Scrolls, at least until you've gained some experience. So, how can you tell if a woman is interested? One of your first cues is how she sets the stage. If, for example, you are invited to her house for dinner, the candles are lit, incense is burning, Barry White is ululating in the background, and there's an extension cord by her bed, chances are she expects you'll *do it* before the night is over. And if she takes off her clothing between the main course and dessert to slip into something more comfortable, like black stockings and a bullwhip, just sit back and enjoy it. Which brings us down to brass tacks —and if brass tacks are your scene, then shame on you. Your second clue is body language. For example, a lot of eye contact can mean one of two things: (a) she is into EST, in which case thank her for dinner, put on your coat, and run, don't walk, to the nearest exit; (b) she is sending you a "signal." The most important thing to remember here is that *women get horny*. All the stage settings and eye contact, the way she brushes your hand lighting your ciga-

rette* really means that she is waiting for you to make a move. Nervous? Well, why not? After all, very few sex manuals tell you how to do it with a woman, and God knows, nobody wants to seem inexperienced. So here are a few easy-to-follow instructions. Read them, practice in the mirror for a few days, and you'll be ready to take on the most formidable ladies of your choice.

Great Opening Lines:

1. The Women's Lib Approach (often referred to as hard-sell CR): Tell her that no woman can truly learn to love herself until she makes love with another woman.

2. The Men-Don't-Know-What-They're-Doing Approach: Tell her you never had a multiple orgasm until you made it with a woman.

3. The Throw-Away-Your-IUD Tactic: Explain that one of the joys of the Sapphic experience is that there's no need to mess with icky rubbers, dangerous birth control pills, sloppy foams and jellies, or any other method of unnatural birth control. Thus she is making a contribution not only to her health but to society as well.

4. The Little-Girl-Lost Approach: Ask her to come over some night and help you with your homework.

*Caveat: A pretty woman never lights her own cigarette.

Easy Instructions Included! And More...

How to Do It with a Woman:
Learning how to do it with a woman is really no more difficult than learning how to do the boy's part to dances, if you follow these simple, step-by-step instructions and diagrams.

Step #1: The Kiss

1. A approaches B with a lateral movement.
2. C moves slightly to right of D. D does the reverse.
3. A and B make a smacking sound in unison.

Step #2: The Hug

In this simple step, A grabs B on the thigh while gazing into her eyes and whispering sweet *nadas*, or *riens*.

Step #3: For spicy photos of Step 3,

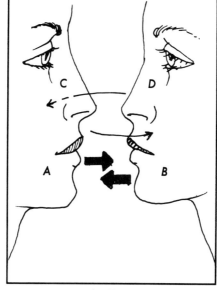

The Kiss

send a check for $10.95 (no stamps please) to Sleazy Mail Drop, P.O. Box 222, Yonkers, New York. Allow three weeks for delivery.

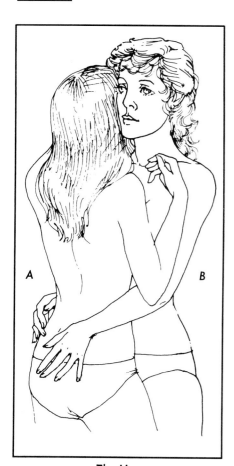

The Hug

Get All the Girls You Want And More...

How to Introduce Her: Now that you have established a happy relationship with the girl of your dreams, it is only natural that you should want to integrate this affair with the rest of your life; and that means *telling* people. Unfortunately, conventional etiquette has not yet devised a graceful way of doing this, and the paucity of our vocabulary makes it damned difficult, too.

Friends: Friends are a snap. You can be frank with friends, otherwise they're not friends and you can do without them, right? Right. And pretty soon you'll get used to the sound of the phone not ringing. Anyway, to friends you introduce her as "my lover." You can even have tasteful announcements made up at Tiffany's that say something about Ms. & Ms. Steer away from terms like "wife." They tend to be off-putting in almost any situation.

Business Associates: Keep a low profile in business dealings unless you can rely heavily on prurience. Otherwise introduce her, and only if you must, as your best friend.

Family: To your family she is your "roommate." If they question this, and they will—after all, what's a thirty-five-year-old woman doing with a room-mate?—mention the skyrocketing rents in your city and the high cost of double beds. Or tell them you feel a lot safer living with someone. When they get a good look at Marlene they'll stop worrying about you getting mugged.

How to Hook a Woman: Will there ever be enough really good women to go around? For every attractive woman you know, don't you know at least *six* available bachelors? How then do you get to be so special that if they offered your girl Charlotte Rampling, for instance, she'd say, "Sorry, I've got a girl"?

Work, love, and energy are required. Oh, granted we all know that there are more important things in life than trying to please a woman, but they're not the same without her. So, until more women miraculously appear, sprung from the head of Zeus *peut-être*, you must act!

- Open a charge account at the florists and spend, spend, spend.
- Rent a house in Bridgehampton this summer.
- Learn her favorite game, be it backgammon or bezique.
- Offer to teach her the latest disco dances.
- Tell her Greta Garbo reminds you of her.
- Learn to cook.
- Install a vibrating showerhead.
- Get her a gift certificate at the Pleasure Chest.
- Keep a bottle of her favorite perfume in your bathroom.
- Don't push marriage/adopting a child.
- Give her plenty of closet space.
- Offer to go out and buy the Tampax once in a while.

Meditations During A Permanent Wave

BY ~ PHYLLIS McGINLEY

Of the small gifts of heaven,
It seems to me a more than equal share
At birth was given
To girls with curly hair.
Oh, better than being born with a silver ladle,
Or even with a caul on,
Is wearing ringlets sweetly from the cradle!
Slaves to no beauty salon,
Ladies whose locks grow prettier when moister
Can call the world their oyster.

Ladies with curly hair
Have time to spare.
Beneath a windy drier
They need not thumb through *Photoplay* each week.
They can look higher.
Efficient, tidy, and forever chic,
They own free hours to cook or study Greek,
Run for the Senate, answer notes, break par,
Write poems, chair the local DAR,
Paint,
Or practice for a saint.

Ladies with curls are kind, being confident.
In smiles their lives are spent,
Primrosèd their path.
Rising, like Venus, crinkly from the bath,
They keep appointments, punctual to the dot,
And do good works a lot.
In crises they are cool. 'Mid floods or wrecks,
Examples to their sex,
Steadfast they stand,
Calm in the knowledge not a hapless strand
Of hair is straggling down the backs of their necks.

However brief their lashes, plump their ankles,
The matter never rankles.
They marry well, are favorites with their kin.
Untyrannized by net and bobby pin,
They seldom cry "Alas!"
Or wring their hands or need divorce attorneys.
They are the girls boys choose at dancing class,
And they are beautiful on motor journeys.

Ah, pity her, however rose-and-white,
Who goes to bed at night
In clamps and clips!
Hers is no face to lure a thousand ships.
Had she been born unwavy,
Not Helen herself could ever have launched a navy.

Candice Bergen for Chanel

Available in what was once considered to be a classy bottle, at fine and not-so-fine stores everywhere.

The Feminish Dictionary

by Deanne Stillwoperone, formerly Deanne Stillman

While women are busy trying to rewrite history and to write and create our own herstory, the language we speak still largely reflects today's male-dominated culture whose hirsute antecedents made up this one-sided lexicon way back when they could get away with it. Except for the minor concessions of bodies of conferences, assemblies, and too few influential newspapers to the use of such now-proper qualifiers as *spokeswoman* or *chairperson* instead of the archaic *spokesman* or *chairman,* there has been virtually no mass acknowledgment of our language's gender problems. There has been no comprehensive reform within new editions of dictionaries. And worst of all, there has been no reform even among the speakers ourselves.

As attempts to define anything must make use of the language and speech that we already know, then the definitions themselves often assume an inadvertent bias. If we as women are to define ourselves meaningfully, then the language itself must be able to accommodate these new definitions; otherwise, the attempt is undermined at the very beginning. In order to facilitate such sorely-needed self-definition, I propose a new women's language, based, of course, on the vocabulary which we already use, but always reflecting *in every aspect* the female object of a particular reference. This new language will be called *Feminish.* In it all references to men will be deleted and replaced with references to either women or all sexes in general when necessary, unless the object of a certain remark is a *self-defined* male, like Frank Sinatra. (If gender is unknown, the unisex rule shall apply.) This means that all syllables like he, male, males, man, men, son, and other more obscure though equally sexist usages of exclusively male references will be wiped entirely from the English language.

We begin at the most obvious point. The very word that man long ago decided to call his counterpart was *woman.* Why *woman?* Because it was merely an extension of the word *man!* We have no moniker that is truly our own! Therefore we must take the next logical step on the road to real self-definition, delete the second syllable *man* and insert temporarily the allegedly nonsexist and currently preferred label *person,* so that *woman* becomes *woperson* (pronounced wo' person). The word *person,* however, has for its second syllable the exclusively male noun *son,* and is therefore unsuitable, so *son* must be replaced by the truly nondiscriminatory noun *one,* so that *person* becomes *perone* (pronounced per own'). Thus *woman* becomes *woperone* (pronounced wo' per own). This new label will be hard to get used to, but after several months' usage, I am quite comfortable with it, and even my friends are beginning to address me correctly. When alone, I practice: I am a woperone, you are a woperone, she is a woperone, and we "women" are all wo . . . people. (*Women,* with the second syllable *men,* is unacceptable.) This change also applies to such nouns as spokesperson, doorperson, seamsperson, layperson, journeyperson, yeoperson, ombudsperson, etc., and even the word female must be altered to the more fair and meaningful term *feperone,* which rhymes with *pepperone,* the sausage that goes on pizza. The transformation of the plural, *females,* would naturally be *fepeople.*

These changes, however, although most basic, are just the beginning. We mustn't forget that *every single noun* applying exclusively to males should and will accommodate the hitherto unacknowledged existence of fepeople, and, more urgently, we must pay attention to our own speech so that corrections begin to come automatically. While comprehensively studying the language, I have discovered that wopeople are inadvertently discriminated against in thousands and thousands of words. To list each and every offender and its new incarnation would consume an entire lifetime, but once you understand the rules, creation of Feminish is as easy as finding your clitoris. Following are just a few examples of our new vocabulary, with a possible manner of usage included with each. As with all languages, there are exceptions to the rule, and they, too, appear herein.

The Feminish Dictionary:
A Guide To Defining Ourselves

Amanda = Aperoneda
Her name is Aperoneda and she comes from Alabama.

amen = apeople
Apeople!

bedfellows = bedsisters, bedbuddies
Politics makes strange bedsisters.

cockatoo = cuntatoo
Feperone cockatoos are cuntatoos.

cockney = cuntney
Cuntneys talk funny.

cockpit = cuntpit, genitalpit
The stewardess and the pilot are getting it on in the genitalpit.

cockroach = cuntroach, or if sex indiscernible, **genitalroach**
Step on that cuntroach!

cocksmanship = cuntswoperoneship
That's cuntswoperoneship!

cocktail = cunttail, genitaltail
I'll have a genitaltail, please, straight up.

Crawdaddy = Crawparent
Crawparent has a new art director.

Adam's Apple = Eve's Apple
She should have that Eve's Apple taken care of.

Frosty the Snowman = Frosty the Snowperone (little girls need to identify)
Frosty the Snowperone was a very funny creature.

Fu Manchu = Fu Peronechu (in case of female offspring)
Don't mess with Fu Peronechu.

Girl Friday = One Friday
Wanted: Versatile and Groovy One Friday!

German = Gerperone
The Gerperone people are a clean people.

hemorrhoids = shemorrhoids
Many lady bus drivers are afflicted with shemorrhoids.

human = huperone (pronounced hup' er own)
The huperone race is near extinction.

hymen = hything
She popped her hything while riding a bike.

"I, a Woman" = "I, a Woperone"
Have you seen *I, a Woperone?*

Isle of Man = Isle of Perone
Several years ago there was a rock festival on the Isle of Perone.

Katmandu = Katperonedu
Many hippies live in Katperonedu.

Landlord, landlady = landperone
Hey, Phyllis, should I answer the door? It's the landperone!

manage = peroneage
My hair is hard to peroneage.

Managua = Peroneagua
Peroneagua, Nicaragua

mañana = peroñeana
The Spanish people never do anything until peroñeana.

Henry Mancini = Henry Peronecini (for his daughter's sake)
Henry Peronecini used to be named Henry Mancini.

mandate = peronedate
The people's peronedate.

mandolin = peronedolin
Someone ripped off my peronedolin.

mandrake = peronedrake
In certain cultures peronedrake root is a cure for lumbago.

Manhattan = Peronehattan
I'll take Peronehattan

Man-o-War = Perone-o-War (gender not obvious)
Perone-o'-War won the Kentucky Derby.

manipulate = peroneipulate
You're just trying to peroneipulate me.

maniac = woperoneiac
Was Lizzie Borden a woperoneiac?

midwives = midhusbands, midspouses
The opposite of midwives is midhusbands.

Alfred E. Newman = Alfred E. Newperone
What, me worry?

menstruation = wopeoplestruation
Wopeoplestruation is a feperone bodily function.

omen = opeople
A full moon is not a good opeople.

shuttlecock = shuttlecunt, shuttlegenital (depends on who's playing)
Badminton is played with a shuttlegenital.

Rumania = Ruperoneia
The national bird of Ruperoneia is the fly.

OCTOBER/1976   Miz VOLUME V, NO. 4

Miz PARODY WRITTEN BY ANNE BEATTS, BLANCHE BOYD, LEE ISRAEL, TRUCIA KUSHNER, CINDY ORNSTEEN, EMILY PRAGER, RAYANNA SIMONS, DEANNE STILLMAN, TRACY YOUNG. ART DIRECTION BY JUDY JACKLIN. ART ASSOCIATE DIANA LAGUARDIA.

COVER BY MARIE SEVERIN

FEMINIST COINS

from the

Dolly Madison Mint.

33mm. Cupro-nickel

Now you can commemorate your own or others' raised consciousnesses with a set of these twelve beautifully-engraved coins, each one symbolizing the indomitable spirit of a different American Feminist:

Elizabeth Cady Stanton,

Emma Goldman,

Abigail Adams,

Harriet Beecher Stowe,

Elizabeth Blackwell,

Sarah Grimke,

Susan B. Anthony
(Betty Ford's choice for "most meaningful American"),

Harriet Tubman,

Sojourner Truth,

Shirley Temple Black,

the first
Mrs. Johnny Carson,
and others.

MAHOGANY CHEST

Enclosed in their own handsome simulated mahogany chest, resting on a bed of ruby red velvet, its color an ever-present reminder of our monthly ebb and flow, these unique coins, cast in a collectible metal of increasing value, were designed by a real artist.

REMOVABLE

The entire collection is removable, attractively framed, and ready for proud display on either wall or table. Or, if you or the giftee prefer, they can be used as currency in feminist restaurants. Only 25,000 sets will be produced, and every one will be hallmarked, numbered, and accompanied with a certificate of authenticity verifying its worth.

LIMITED EDITION

Due to the extremely limited edition, orders will be filled according to the earliest postmark.

DISCOUNTS

Allow 10 percent discount for Daughters of Bilitis and members of other accredited feminist groups.

- **UNIQUE COLLECTION**
- **LIMITED EDITION**
- **ONLY 25,000 SETS**
- **ORDER NOW**
- **FREE DISPLAY CASE**

THE DOLLY MADISON MINT
Please send me the following number of Feminist Coin Sets:

Number ordered_____at $475.00 each set

My name_____

Address_____

City_____State_____

Zip_____

I enclose my check for $_____

I prefer to charge my order. Bill my account with
Bank Americard ☐   Master Charge ☐   Diners Club ☐
Mistress Charge ☐

(Please allow 30 to 60 days for delivery. Insurance and postage will be paid by sender.)

LETTERS

Dear Miz:

I read with interest your recent article entitled "You Name It, I've Had It," on venereal disease and genital infections. Having just recovered from a nasty bout of monilia, I would like to pass on to your readers an herbal remedy which I found very effective:

Bone and flatten 2 chicken breasts until ¼" thick. Dredge lightly with flour, sprinkle with salt and pepper. Heat ⅓ cup olive oil in shallow pan and sauté chicken along with 2 cloves minced garlic. Cook gently until brown on all sides. Pour ½ cup dry red wine over chicken, cover, and cook another five minutes. Meanwhile, simmer 1 cup of Italian tomato puree with 1 tsp. dry basil. Cook five minutes and add to chicken mixture. Turn chicken and bathe it thoroughly in sauce. Cook until tender. Place mixture in blender. Puree. Spoon small amount onto tip of tampon and insert.

I think monilia sufferers will find this an effective method of reducing itching and local soreness. Leftover portions may be served on crackers as an hors d'oeuvre. Garnish with radish roses.

Miz Barbara Rezucha
2900 Ocean Parkway
Brooklyn, N.Y.

Dear Miz:

Dr. Seuss is a sexist pig!

Miz Jessica Adams Wedgewood
Okmulgee, Oklahoma

Dear Miz:

My husband disappeared over 20 years ago. Yet he still gets all the publicity. Why?

Miz Judge Crater

Dear Miz:

I have decided to change my name to Della Highway.

Sincerely,
Miz Della (Street) Highway

Dear Miz:

My question is: Modess—why? Why conceal the biological reality that we all bleed fairly regularly? We're not just denying our identity by stuffing our vaginas with ugly penis-shaped tampons and/or covering them with bandage-like sanitary napkins, as though they were wounds or something; we're also helping to support sexist profiteers in male-dominated industries, giving them money that could be far better spent for Movement projects. By just letting the blood flow unchecked down our legs we can assert our sisterhood unequivocally at least once a month! Just let it bleed, sisters—be a "Redstocking" *worthy* of the name!

Miz Rosalie Eleanorchild
Paducah, Ky.

> **Not only must fetuses be accorded simple human rights as living beings within other living beings, they must also be accorded the God-given right to vote, smoke, and join the country club of their choice.**

Dear Miz:

Click!

In sisterhood,
Miz Earleen X. Washington
Fayetteville, N.C.

Dear Miz:

I had an orgasm today.
Thanks.

Sincerely,
(name withheld by request)

Dear Miz:

I just finished reading "Lost Women: Mme. Nhu—Down and Out in Paris and Cannes," and it made my day. It was only too easy for me to sympathize with such tragic victimization as I too am an exile—from my motherland, Uganda. I won't go into the struggle and hardship I've endured at the hands of a certain racist, sexist "village tyrant," nor will I mention the outrage and humiliation I've suffered as a result of an unfortunate incident involving a men's room at Orly (a highly misinterpreted attempt on my part to improve Anglo-Ugandan relations). Suffice it to say, if I hadn't had the good sense to turn sideways and thus slip through the fingers of tne station police, I might never have hopped a 4:40 freight to Zaire (which is where I'm holed up at present).

Since then, I've taken time to look into myself. I've suppressed all male-oriented urges. I've given up government and modeling, and at present am devoting full time to the Village Women's Consciousness-and-Yam-Raising Group which I founded upon arrival. It's been a beautiful and sensitive growth experience for me. I have managed to institute several liberated reforms: local bride-price has been raised from 10 to 25 cows, in advance; age for clitorectomy is now 15 instead of 11, and with a pen knife as opposed to a cheetah tooth; and the doorway of the menstrual hut (and of this I am proudest) now faces the interior of the kraal, whereas before it stood open to the surrounding jungle, a sanguine prandial invite to every passing carnivore. I still haven't solved the problem of the Congolese mercenary and the nun, but I'm working up a list of demands.

In closing, I would like to say that *Miz* is a constant source of inspiration to those of us out here in the baboondocks. Keep up the good work!

Miz Princess Elizabeth of Toro
Two days' journey by
dugout canoe from
Kinshasa, Zaire

Dear Miz:

If the Women's Movement is so important, how come Gloria Steinem hasn't been assassinated yet?

Michael O'Donoghue
New York, N.Y.

Dear Miz:

After reading many tedious articles in your magazine discussing the development of a lingua-franca or nonsexist pronominal terminology, I'm ready to spit! Why not forget all this "ter and tem" hooey, and adopt the patois of my Bushman forebears: *xclikxebxa* and *xclikxabxa*. To wit: one who buttons on the left, and one who does it the other way.

Miz Miriam She-Who-Marries-
Black-Revolutionary-And-Moves-
To-Land-of-Bushman-Forebears
Ganja, Liberia

(continued on page 83)

OUR LABIAS; OUR LOBES

THE FIRST INTERNATIONAL WOMEN'S ORGASM ROUND TABLE

We recently asked four women—each representing a corner of the earth—to participate in a symposium dedicated to a universal feminist concern: orgasm. Joyce, a keypunch operator from Toledo, Ohio; Nguyena-Thu, a worker in a North Vietnamese factory that converts American munitions into speculums; Nanook, the only educated resident of Frobisher Bay, Canada; and Juba Matuba, a Botswanaland mother, all agreed that orgasm has for too long been denied womankind.

JOYCE: My first orgasm occurred when I was six. I was an early reader and one day was reading *Peyton Place,* the scene where a woman performs fellatio on Rod while he is driving. I felt a throbbing sensation in my pubic area and my hand seemed to gravitate toward my clitoris. I started rubbing it. Of course, I didn't know what I was rubbing at the time, but it sure did make me feel good. Pretty soon my legs shuddered and I guess that was my first orgasm. Years later, after reading much of the more modern orgasm literature, I decided that I subscribe—or is it *ascribe?*—I never can get those two words straight—

MIZ: It's not important. Women have been denied a proper education.

JOYCE: You're all so supportive . . . I'm overwhelmed . . . it's wonderful . . . I guess I was trying to say that I believe in clitoral orgasm. I don't believe in vaginal orgasm and I've never had one.

NANOOK: While growing up in an Eskimo village where patriarchy is a strict religion as well as a way of life, I never had an orgasm because I didn't even know

there was any such thing. Women were supposed to engage in sex to have babies, and that was it. I'm lucky that I was awarded a scholarship to the University of Saskatchewan, where I learned many things. I met some members of a women's C.R. group and joined. We became very close. One day during an anthropology class, a man called me "Nan Nooky." I didn't know what he meant, but all the men were laughing. That night I had a C.R. meeting and discussed the incident with my sisters. They told me what he meant. It made me mad. They gave me books to read. I read of the trials and tribulations of women down through the ages—Anais Nin, George Eliot, Madame Bovary, Kate Chopin, Cherry Ames. I decided that I really didn't like men,

JUBA MATUBA: I suppose I really shouldn't be here and you probably wouldn't have asked me to attend had you known that as a child I was forced to have a clitorectomy.

MIZ: We'll draft an anticlitorectomy statement immediately and send it to your hillside.

At this point, it seems appropriate to present the findings of our orgasm research cadre. Copies of the report will be circulated, but for the record *Miz* will read aloud that section of the report written by Erica, a member of the orgasm research team.

Erica writes: "For the past 12 months, I have sequestered myself in a sound-proof pleasure chamber equipped with every conceivable arousal accoutrement known to humanity. For alimentary satisfaction, I supped on the finest steaks and red wines; my relaxation included a water bed,

a double bed, and a bed of lettuce. I listened to the quadrophonic melodies of Mantovani and Hot Tuna, and I toyed with vibrators in all sizes and shapes whenever I fancied. For added excitement, I had at my disposal an array of aphrodisiacs, a photograph of Jim Bouton, and a small silver handbell with which to summon my sexual partner. During the entire 12 months, I did nothing but masticate, fornicate, masturbate, and fantasize, while maintaining a detailed log of my orgasmic experiences. I am now happy to report my discovery, the pineal orgasm, which I blundered upon one evening as I mistakenly grazed my forehead against the television console."

NGUYENA-THU: Television console! Then this kind of orgasm can only occur in capitalist societies!

MIZ: Erica continues: "I brushed up against the TV with my forehead. A tingle of excitement such as I have never known surged through my body! As soon as I regained consciousness, I looked up the excited area of the head in an anatomy book and learned that my newly-found pleasure center was the allegedly nonfunctional pineal gland. It is located in the forefront of the brain and, upon further investigation, I discovered that the pineal gland is the "third eye" of many mystical cults and has been known to react with a wondrous spurt of phosphorescent juice when touched in a particular manner. I would certainly describe the pineal orgasm as cosmic."

JOYCE: I'm sorry, but I just don't believe Erica. I'll stick with my clitoris, if you don't mind.

FOUND, LOST, AND MISPLACED WOMEN

ILSE KOCH, THE RED WITCH OF BUCHENWALD

Ingeborg Night

Joseph Goebbels considered that "the mission of woman is to be beautiful and to bring children into the world." For the most part, the women in the man's world of Hitler's Third Reich devoted

themselves to "Kinder, Kuche, Kirche," as was the will of Der Führer. But, here and there, an exception stands out. This attractive, energetic, red-headed woman started out as a typical "good German wife" when she married Colonel Karl Koch, an ambitious young SS officer.

It was not until Colonel Karl Koch was appointed camp commandant at Buchenwald that Ilse's innate abilities came to the fore. Tired of sharing coffee and gossip with the other officers' wives, Ilse determined to take as active an interest in camp life as her husband did. Perhaps she was initially motivated by a desire to "beat him at his own game," distasteful as that game may or may not have been to her. Lacking any strong female role model, she could not help but emulate her husband's misdirected aggression. It is surely a tribute to her strength of character that in many instances she was to surpass him at his best, or worst.

In any case, from the workshops

to the quarries to the vegetable gardens, the petite woman with the flaming hair was soon a familiar figure to guard and inmate alike. She brought to her work an intensity that some found terrifying. Her energy knew no bounds; she was tireless in her enthusiasm for the project at hand, an enthusiasm which she communicated to the prisoners by any means possible. At first, conditioned as she was by her traditional strict German upbringing, Ilse made discipline and the maintenance of morale among the prisoners her special concern. Her unceasing efforts in this direction included the establishment of a "cottage industry" for the production of gloves, purses, lampshades, and other ornamental household articles.

Later, grown more sure of herself and her "success" on masculine terms, she undertook the ordering and supervision of more ambitious projects, such as the construction of an elaborate riding hall, at an estimated cost of 250,000 marks. There she exhibited her talents as an equestrienne for the edification of select prisoners, to the accompaniment of the camp orchestra. Obviously, Ilse had overstepped the accepted female role of the day—and at the same time, she was compelled by social forces to submerge her true, healthy femininity in male-oriented games of dominance and submission.

Other public-spirited German citizens with an equal stake in the prisoners' welfare, like Dr. W. Hoven, an expert in alkali poison

research, were attracted to Buchenwald in large part by the hospitable atmosphere which Ilse created, and soon became part of her circle. In her efforts to match her husband's zeal, which itself

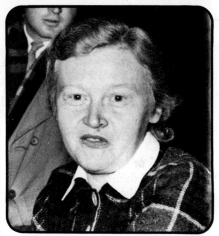

was not inconsiderable, Ilse displayed an almost superhuman devotion to the task of prisoner rehabilitation. During the years in which her husband served as camp commandant, she is reputed to have taken a personal interest in the suffering of over 180 prisoners, an estimated 135 of whom survived her attentions.

Sad to say, she competed in the only area open to her. It is further indication of the unique character of Ilse Koch that after the war she was the only woman among the thirty-one defendants accused of war crimes at the "Buchenwald Trial"—truly an example of a "woman who made it in a man's world."*

*This is not to say that the Third Reich was a desirable world. However, we at *Miz* feel that any woman, however misguided, who successfully combats chauvinism is to be saluted.**

**As you may have noted, we are running out of women to salute in this section. Have we missed anybody? If so, please submit suggestions to "Lost, Found, and Misplaced Women," c/o *Miz*, Unpretentious Business Address, New York, N.Y.

Edited by Susan Dowdy

GABFEST
NEWS FROM JUST EVERYWHERE

KEEPING ABREAST OF THE TIMES

Dr. Gail Livingstone was the keynote speaker at the inaugural meeting of the Conference of Women People Who Have Undergone Radical Mastectomies (WPHURM) held recently in Vandalia, Illinois. Said the distinguished sex therapist (and cofounder of the WPHURM): "In the first months after my own breast surgery, I felt de-feminized, isolated from my double-breasted sisters. I confess I began drinking to cope with my pent-up feelings of unequal representation. And then, one afternoon, as I yanked the cork from a wine bottle between my knees, I came to a startling realization: that action, once a fear-provoking confrontation between fast-moving fist and stationary breast, was now as unhazardous for me as for any male sommelier. I no longer thought myself in a state of 'half-womanhood,' but rather in one of 'unilateral liberation.'

Throughout the conference, women from all social strata confirmed Dr. Livingston's experi-

ence, speaking of the physical and psychological elbow room one-breastedness provides. A Los Angeles policewoman told of her promotion to detective rank as a direct result of her new-found ability to employ the shoulder, instead of the ankle, holster. A professional golf person described the increased power of her now unimpeded downswing, claiming that she owed it to her handicap.

Women celebrated, again and again, their increased facility in carrying children and groceries, cleaning out bathtubs, applauding at concerts. "I rarely come up against 'mashers' in the subway rush, now," said one woman, "and intercourse with my husband is no longer a crushing burden."

But the spirit of the conference was best summed up by an Omaha, Nebraska, housewife, who mused, "I really feel as if I have the best of both worlds. I mean, now that I have only one breast, I don't know why I ever needed two." —*Emily Prager*

"I realize how silly this looks now," says editor Gloria Nobody.

THE LESBIANS OF ROSELAND

More than 800 women gathered last month at Roseland in an attempt to demonstrate that allegations of separatism, splinterism, and street beatings within the feminist ranks are wholly and insidiously the creation of the male-dominated media.

Noticeably missing from the mammoth dance hall were many straight feminists who refuse to ally themselves with lesbian-feminists, and a newly formed splinter group of realradicalesbianseparatist-

continued on page 154

Attend the First Annual Conference to Divide Women! To be held in a field twenty-four miles from Hays, Kansas (the geographical center of the U.S., disregarding Hawaii and Alaska), during the summer solstice (1977). Sign up now for:

Personality Workshop. This workshop will teach new techniques for smashing the male concept of personality. Learn to rid yourself of those quirks, those idiosyncrasies that make you different from other women!

Horizontal Hostility Workshop. The Boston HH will introduce a new ritual devel-

oped in Boston which involves the blood sacrifice of one member of the group per hour. This technique does wonders to ease tensions and allows for a constant flow of new members in the group.

PLUS: The Camden, N.J., Liberation - Army - Leaf - Diet - Lesbian-Feminist-Guerrilla-Theater will give a short performance on the hows and whys of living on leaves. Leaves will be provided.

Write to: Elizabeth Milliedaughter, c/o Mrs. Millicent Katherinedaughter, P.O. Box 192285, LaJolla, California.

—*Blanche Boyd*

...AND SHE IS DIVINE...

Her disciples refer to her as the "15-Year-Old Perfect Mistress." She is Maharini Guru Gee of Bombay, India, the world's first female guru. Maharini Gee, who will be 16 next month, combines the teachings of Lao-tze, Confucius, Buddha, and Alan Watts with the philosophy of Betty Friedan.

Last month, at the First Annual Guru's Caucus in Chambersville, Pennsylvania, the Maharini told a room overflowing with followers (mostly women), "The true light, supraconsciousness, or the essence of cosmic being, is like the beads of the ocean spraying across the universe, like the bubbles that emerge from a sparkling pond, like the head of a boil about to burst. This true light, the level of true knowing, will come from the women of the world, the holy celestial sisterhood of knowledge."

Maharini Gee is president and chairperson of Bliss, Inc., whose $2.5 million annual income comes from Blissed-Out Products, a line of oils, incenses, hash pipes, Ben-Wa balls, and other items related to attaining a state of gyno-alphic consciousness. She also edits *Lady Divine*, a monthly publication sold through her *ashrams* (dormitories) around the country. The *ashrams* are matriarchally run, with male followers tending the children and serving and cooking the meals. Males are permitted to engage in sexual intercourse only at a woman's request or for procreational purposes. Above the doors of all *ashrams* is inscribed the watchword of the Maharini: "We will show our brothers the path, but they cannot lead us as they were born without ovaries."

The 15-Year-Old Perfect Mistress has just completed a hectic 12-week/28-city tour across the United States and is currently "recharging her yonic energies" at her retreat in Ibiza.

"A woman's body is like a car," explains Maharini Gee. "When there is fuel line freeze-up, it's time for an overhaul."

—*Cindy Ornsteen*

continued from page 153

tists who eschew absolutely any involvement with "heterosexual men, faggots, nonlesbian feminists, and orange cats."

Withal, the Roseland Unity Fête-à-Tête was a joyous day of dance and dialogue. Brief position papers were read, and music was provided by three outstanding groups: Sappho Was a Right-On Woman Street Flashers, Hot Combs, and the Breasted Shandas.

The women attending were encouraged to represent themselves by wearing a label. Some of the outstanding designations, exhortations, and exclamations included: "Unreconstructed Diesel Dyke," "Media Transsexual Will Travel," "Change of Life Child," "Feminist Fatale," "Kiss Me Quick, I'm Polymorphous Perverse," and "Edna St. Vincent Millay / Boom! Boom!"

The day was not without its disruptions. Shortly after 1 P.M., Tie Dye, the mesmeric, ultramilitant lesbian syndicalist who has been arrested twice for sending letter bombs to Burt Reynolds, flattened the Hot Combs' lead singer with a rabbit punch, commandeered the microphone, and delivered a searing philippic. She harangued the conference as "a council of worms ...a racist, elitist, co-opted asshole affair masterminded by David Susskind."

One of the most invigorating position papers was read by Barbie X, a California stenotypist presently embroiled in an all-out battle with the AMA on the question of medical self-help for women by women. Miz X and various members of the steno-typist pool of the Los Angeles insurance company for which she works have performed at least eight voluntary hysterectomies during the last year upon women who have "sought to extricate themselves from the oppressive, bloody, vengeful monthly menses."

"The Man in the Moon is no misnomer," Miz X proclaimed. "He is out to get you and me. The only answer is hysterectomy on demand! Hysterectomy for liberation! Hysterectomies performed on women by women!"

But the high-point of the confab was the speech by jill lowercase who insisted on speaking, not from the bandstand, but from a level place. Glowing with evangelical fervor, speaking with unusual lucidity, jill began her plea for communality by paraphrasing what she called her "favorite rap: the serwoman on the mount." All the crowd sought to touch her or her bike, lesbians and gentiles alike.

She began, speaking without notes, hands outstretched: "Blessed are u when men hate u & when they ex-glued U and cast out your maiden name as evil that scene is known to me on accounta i was tripping that way four years and making It with every tomdick&hairy whilst lusting after Gertrude in Paris and even or especially Alice Beatitude Toklas who was me even then as i am her now, tho it's harder for a straight woman (sic) to enter the queendom of ecstasy than for two humping camels to pass thro the needles' i is no reason for us dykes to think we're hotshit even tho we are."

—*Lee Israel*

TSK! TSK!

Even the Fighting Irish who, it seems, should be above . . .

from a football program, submitted by Sister Ignatius Loyola.

NO COMMENT

from *Ms.* magazine, March, 1976, submitted by Patricia Saturday Night Special, New York, N.Y.

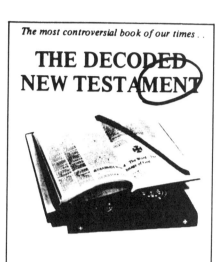

The most controversial book of our times . .

THE DECODED NEW TESTAMENT

JUST PUBLISHED
By Gene Savoy
Author of "Antisuyo" . . .
Feathe . . .

from *Watchtower,* May 6, 1976, submitted by Mrs. Helen Putnam, Ogunquit, Me.

from a playbill, submitted by Maura K. Wedge, New York, N.Y.

A priceless Picasso masterpiece, titled Mother and Child, was reported stolen from the Long Island home of the painting's owners, Mr. and Mrs. Alex R. Hamill, late yesterday. According to reports, the thief forced his way through the fence that surrounds the property and climbed in through the kitchen window at the back of the house. The incident occurred in broad daylight, under the unsuspecting noses of the security guards who patrol the grounds regularly. In addition to the guards, the Hamill's housekeeper, who had gone down to the basement to do the laundry at the time police say the robbery took place, claims to have heard nothing. Police are questioning several suspects, and a thorough investigation is under way.

from the Sioux City *Times-Ledger,* July 31, 1976, submitted by Marjorie Gross.

from the Manhattan Telephone Directory.

CLASSIFIED

Black Widow: An Autobiography. "A heart-rending story of a black woman's struggle to cope with the fact that her husband died instead of deserting her."—Unwed Mothers Newsletter. FH/622. $3.95. Little Black Books. Please do not send cash.

"How to Throw Like a Boy." Solid advice from nationally known experts in issue #1 (Aug. '75) of *Women's Practical Digest.* Issue #2 features dialogue between Betty Friedan and Simone de Beauvoir—"Which to Buy: Boy's Bike or Girl's?" $15 per year. Checks only. P.O. Box 11123, Lansing, Mich. 00068.

Do your clothes make a political statement or just hang on your body? Let your T-shirt show the world where your consciousness is at. **"Rape Is Wrong," "Nonsexist Childraising,"** and **"Don't Be a Chauvinist"** in bold lettering on soft, washable cotton. Militant Olive, Peaceloving Blue, or Radical Russet, all with white. Sizes small, medium, and butch. $5. Checks only, no pig cash. Politically Correct Clothing Company, Box 14758, Tacoma, Wash.

Poster $2, bumper stickers 2 for $1. P.O. Box 2185, Grand Rapids, Mich. No cash please!

No Viet Cong Ever Called Me Honey!

Burning Bra Cigarette Lighter. Snazzy butane-fueled lighter with flip-up bra cup top and replaceable flints. Comes in black, white, red. Also specify A, B, C, D, DD cup. $2.50. Please do not send cash. P.O. Box 36, Madison, Wisc.

Feminist Cookbook. Tired of eating the same old macho meals? Send now for the first Feminist Cookbook and learn how to prepare politically correct meals like "Swedish Meat Ball-less" and "Hershey Bars w/o Nuts." Kosher suggestions also included. Send $4.98 (checks only) to P.O. Box 34, Butte, Mont.

Whistle While You Work—Singing Vibrator. Battery powered Stim-Fem vibrator plays "I Am Woman" every time you turn it on!!! Your choice of pink, white, black, or purple. Free catalogue of tape cassettes available. Send $12.50 to Singing Vibrator, Box 10, M Street, Taiwan. Please do not send cash.

Bicentennial Douche Bag
Celebrate the birth of your nation. Red, white, or blue rubber bag covered with dime-size portraits of the 38 Presidents. Order now and get silver-plated clip shaped like Liberty Bell. Yours for only $5 plus postage (no cash, please!). Write Bi-Products, P.O. Box 522, Tenafly, N.J. 22093.

Free Brochure: Non-Sexist Child Abuse. Referral service also available. We help families replace abused children. All inquiries confidential. Write: Punch Judy Foundation, 72 Main St., Albuquerque, N. Mex. 92856.

Liberated Ironing Board Covers. Equality symbol in bold red, fits all sizes. Order now. Send check for $2 to Liberated Novelties, Box 13, Anaheim, Calif. 90004.

International Women's Year Dinner Bell Chimes for the truly liberated woman. Silver, gold, or stainless steel. Send for price list. Barbara R. Bender-Crest, 11 North View Grove, Darien, Conn.

Women's Suicide Prevention Bureau. Will handle all your needs. Phone for a recorded message now. Don't hesitate. (212) 999-3838. If busy, keep trying!

Read "Pejorative Retort"—the weekly lowdown on how we get fucked over; regular columns dealing with cystitis, monilia, vaginitis (nonspecific and otherwise); features by paramedics, paralawyers, parawriters. Special 9-month "gestation" offer. $10 to PR (checks only). 3 Emma Goldman Mews, N.Y., N.Y. 10099

Gay Luau: Join your lesbian sisters in Hawaii next summer for the first annual male chauvinist pig roast. Communal surfing and snorkeling. Lots of love! For further info write Erika Kamehamehamehamehamehamehameha, P.O. Box 33, Maui.

Handicapped Amazon? Center for gay amputees and other sisters with physical shortcomings offers therapy, support, companionship, and special toilets. Serving the Middle Atlantic states. Call toll-free number (800) 555-5843.

Women in Hibernation! Calling all members of the female race who are sick and tired of all the bullshit! We are going into hibernation beginning Feb. 1, 1977, and we're not coming out until sexism is totally eradicated! Join us! WIH, P.O. Box 788, Cleveland, Ohio 44106.

La Leche tote bag and color-coordinated "Mamouflage" T-shirt. At last, liberation for leaking lactaters! Eliminate the problems of telltale teat trickle with our pre-stained nursing T-shirt. $4.50. Sizes L/XL/XXL. Tote bag $15. Send checks only to: La Leche League, Box 618, N.Y.

Home Mastectomy—$15. For women who are fed up with the male-dominated medical establishment and realize that the butchers of the AMA cannot be trusted. Kit includes self-diagnosis test, kitchen biopsy instructions, etc. Limited offer. Do not send cash. Write: Our Breasts, Our Selves, 57000½ Galt Ocean Mile, Ft. Lauderdale, Fla.

Sick of powder room rip-offs? Tired of compulsory "sit-downs"? Stiff from squatting? With what you'll save on pay toilets alone you can easily afford our $30.00 fee for twelve sessions of Vertical Urination Training. We guarantee you'll be able to pee standing up anywhere or tuition cheerfully refunded. Write: The Institute for Micturitional Equality, 80 St. Marks Place, N.Y., N.Y.

Feminist chefs! Liberate the backyard barbecue and fan the flames of controversy in your Nonsexist Chef's Hat and Apron, stenciled with humorous Feminist sayings. Only $14.95, or $17.95 with matching barbecue mitt. HiJinx Products, Inc., Dept. 8-H, Minneapolis, Minn. 55403. (Checks only.)

Liberated penwomanship! Still using sexist ballpoints? Switch to our refillable flow-tip pens, ideal for jotting down notes, manifestos, letters of protest. $10 a doz., red only. Order now from Anti-Pig Pens, Hi-Jinx Products, Inc., Dept. 8-H, Minneapolis, Minn. 55403. Checks only.

Feminist Leather. Black hood with blindfold, zipper-mouth, antiqued brass women's symbol buckle. $24.95 plus $1.25 postage. Also matching body harness, wrist and ankle restraints with women's symbol. $50 the set plus $2.50 postage. N.Y. residents add tax. (No cash, please!) The Pain Chest, 23½ Christopher St., N.Y., N.Y. 10014.

"How to Find Your Clitoris." Up-to-date instructions, diagrams. New, sensitively written, illustrated sex manual for women who know something is missing from their sex lives but just can't put their finger on it. $4 postpaid. Send check only. Betty Doddaughter Press, P.O. Box 1925, N.Y., N.Y. 10021.

Liberated Speed Reading! Learn to scan, speed read newspapers, mags, books for sexist content. Thousands of words in *minutes!* Invaluable to students, scholars, movement militants, and injustice collectors. Call to arrange free trial lesson. The Women's Reading Institute, 376 Bleecker St., N.Y., N.Y. 10011. (212) KL-5-1334.

"The Isles of Greece, the Isles of Greece/Where burning Sappho loved and sang!" *Cultural-social Lesbian cruise of Greek isles. Together we will retrace the movement of Sapphic civilization in the Blue Aegean. Tour under the direction of Carlotta Rimbaud-Rutting (Ph.D, Amazon Studies, University of Dorking). For further info write: The V. Sackville-West Foundation for Lesbian Research, 1 Maidenhair Lane, West Carnivore, England.*

Liberated duck calls, buck lure. Feminist hunters! Declare open season on male game with "Eau de Doe." Just a dab of our patented musk behind each knee—and you'll get your buck. Guaranteed irresistible. Also available: nonsexist side-zip waders. Junior, misses sizes 5–14. Write for free catalog to Virginia's Rods 'n' Reels, Box 56, Brattleboro, Vt. 00413. Discounts for service-persons.

Lesbian Wedding Invitations. Samples: $1 (refundable). Do not send cash. Lavender Ink, Inc. Glendale, Calif. 94022.

Bisexual hoedown! Every Saturday night at 9, bi's of many nations, creeds, religions meet at the New Frontier Talk House and "swap" ideas, etc. 8222 Ninth Ave., N.Y., N.Y. 15th floor. No curious straights, please.

Speculum riot!!! Self-help group has lost its lease and *every item has to go!* **Speculums** . . . **cervical mirrors** . . . **vaginal jellies!** All sizes, shapes, and makes! Write, phone, or check out these *unbelievable* savings for yourself! Jane Addams Hospital Brigade, 9091 North Michigan Ave., Chicago, Ill. (315) 555-7877. Hurry . . . supply limited!

Miz Potato Head—Finally kids can learn equality from a female spud. Demand this revolutionary new game at your local store or write Parker Sisters, 42 Artichoke Way, Castroville, Calif.

Death Be Proud. Call your afterlife your own and reserve a plot now in the Feminist Cemetery. Choose from a wide selection of beautiful tombstones. Cremation services available on request. All inquiries will be handled with discretion. Write to: Fem-Cem, P.O. Box 55, Forest Hills, N.Y. Special rates for poets.

IMMACULATE CONCEPTION WORKSHOPS: Throw off the yoke of penile necessity, learn about unnatural childbirth as it was practiced almost 2,000 years ago. Join nondenominational feminists from all over the country this summer at our thrilling two-week workshops held in beautiful Big Miz, California. Room, board, and rites, $1,500 inclusive. Sign up today. Space limited. Write ICW, P.O. Box 0, Big Miz, Calif.

How to make your own IUD out of a roach clip. Hundreds of other useful tips, insights, in "Splitting the Counter-Revolutionary Counterculture" by Andrea Femaleperson. $5 (no cash). Box 3482, Cambridge, Mass.

Carry your beliefs into the bathroom with nonsexist Ter and Ter towels, also oversized "Tey" bath sheets. Available in a full range of colors from the Bath Boutique, 1490A Lexington Ave., N.Y., N.Y. 10021. SAE brings free catalog.

Elizabeth Bennett

Are You a Man or Woman?

by Mary Cantwell and Amy Gross

The big thing now in the world of science is to investigate the differences between men and women. Which means to us that the world of science does not know what these differences are. How, then, can we? You might assume carelessly that a simple mirror-test would resolve any doubts. Not so fast. All a mirror proves is that nature or possibly a triumph of medical technology has endowed you with certain primary sexual characteristics. Maybe even secondary sexual characteristics. This might be enough proof for the average person, but those of higher, finer sensibility will not rest until they have a grasp on those all-important tertiaries. This is not to say that you should overlook the primaries and secondaries (see *Sports, Hairy Ears, How Much Can You Trust Your Doctor, etc.*), but the genuinely resourceful investigator will not halt at surface delineations. Or bumps. The genuinely resourceful investigator will go for the gut. And this is where we come in.

We have just completed a massive study of at least 500 persons. They did not tell us what sex they went by. As they walked slowly past us, we asked them many pertinent questions aimed at developing criteria for gender definition. On the basis of these criteria we then sorted our sample into males and females. A jury of 20 other persons was subsequently assembled, supplied with our criteria and instructed to use them for independent testing. The results were gratifying. In almost every case, the jury's findings paralleled our own. We now feel confident that we have established a reliable means of discerning gender, assuming of course that the testee responds to these questions with neatness, precision, and aptness of thought. And, most important, with an open mind: It is essential that the testee relinquish at the onset any preconceived, not to say stubborn, notions about its sexual identity.

Your occupation may be a clue

Are you a (check one):

a. secretary ☐ yes ☐ no
b. telephone operator ☐ yes ☐ no
c. pantyhose salesperson ☐ yes ☐ no
d. nurse ☐ yes ☐ no
e. mugger ☐ yes ☐ no
f. truckdriver ☐ yes ☐ no
g. ladies room attendant ☐ yes ☐ no
h. athletic coach ☐ yes ☐ no
i. hairdresser ☐ yes ☐ no
j. nun ☐ yes ☐ no

Only c., g., and j. are useful clues. If you are any of these three, it is safe to say that you are probably a woman.

157

How to tell from your outfit

It's hard. For instance, one of us authors is wearing a Shetland sweater, gray flannel pants, woolen socks, and clogs. It feels pretty safe in its claim to be a female because it is also wearing a bra. Frankly, however, it doesn't need a bra. The other author, being braless, must base its claim to femaleness on the fact that it is wearing a skirt. But this author could be a Scotsman.

Hairy ears

There is only one characteristic transmitted via the male chromosome. Here's where a mirror is useful. Do you have hairy ears? If so, you have found your sex. *Mazel tov.*

Method of suicide

Sit back. Relax. Close your eyes. And imagine committing suicide. How would you do it? Would you shoot yourself in the head? Slash your throat? Jackknife from the thirtieth floor? If so, statistically speaking, you are a man. If, however, you would opt for pills or the ultimate fem out, the oven route—if, in short, your method is fallible—you are probably a woman.

Sports

Are you the best floater in your pool? If so, you are either a woman or an overweight man. While you are in the pool, take this opportunity to check your bathing suit. Look closely at it. Does it have net underpants? If so, your suspicion that you are an overweight man is confirmed.

Blood will tell

If you menstruate, you are a woman. Definitely. If you do not, you may be a man, a *very* young woman, an older woman, or a pregnant woman.

Check your birth certificate. If you were born before 1925 or after 1963, sorry, the question is still moot. If, however, you were born *between* 1925 and 1963, you are either a man or pregnant. If you are pregnant, you are unquestionably a female.

Research

See if you can get in touch with the doctor who delivered you. Ask him/her if he/she remembers saying either "It's a boy" or "It's a girl" when you emerged.

How much can you trust that doctor?

Your doctor when saying "It's a boy" or "It's a girl" was relying on visual evidence. This, as we've indicated, is inconclusive. Also, the doctor's memory may be going.

How much can you trust your birth certificate?

Not so much. The sex identification checked off there is, as we have stated previously, only your doctor's hasty first impression. The real value of your birth certificate is that it tells you your birth year and, more importantly, it provides the information necessary to calculate your sun sign and rising sign.

Average number of hours slept

No clues here.

Do you cry once a month?

You are either a highly sensitive male, a Latin of indeterminate sex, or a female who suffers from premenstrual tension.

Re the above statement

We can't believe we really said that. As people who suspect themselves to be women, we extend our apologies to Sisterhood. Which is powerful. And scares us.

Are you a mental defective?

Statistics indicate you are probably a man.

A few simple experiments to conduct at home

Next rainy afternoon, invite a few hundred friends over to the house. Test their pain thresholds, hearing acuity, vision, and sense of smell. (You may disguise these tests as party games.) *Results* re pain: those with lower pain thresholds are more likely to be women. Re hearing: those who hear better are likely to be women. Ditto with those who smell better. Those who see better, however, will tend to be men.

Paying restaurant bills

If you are dining in a restaurant with others of your presumed sex, is the paying of the bill a complicated series of mathematical computations, resulting in everyone being asked to chip in $6.64 apiece with the exception of yourself who owes an extra 50¢ for a second cup of coffee? Not forgetting the one who owes $1.50 because it had a shrimp cocktail, which was not listed in the appetizers included in the prix fixe lunch? If so, you are almost certainly all women.

Are you in therapy?

Yes? Statistically speaking, you are a woman.

Formerly reliable indicators

The genuinely resourceful investigator must take pains to avoid jumping to conclusions based on the following formerly reliable indicators of sexual identification:
Earrings
Possession of hair dryer
High heels
Needlepoint kit
Superior position *au lit*

Conclusion

If your answers to these questions indicate that you are more likely to be a female than a male, or conversely, a male than a female, you are safe in assuming that that is indeed what you mostly are. This conclusion, however, should not bind you in any way to any one, necessarily limited, sexual identity. Science is not a tyrant but a teacher: it gives you the information, yes, but it can not dictate choice. In the end, the decision—are you a man or are you a woman?—rests with you.

EVERYONE REMEMBERS CERTAIN NIGHTMARES FROM CHILDHOOD — HORRIBLE, GRIPPING EVENTS WHICH ECHO THROUGH OUR LIVES. THE VERY MENTION OF A KEY WORD AND COLD FEAR GRIPS THE HEART. WITH SOME IT MAY BE "DOLLY" OR "MOTHER," SOMETIMES "HALL CLOSET." BUT FOR MANY, THE SMELL OF SWEATY SOCKS, TRILL OF A WHISTLE, OR BOUNCE OF A BALL MEANS TERROR, AGONY... MEANS "PHYS. ED."!

Phys. Ed. Phunnies

DONE IN BY LEE MARRS

AT THE VERY TIME WE WERE MOST SELF-CONSCIOUS ABOUT OUR BODIES, THERE WE ALL WERE: DRESSING OUT! EXPECTED TO -SHUDDER- CHANGE OUR CLOTHES ALMOST IN PUBLIC!

EXPOSED TO RIDICULE FROM "THEM"...

WE LEARNED WHAT IT WAS ALL ABOUT: TORTURE!

EVEN WORSE, ALREADY AGONIZINGLY SELF-AWARE, WE HAD TO FACE CLASSES WITH RATTY APPEARANCES.

·THIS STORY IS DEDICATED TO THE MONTGY. ALA. 1958 GIRLS ALL-CITY CHAMPIONSHIP BASKETBALL TEAM·

AND REMEMBER THOSE ROTTEN GYM TEACHERS? THEY FELL INTO ONE OF 3 CATEGORIES:

YEP, IT WAS FROM THOSE SWEETIES WE FIRST LEARNED HOW THE WORLD REALLY FUNCTIONED!

DESPERATELY, WE LEARNED TO SURVIVE, TO COPE, TO GET ALONG, TO GET AHEAD AS WE COULD.

AND IT WAS THROUGH PHYS. ED. THAT WE FIRST BECAME AWARE OF A CERTAIN... UH... SITUATION:

THE NEW STADIUM WILL BE DONE BY FALL.

I'M NOT PLAYING IN THE SOUTH FIELD AGAIN! YESTERDAY THE QUICKSAND ATE MARSHA! AND THE MOSQUITOES..

CONGRATULATIONS! TOMMY— THE PODUNK COUNTY TIDDLY-WINK CHAMP FOR THE WHOLE LAKESIDE DISTRICT!

CLAP CLAP CLAP CLAP CLAP CLAP

JUST GOT THIS IN THE MAIL. YOU'RE THE NEW U.S.A. JUNIOR HIGH JUMP CHAMPION. CAREFUL—I THINK IT'S FOOL-SCRAP.

PANT ?

NOT ONLY DID SOCIETY FAVOR THOSE CRUMMY BOYS — BUT TRAITORS DWELT WITHIN OURSELVES...

WAP!

WOW! YOUR FOURTH HOMER IN A ROW!

GO SLUGGER!

HUP HUP KEEP UP, MEN..

SAY, SWEET STUFF, DON'T CHOKE UP ON THE BAT... MOVE YOUR GRIP DOWN..

I BLUSH

CHEEZ.

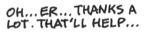

OH... ER... THANKS A LOT. THAT'LL HELP...

WHAT CAME OVER ME? WHY DID I SAY THAT? ER, HMM... HE WAS SO CUTE! KNOWS NUTHING ABOUT BASEBALL... WONDER IF.. HM... I DON'T UNDERSTAND EXACTLY...

GULP

C'MON "SLUGGER" WE AIN'T GOT ALL DAY!!

LATER ON, WE DIDN'T EVEN GET TO PLAY REAL SPORTS — INDOCTRINATION HAD BEGUN. THE MIND WARPS WORKED WELL — BY COLLEGE, WE HAD FORGOTTEN EVERYTHING WE COULD ONCE DO.

OW! OUCH! WHAT GOOD IS THIS SINCE THE BOYS DON'T LEARN HOW TOO?

GIRLS! PAY ATTENTION GIRLS!

ONE-TWO-THREE- I, II, III.

STOP ENJOYING YOURSELVES THIS VERY MINUTE!

OH OH OH

...TO THE CASBAH!

OH, YOU BOYS JUST GO PLAY! WE'LL WATCH GRACEFULLY FROM THE KNOLL WITH THE BEER, TEE HEE.

ALL THAT EMBRYO SKILL- GONE AND FORGOTTEN. >SIGH<

AT LEAST, I THOUGHT WE HAD FORGOTTEN. BUT PHYS. ED. SEEMS TO...UH... LINGER ON — IN STRANGE ECHOES... FUNNY HOW THINGS COME BACK TO YOU... AT THE ODDEST TIMES.

ELOISE HAS AN ASTHMA ATTACK OVER GYM SHORTS...

AND WHEN ALICE FINDS LIFE TOO HECTIC, THERE ARE DREAMS...

OF COURSE, THIS IS ALL QUITE SILLY. HAPPENED LONG AGO — ALL THAT SADISM, COMPETITION, ETC. I'VE COME TO TERMS WITH IT, MYSELF. THINGS ARE CHANGING IN PHYS. ED. TOO. BETTER PROGRAMS, NON-SEXIST, TRAINED PERSONNEL, ALL SORTS OF NEW...

RESTLESS REVERIE

Diane Noomin

HEDY the hooker

BY TRINA ROBBINS

HEDY'S "BUST-INTEREST" MINI BY LAVERNE VALENTI, CHICAGO, ILLINOIS.

HEDY'S "PLUNGING NECKLINE" MINI BY RUBY WASHINGTON, LENNOX AVE., NEW YORK

HEDY'S SPARKLE KNIT HOT PANTS OUTFIT AND VELMA'S STUDDED ROMPERS BY CORABELLE JOHANSEN, LOVELOCK, NEVADA

GIRLS 'N' BOYS! THROW AWAY THOSE MESSY CREAMS AND LOTIONS. EAT CHOCOLATE, WHIPPED CREAM— EVEN **PIZZA** – AGAIN. WHY FIGHT A BASIC FACT O' LIFE? THE COMMON PIMPLE IS HERE TO STAY. SO LEARN TO **LOVE** THE LITTLE BUGGERS. LEARN THE **FINE ART** OF *Zit Picking*

by shelby

"EVERYBODY'S TRUE STORY"

MY FIRST ZIT APPEARED AT THE TENDER AGE OF 11. I WAS SPENDING THE SUMMER AT THE BEACH WITH MY COUSIN.

WOWEE, KIDDO! IT'S A REAL **BLOSSOM OF GLORY!** NEXT THING YOU'LL BE GETTIN' THE **CURSE** AND MAYBE EVEN **BOOBS!**

THIS WAS NOT ENTIRELY NEW TO ME. MY MOM OFTEN PLUCKED STRAY HAIRS & SQUEEZED BLACKHEADS. I NOTICED HOW THE PLUGS FROM PORES AROUND HER MOUTH WERE TINTED WITH HER LIPSTICK.

DUMB KID!

ARE YOU **SURE** IT WON'T **HURT**?

THAT'S IT! NOW JUST GIVE IT A **HARD SQUEEZE!**

SHE TAUGHT ME THE RITUAL OF PORING OVER MY FACE FOR THE TINY BUMPS WHICH, PROPERLY PUSHED, YIELDED AN OFF-WHITE GLOB OF MATTER.

OOH! IT LOOKS LIKE A LITTLE TIT! DOES IT **HURT**?

MY DAD WAS ONCE VISITED WITH THAT TIME-HONORED BIBLICAL AFFLICTION – **BOILS.** THE PAIN THEY CAUSED, AND ITS RELIEF WHEN THE DOCTOR LANCED THEM, REMAINED VIVID IN MY MIND.

WITH EXPERIENCE, OF COURSE, CAME EXPERIMENTATION, THEN REFINEMENT.

I DISCOVERED THE BATHROOM MIRROR. LIT FROM ABOVE, IT CREATED A LUNAR LANDSCAPE OF MY YOUNG CHEEKS, HIGHLIGHTING THE PITS AND BUMPS THAT MIGHT YIELD UP THEIR CONTENTS TO MY PROBING FINGERTIPS.

"GOOD LIGHTING IS THE BASIS OF GOOD PICKING"

· TOOLS OF THE TRADE ·

THE **MAGNIFYING MIRROR** GROTESQUERIE UPON GROTESQUERIE!

BUT I ALWAYS CAME BACK TO THE NATURAL ORGANIC METHOD— THE RELIABLE **FINGERTIPS**. GOOD STRONG FINGER-NAILS ARE A **MUST**— SO DRINK UP THAT GELATIN, KIDS! SPECIALIZED TECH-NIQUES INCLUDE:

THE ALL-PURPOSE SQUEEZE

STRETCH

PUSH

THE NAIL-TO-NAIL METHOD

PUSH   PUSH

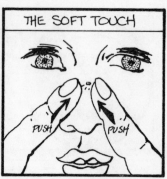

THE SOFT TOUCH

PUSH   PUSH

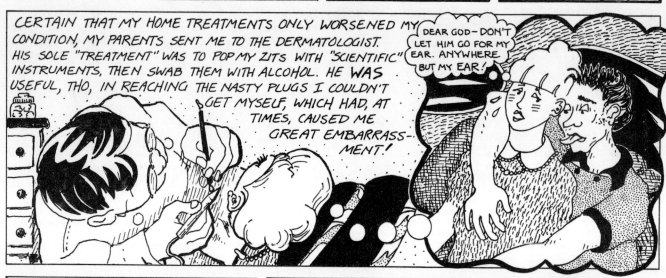

CERTAIN THAT MY HOME TREATMENTS ONLY WORSENED MY CONDITION, MY PARENTS SENT ME TO THE DERMATOLOGIST. HIS SOLE "TREATMENT" WAS TO POP MY ZITS WITH "SCIENTIFIC" INSTRUMENTS, THEN SWAB THEM WITH ALCOHOL. HE **WAS** USEFUL, THO, IN REACHING THE NASTY PLUGS I COULDN'T GET MYSELF, WHICH HAD, AT TIMES, CAUSED ME GREAT EMBARRASS-MENT!

DEAR GOD— DON'T LET HIM GO FOR MY EAR. ANYWHERE BUT MY EAR!

ONCE, A CHANCE TUG OF THE SKIN REVEALED A **HUGE CLOG** JUST UNDER THE JAWLINE.

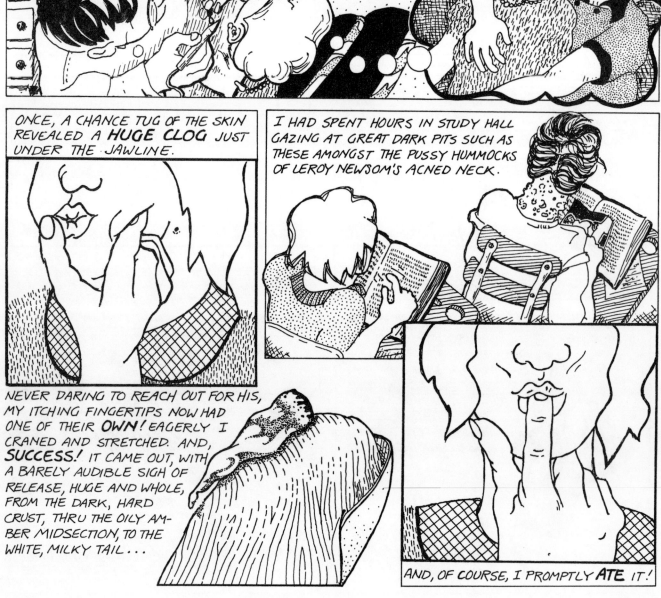

I HAD SPENT HOURS IN STUDY HALL GAZING AT GREAT DARK PITS SUCH AS THESE AMONGST THE PUSSY HUMMOCKS OF LEROY NEWSOM'S ACNED NECK.

NEVER DARING TO REACH OUT FOR HIS, MY ITCHING FINGERTIPS NOW HAD ONE OF THEIR **OWN**! EAGERLY I CRANED AND STRETCHED. AND, **SUCCESS**! IT CAME OUT, WITH A BARELY AUDIBLE SIGH OF RELEASE, HUGE AND WHOLE, FROM THE DARK, HARD CRUST, THRU THE OILY AM-BER MIDSECTION, TO THE WHITE, MILKY TAIL . . .

AND, OF COURSE, I PROMPTLY **ATE** IT!

AS I GREW OLDER, THE TYPE AND LOCATION OF MY BLEMISHES SLOWLY CHANGED. THE "BLOSSOMS OF GLORY" OF PUBERTY SOON BECAME A CONSISTENT SPOTTING OF THE FOREHEAD, NOSE, AND CHIN, ACCOMPANIED BY LIGHT, OILY BLACKHEADS. BY AGE 14, THEY WERE SPREADING OUTWARD, A PROCESS WHICH CONTINUED UNTIL STABILIZATION AT ABOUT AGE 18.

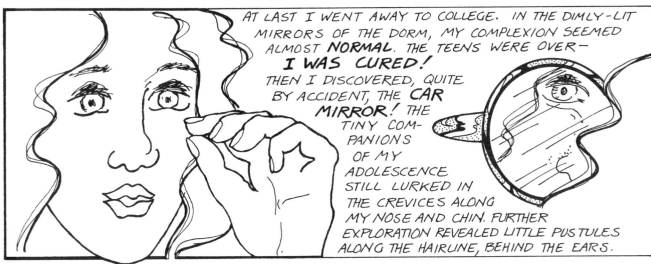

AT LAST I WENT AWAY TO COLLEGE. IN THE DIMLY-LIT MIRRORS OF THE DORM, MY COMPLEXION SEEMED ALMOST **NORMAL**. THE TEENS WERE OVER— **I WAS CURED!** THEN I DISCOVERED, QUITE BY ACCIDENT, THE **CAR MIRROR!** THE TINY COMPANIONS OF MY ADOLESCENCE STILL LURKED IN THE CREVICES ALONG MY NOSE AND CHIN. FURTHER EXPLORATION REVEALED LITTLE PUSTULES ALONG THE HAIRLINE, BEHIND THE EARS.

THERE ARE MANY VARIATIONS ON THE BASIC ACT OF ZIT PICKING. LIKE SEX, THERE ARE AS MANY VARIATIONS AS PEOPLE WHO INDULGE. SOME OF MY FAVORITE EMBELLISHMENTS ARE:

COLLECTING A BUNCH OF OILY BLACKHEADS ON THE FINGERNAIL THEN SMEARING THEM, COMET-LIKE, ACROSS THE MIRROR...

MAKING LITTLE FLOWER OR STAR SHAPES ON THE MIRROR WITH A PARTICULARLY LARGE LUMP OF PUS...

AND TRYING TO PREDICT, BY SIZE AND SHAPE, WHICH PIMPLES WILL BE LEAKERS OR BLEEDERS.

YOU CAN CREATE YOUR OWN!

WHEN I WAS 14, THEY SAID, "YOUR SKIN WILL CLEAR UP BY 16." WHEN I WAS 16, THEY SAID, "YOU'LL GROW OUT OF IT BY 18." WHEN I WAS 18, THEY DISCREETLY STOPPED TALKING ABOUT IT. NOW, I'M 33, AND OFTEN ASKED FOR I.D. EVEN TO BUY CIGARETTES. WHEN ASKED MY SECRET FOR KEEPING THE COMPLEXION OF A TEEN-AGER, I SMILE AND REPLY— JUST **PICK YOUR ZITS!**

END.

172

I CAME TO THE NEXT MEETING DETERMINED TO TELL MY WOMEN FRIENDS I WAS LEAVING THE GROUP. BUT AN ANGEL OR DEVIL GOT THE BEST OF MY GOOD INTENTIONS.

HE'S **SO** WONDERFUL...

YES, MINE IS WONDERFUL, TOO.

SHALL I ??

GO AHEAD.

ON THE COUNT OF THREE, TELL US YOUR BOYFRIEND'S NAME ~ ONE, TWO, **THREE!**

TED!

ANGELA AND BERNADINE FELL INTO EACH OTHER'S ARMS. FOR A BRIEF TIME, SANITY AND SISTERHOOD WERE RESTORED.

OH, I WAS SUCH A FOOL! I NEVER LIKED HIM AS MUCH AS YOU.

YOU KNOW, HE WAS REALLY A LOUSY LOVER, ANYWAY.

BUT AT THE VERY NEXT MEETING MY FRIENDS GREETED ME WITH SUSPICION AND ANGER.

IF YOU WANT TO BE SO COLD AND MANLIKE, YOU DON'T BELONG IN A WOMEN'S GROUP.

YOU'RE TOO AGGRESSIVE AND AMBITIOUS.

WOMEN SHOULD GIVE LOVE, NOT CRITICISM!

ANYWAY, I **STILL** THINK TED'S GREAT. HE TOOK ME OUT SUNDAY AND ANGELA TUESDAY-HE'LL JUST HAVE TO CHOOSE BETWEEN US.

DON'T FORGET, WE'RE YOUR **SISTERS!**

I CAME HOME AND CRIED ALL NIGHT AND NEVER RETURNED TO THE WOMEN'S GROUP.

DEAR DIARY: I GUESS WOMEN CAN BE AS DIFFICULT AS MEN.

END

173

A DAY AT ST. CLARE'S

WRITTEN BY
DENNY DILLON
DRAWN BY PATY

WRITER:
JANIS HIRSCH

ARTIST:
NORMA ASBORNSEN

SOMEWHERE I HAD READ THAT THE MOST IMPORTANT THING TO LOOK FOR IN A MAN WAS A SENSE OF HUMOR, SO I LOOKED.

IN THE FOURTH GRADE, ARTHUR TOBIN WAS CONSIDERED TO BE THE PARKWAY SCHOOL WIT.

ARTHUR TOBIN, DID YOU WRITE THIS?

LUCKY ARTHUR IS A CARELESS PENMAN.

BUT ONE DAY I FELT SOMETHING TRICKLING DOWN MY BACK...

WHAT'S THAT ARTHUR? WHAT'S THAT WATER? WHAT'S THAT ALL OVER MY GYMSUIT AND MY SHOELACES AND MY RULER? AND WHY ARE YOUR PANTS... OHH MY GOD! MY GOD!!

VERY LITTLE ARTHUR DID AMUSED ME AFTER THAT. LATER ON, THERE WAS WILLY LEW CATHCART. WILLY LEW HAD A THING FOR LITTLE RUBBER ERASERS SHAPED LIKE HIPPOS.

HIPPEE! HIPPEE! MY HIPPEE!

IN OUR SIXTH GRADE GRADUATION PICTURE, WILLY LEW CROSSED HIS EYES BECAUSE HIPPEE TOLD HIM TO...

ONLY ONE THING BLIGHTED OUR RELATIONSHIP. WILLY LEW BIT. I WANTED A MAN WHO COULD KEEP ME LAUGHING AND DIDN'T BITE. I USED TO SPEND HOURS READING BENNETT CERF'S "OUT ON A LIMERICK" AND "MORE LAUGHING OUT LOUD WITH MYRON COHEN," DREAMING THAT I'D MEET SOMEONE AS FUNNY...

I WONDER IF ALAN KING HAS A SON?

IN EIGHTH GRADE THERE WAS EUGENE GUNDERMANN. HE HID UNDER THE TEACHERS' DESKS AND LICKED THEIR KNEES AS THEY SAT DOWN. HE PULLED CHAIRS OUT FROM UNDER PEOPLE. HE STUCK NO. 2 PENCILS UP HIS NOSE. HE WAS THE MAN FOR ME.

SIGH!

I BET DONNA REED'S SON WOULDN'T PICK HIS DATE UP IN A TRUCK!

I INVITED EUGENE TO A SADIE HAWKINS PICNIC. HIS MOTHER PICKED ME UP IN A TRUCK.

EUGENE GUNDERMAN

IN COLLEGE, MY SORORITY SISTERS TOLD ME THAT FRATERNITY MEN WERE THE FUNNIEST. I BOUGHT SWEATERS SO THAT WHEN I GOT PINNED I WOULDN'T RUIN MY BLOUSE. I STOPPED CHEWING MY CUTICLES SO THAT WHEN I GOT ENGAGED, MY FINGERNAILS WOULDN'T BE BLOODY. WHAT I DIDN'T KNOW WAS THAT "FUNNY" MEANT "DRUNK."

I WAS SO DRUNK LAST NIGHT I TOTALLED MY PORSCHE! HA! HA!

I WAS SO DRUNK LAST NIGHT I THREW UP ON MY DATE! HA-HA!

I WAS SO DRUNK LAST NIGHT I PUT EX-LAX IN THE PLEDGES' PIZZA! HO! HO!

WHAT KIND OF PEOPLE LAUGH HA! HA! HO! HO!?

THEN ONE DAY MY DREAMS CAME TRUE. I GOT A JOB AT A MEN'S HUMOR MAGAZINE.

I TOOK EX-LAX AND THREW UP ALL OVER MY PORSCHE!

WHO WROTE THIS?

HIPPEE MADE ME DO IT.

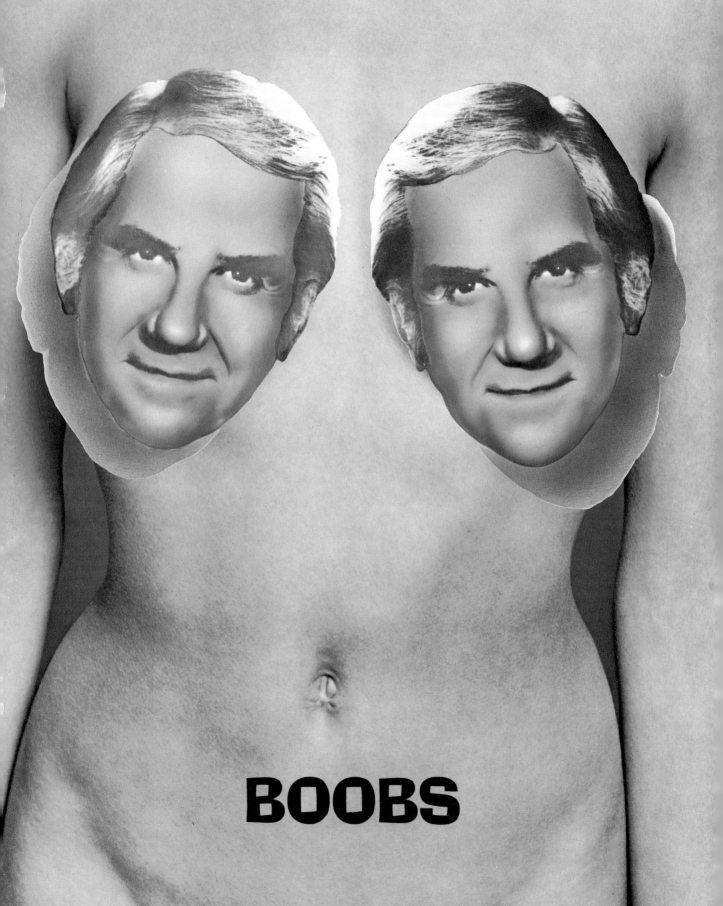

BOOBS

☐Bake little notes to yourself into your food: "You pig!" "Kate Smith phoned. She wants to know if she can borrow your dress."

☐Eating is self-punishment: punish the food instead. Strangle a loaf of Italian bread. Throw darts at a cheesecake. Chain a lamb chop to the bed. Beat up a cookie.

Gilda Radner's Diet Tips

☐Chew every mouthful a hundred times and then spit it out afterwards.

☐Always wear clothes that are too tight and will ride up into your crotch if you overeat.

☐Mail all your food to Europe.

☐Only eat airline food: strap yourself into your seat and turn on an electric fan to create turbulence. Leave an air sickness bag out where you can see it.

☐Shoot up with crystal methedrine right before dinner.

☐Eat everything out of a dog bowl.

☐Chew gum while you're eating.

☐Enter restaurants through the kitchen.

☐Think about what happened to Mama Cass.

☐Really make fun of fat people by giggling when you pass them on the street, offering them chocolate and ice cream cones and running after them and forcing them to eat in front of you.

☐Hire someone to play tricks on you by putting rubber spiders and other joke items in your food.

☐Stub out your cigarette in your food before you've finished eating.

☐Use rusty silverware.

☐Have a picnic near a car accident.

Photography by Jill Mariani and Fran Heaney

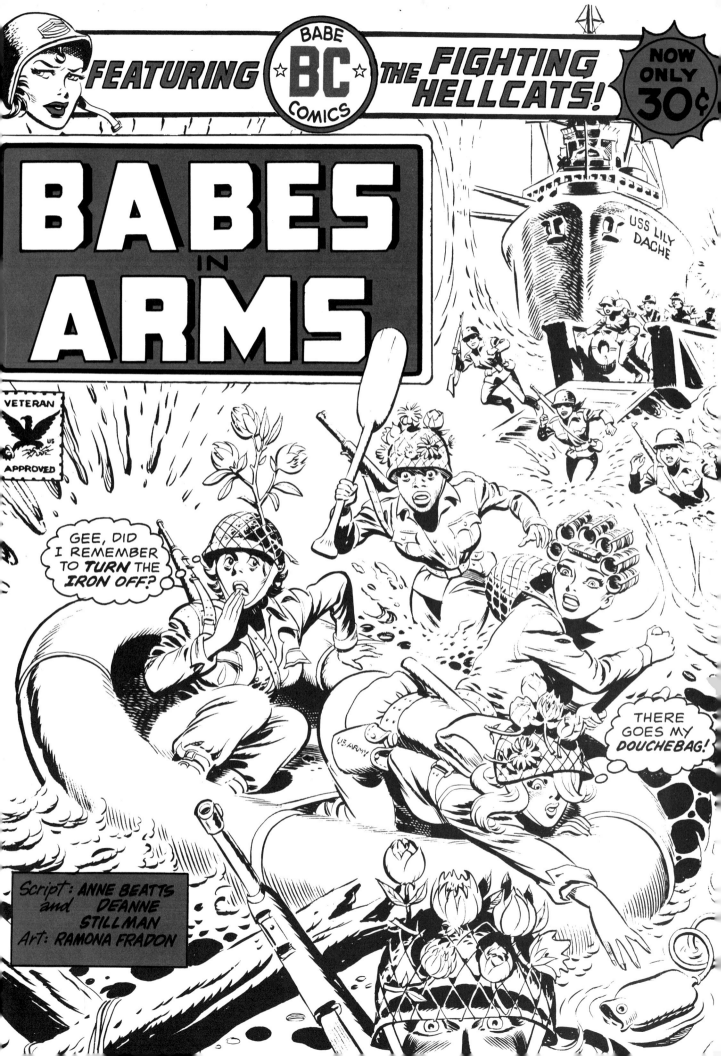

*ADD ½ CUP BRANDY, 1 TBLSP. SUGAR, AND 1 TBLSP. CORNSTARCH TO TWO CUPS COOKED CHERRIES. SERVE FLAMING.

THE HELLCATS SEIZE THEIR CHANCE...

WAS IS LOS?

SPRECHEN ZIE DEUTSCH?

YOU VILL ALL BE *SHOT* AT *DAWN!* UND YOU, *GOLDSTEIN,* VILL BE SHOT *TWICE!*

BUT FIRST, TURN THIS *PIGSTY* INTO *QUARTERS* FIT FOR AN *OFFICER* OF THE *SS!*

BUT THE *KILLER HUN* HADN'T FIGURED ON THE *SAVVY* OF THE *AMERICAN FIGHTING GAL!*

THIS ONE'S FOR *BIG JERRY!*

NOW THAT WE'VE *CLEANED UP* THE *HOUSE,* IT'S TIME TO *CLEAN UP OURSELVES!*

IF I'M GONNA *DIE,* I WANNA *LOOK PRETTY!*

ACH DU LIEBER!

SCHWEINHUND!

GOTT IN HIMMEL!

ACH! WAS IS LOS!

BLITZKRIEG!

LEBENSRAUM!

O TANNENBAUM!

RAISINETTES?

MILK DUDS?

WASH-INGTON, WHY DID YOU *WRITE* THAT?

I DIDN'T KNOW *HOW* TO *SPELL PIERRE!*

THE CHOCLATE BAR KID

THE END.

My Beauty Secrets, or Never let a whale bite your leg off

by Chris Chase

There are certain differences between me and Mark Twain.

Besides the obvious one of gender, and his being a riverboat pilot.

His cynicism is what I refer to.

"I hate to take advice from some people," he said, "when I see how bad they need it."

I'm nothing like that. I take advice from anyone, and I believe I should be empowered to dole some out too. If you accept the old saw about "Those that can, do; those that can't, teach," you'll also have to accept that my ignorance qualifies me to instruct people in many subjects.

I can't speak Chinese, ride a horse, play golf, shinny up a flagpole, make change, or ask a cop a question.

I also can't ski, stand up straight, set my hair, grow an avocado, or kiss good. (There have been complaints about the last one.)

So, if I were venal, I would instantly open an academy for the illumination and indoctrination of almost everybody in almost everything, and the money would start rolling in.

But I don't operate that way. If you want advice from me, just come around. I give it free.

I frequently say this to people, yet nobody asks my opinion, not even about my beauty secrets. This bothers me *au fond* (I couldn't teach French; I'm too much of a crackerjack at it) because all us important actresses are lookers. In my profession you got to be lovely, and never mind Sarah Bernhardt was plain—have you seen her in a movie lately?

Anyway, I am as beautiful as the next one. (The next one is my husband, and his face may be prettier, but his expression isn't so sweet.)

I try to collect all the beauty tips I can from *other* beauties—a woman cannot be too delectable, especially when she doesn't kiss good—but much of the counseling you get elsewhere is of no earthly use.

Why, I remember reading interviews with nineteen supermodels, and those models' recommendations were pitiful.

One girl named Cheryl Tiegs came out for "the clean look," and she had "small, sparkling white teeth, as even as ivory beads."

Well, what good did it do me to know that, when my own look is somewhat lived-in and my front teeth are all different colors?

A great huge model named Veruschka was a bust, too, when it came to guidance. "If I am in the mood to look very young," she said, "I put to my freckles some more with a brown pencil."

I wouldn't like to tangle with Veruschka—she's bigger than a boxer, let alone a breadbox—but I put to my

Miriam Wosk

freckles some more with a brown pencil on a day when I was looking middling old, and I wound up looking middling old with measles.

There was a model who stuck "single false lashes" in among her own natural feathers. One at a time. I tried it. It was terrific. The only hangup is it took twelve hours. By the time I was ready to go out, my husband was already in bed inquiring about when was I going to turn off the bathroom light?

There were other tips in that bunch, too. One model used mustache wax, and one model concentrated so hard on applying her makeup that she sometimes fainted in the process.

I see no value to any of this, except the hint about fainting, which is sound, since when you faint you fall down, and falling down brings blood to your head and gives you a glow.

Most of those nineteen supermodels said they used no cosmetics—"just a little eyeliner and a blusher"—but this is not a good tip either, what with its being a flat-out lie. Else why do they carry those satchels full of paint around with them and why, if you accidentally slap a model in the face, does a piece of her cheek chip off?

No matter. If you're dubious about making a pleat near your eye with surgical adhesive, you've come to the right place. You think I'm making it up about the pleat, but *Glamour* magazine once recommended it as a way of opening up the outside of your eye.

"With a toothpick, apply a dot of adhesive to the base of the false lash at the outside corner. Now place the toothpick below your own lashes at the outside corner and another toothpick about a hairline above the dot of adhesive, and press together, forming a tiny pleat."

I studied that over about nineteen times, and then I tried it and I thought I got it just right, but when my husband came home he said, "Why have you pasted toothpicks in your eyes?"

Enough. I am going to give the women of America, whether they want them or not, my beauty secrets, at absolutely no cost to themselves. Which is more than Luella Cuming did for me.

The reason I mention Luella Cuming is she is a lady who acted like she was going to tell *me* a lot of secrets, but then it turned out she wanted $14.95 for them.

She came on like she was anxious to learn me—and a few other hand-picked clients—about "social awareness, poise, and gracious living."

How I knew she'd picked me out special was the brochure she sent was addressed to "Occupant, Apartment 3A," and that's where I live.

"Frankly, this course is not for everyone," she wrote, "but for those whose interests and activities indicate they have the potential for further social advancement."

It was exciting that Luella believed in my potential, because I hadn't given her any good reason to do so. Perhaps she had seen me crouching beside the stove in some fashionable East Side kitchen one night, while others were in the living room drinking and laughing it up. I just don't know. But the brochure said she was going to sit down with me and give me "the same individual guidance she gives the top executives, society women, diplomats, and other important people who attend her course in New York."

The brochure said Luella's students gladly paid high fees to acquire graces, among them being "how to act toward your escort, how to get a good table without waiting, how to catch the waiter's eye, and how to order food and drink that mark you immediately as a person of superior taste."

I'd seen some top executives and society women ordering food and drink, but I never knew where they learned it until I got the brochure from Ms. Cuming. When I was playing in a soap opera at CBS, I took a great interest in Mr. and Mrs. Paley (an executive and a society woman sans peer), but before the brochure came, I thought they drank in all that good breeding with their mothers' milk.

Ms. Cumings promised I'd never again feel nervous or embarrassed, "even in the plushest places," and that I'd be able "to command the center of interest in any group."

Then she broke her pick with me.

She said she was going to divulge the answers to such tricky social problems as:

1. How to reply to an extremely personal question.
2. The best way to "break the ice" with a new acquaintance.
3. The tactful way to get rid of a guest who overstays his welcome.

What's tricky about *those* problems? What's the matter with time-tested answers like:

1. None of your beeswax?
2. How are they hangin'?
3. Haven't you got a home?

Ms. Cuming also said she would give her pupils insights into the relationships between men and women—"You'll discover what a man looks for and expects in a woman"—and that sounded promising, too, until she clued me in that it had to do with being a person of "refinement and warmth."

I thought about it. And I realized Marlon Brando in his whole life was never attracted to a person of refinement and warmth. He just likes those girls with long dark hair and a flower behind their ear. And I decided the hell with good taste; it's back to beauty for me.

It's true enough that one can't share *all* the mysteries of one's bloom with one's readers, because one has certain attributes that are a direct gift from the Creator.

I mean, how can I tell people a way to get flat feet? You're either born with 'em, or forget it.

I did have something to do with the fact that the caps on my front teeth are all different colors. The secret of this is to go to all different dentists, each of whom will assure you he can match your caps perfectly, but each of whom is lying in your teeth.

What happens is your cap always breaks in a strange city. You will be in Boston's Chinatown, daintily nibbling on a sparerib, when your front tooth disengages itself, and the director of whatever disaster you're traveling with won't let you go home to New York, and you can't go onstage without a front tooth because the rest of the cast will think you're trying to be smart, so it's a nice glass Boston tooth (ivory) in a line of New York's finest porcelains (white) and that's simply the beginning. Add a Hollywood molar (beige) and you get part of the picture. The reason I write is I don't like to talk too much because of having to open my mouth.

Now that I look this over, my caps don't sound like a good secret. Maybe the secret is not to eat spareribs. Or Good Humors. I once broke a cap on a Good Humor. After that I had my caps angled so far forward I keep nibbling on my lower lip, but it isn't the same as having Marlon Brando do it. I bet.

However, before I leave the subject of loveliness, I have a few really urgent words to the wise.

Stay cheerful. Suffering makes lines in the face. Another way of saying this is, Never let a whale bite your leg off. I saw a production of *Moby Dick* in which Rod Steiger played Captain Ahab, and one sailor said to another sailor, "Ever since he lost that leg, he's been kinda moody."

Moodiness will make lines in the face as quick as suffering.

Eat plenty of potatoes. This produces a firm, round, unwrinkled appearance exactly like Elizabeth Taylor's.

Eat plenty of garlic. This guarantees you twelve hours of sleep—alone—every night, and there's nothing like rest to give you shining orbs (poetic), peepers (colloquial), or lamps (slang). A diet of potatoes and garlic leaves you oodles of time for reading *Roget's Thesaurus in Dictionary Form,* too.

Never admit you're thirty-one. A couple of years ago, four airlines in this country had policies requiring stewardesses to retire soon after they hit thirty, and when a newspaper asked why, an airline executive declared, "It's the sex thing. Put a dog on an airplane, and twenty businessmen are sore for a month."

One of our representatives in Congress, looking into the whole sorry affair, said the airlines needed "to be educated to the fact that they're not operating flying bunny clubs," and another congressman quoted Benjamin Franklin, who'd said that in middle age, feminine allure and sensitivity were enhanced "as in vintage wine."

Vintage eyewash. Never admit you're thirty-one.

There, I've done my best. Told all I knew, and a few things I've only guessed at.

In the end, the master, Cary Grant, whose own beauty is limitless, may have given us the best steer.

"We should all just smell well," he said, "and enjoy ourselves more."

by Emily Prager

Man, Oh Man!

Something of a sentimentalist, Dirk is especially fond of a conch shell he picked up during a brief stint as a water-ski bum in Hawaii.

Put together a passion for backgammon, a brooding magnetism, a dynamic powerhouse of a body, a private vulnerable side, a keen mind, and three German shepherds named Aquarius, Libra, and Scorpio; and what have you got? An engaging, sexy combination known around the San Francisco Plum, where he tends bar, as Dirk Dougherty. A mellow thirty-three, Dirk says he has learned that the fruits of life must be left to ripen on the vine and plucked only when ready, i.e., he appreciates older women. Of course, the lady of his choice must also share his passion for watching cop shows on television with the lights out, walking in the rain, sleeping in satin sheets, German shepherds, and backgammon. "But I wouldn't kick her out of bed if she didn't dig those things," Dirk hints slyly. "If I could just find a chick who could learn to love backgammon, I'd stop messing around."

Created by Pat Oleszko

Photographed by ROBIN SCHWARTZ

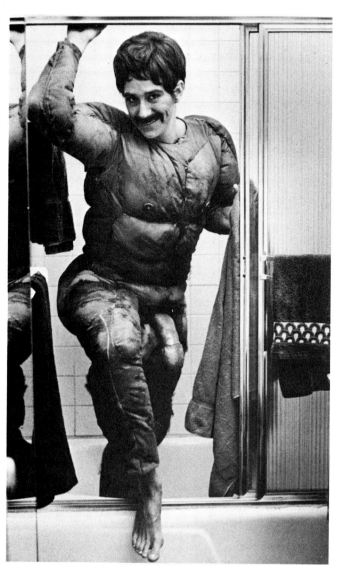

"I hate to bathe alone," Dirk says, as he playfully invites our lens-woman to join him for a frolic in the tub.

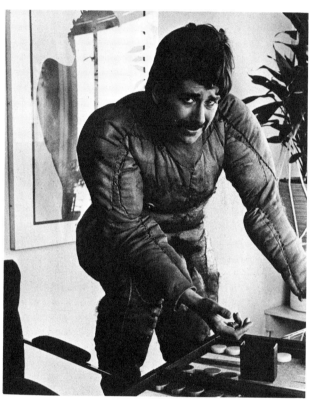

Dirk's hottest current enthusiasm? Backgammon, which he plays with insouciant flair. "I love backgammon," says Dirk. "Mainly, it's the competition."

"I never finished school," Dirk shrugs. "I learned everything I need to know from this little ole book called Webster's."

ACKNOWLEDGMENTS

ART ASSISTANTS

June Bennett, Davida Dale, Diana Feldman, Jean Hipp, Diana LaGuardia, Anne Lee Litterman, Gail Miller

COPY EDITORS

Louise Gikow, Jane Herman

PRODUCTION

Wren D'Antonio, Rusty Gutwillig, Jim Lepper, Don Longabucco, Helen Mills, Penny Sommer

LOCATIONS

Ron Brawer, Gene and Jane Kazlow, Mary-Jenifer Mitchell, Gilda Radner, Mr. and Mrs. Michael Secunda, Sheri Secunda

MAKEUP

Carl Fullerton, Fran Kolar, Mary Wilshire

MODELS

John Belushi, Amy Boisseau, Dana Bree, Gay Bryant, Rhonda Coullet, Sidney Davis, Cecelia Dennie, Delia Doherty, Sharon Francis, Fran Heaney, Trucia Kushner, Anne Lee Litterman, Mary-Jenifer Mitchell, Andra Mooney, Kristin Mull, Michael Nouri, Sara Nicholson, Cindy Ornsteen, Pavla Partch, Emily Prager, Gilda Radner, Nano Riley, Roger Rubin, Dona Sadock, Barry Secunda, Anna Uppstrom, Francesca Vignola, Tracy Young, Maria Zannieri

PHOTOGRAPHY

The photographs on pages 83, 94, 95, 122, 123 appear by courtesy of United Press International

SPECIAL THANKS

The Marshall Baer Group, Carol Belsky, John Belushi, Michael Denneny, Marjorie Gross, Michael Gross, Janis Hirsch, Peter Kleinman, Michael O'Donoghue, Ben Pesta, Mrs. Helen Putnam, Beth Rashbaum, Regina Ryan, Barry Secunda, Rex Weiner